anarchic **dance**

Liz Aggiss and Billy Cowie, known collectively as Divas Dance Theatre, are renowned for their highly visual, interdisciplinary brand of dance performance that incorporates elements of theatre, film, opera, poetry and vaudevillian humour. They have created dance theatre, cabaret, live art, single and multiple screen dance installations, and live performance installations.

Available in one package for the first time, *Anarchic Dance*, consisting of a book and DVD-ROM, is a visual and textual record of the work of Divas Dance Theatre. The DVD-ROM features extracts from Aggiss and Cowie's work, including the highly acclaimed dance film *Motion Control* (premiered on BBC2 in 2002), rare video footage of their punk-comic live performances as The Wild Wigglers and reconstructions of Aggiss's solo performance in *Grotesque Dancer*.

These films are cross-referenced in the book, allowing readers to match performance and commentary as Aggiss and Cowie invite a broad range of writers to examine their live performance and dance screen practice through analysis, theory, discussion and personal response. As much as their practice is hybrid, maverick and hard to define, the various theories presented are equally challenging, lively and fresh.

Extensively illustrated with black and white and colour photographs, this beautiful multi-media package is a celebration of Divas' boundary-shattering performance work. *Anarchic Dance* provides a comprehensive investigation into Cowie and Aggiss's collaborative partnership and demonstrates a range of exciting approaches through which dance performance can be engaged critically.

anarchic **dance**

edited by liz aggiss and billy cowie
with ian bramley

Routledge
Taylor & Francis Group

LONDON AND NEW YORK

First published 2006
by Routledge
2 Park Square, Milton Park, Abingdon, Oxon OX14 4RN

Simultaneously published in the USA and Canada
by Taylor & Francis Inc
270 Madison Avenue, New York, NY 10016

Routledge is an imprint of the Taylor & Francis Group

Typeset in Joanna by RefineCatch Ltd, Bungay, Suffolk
Printed and bound in Great Britain by
MPG Books Ltd, Cornwall

British Library Cataloguing in Publication Data
A catalogue record for this book is available from the British Library

Library of Congress Cataloging in Publication Data
Anarchic dance / edited by Liz Aggiss and Billy Cowie with Ian Bramley.
     p. cm.
   Includes bibliographical references and index.
1. Dance criticism. 2. Aggiss, Liz – Criticism and interpretation. 3. Cowie, Billy –
Criticism and interpretation. 4. Divas Dance Theatre. 5. Choreography. 6. Modern
dance. 7. Dance in motion pictures, television, etc. I. Aggiss, Liz. II. Cowie,
Billy. III. Bramley, Ian, 1968–
   GV1600 .A53 2006
   792.8 – dc 22   2005019860

ISBN10 0–415–36516–3 (hbk and DVD-ROM)
ISBN10 0–415–36517–1 (pbk and DVD-ROM)

DVD-ROM Catalogue Number: ANDA365163

This book is dedicated to us, Liz Aggiss and Billy Cowie, to mark our long-term collaboration and friendship.

contents

list of illustrations

Cover photographs

Front cover

'Red Dress' – Liz Aggiss in *Motion Control*

Inside cover

'Variation 3' – Liz Aggiss in *Anarchic Variations*

Back cover

'Variation 1' – Liz Aggiss in *Anarchic Variations*

Plates

Figures

notes on contributors

Liz Aggiss is a performer/choreographer/film-maker. She works principally with Billy Cowie in the area of dance/theatre/live art performance, screen dance and installation. They have made over thirty live performance pieces for their company Divas, have toured Europe extensively and completed five major dance screen projects (two BBC Dance for Camera commissions and three Arts Council England Capture projects). They have created commissioned work for Extemporary Dance Theatre, Mantis, Transitions, Intoto, Carousel and High Spin. Liz Aggiss has written for *Dance Theatre Journal* and *animated*.

Liz Aggiss has received numerous awards including: Bonnie Bird Choreography Award (1994), Arts Council Dance Fellowship Award (2003). Aggiss/Cowie's dance screen work has received numerous international awards including: Czech Crystal, Prague Golden Film Festival (2002); Special Jury Golden Award, Houston (2003); Best Female Film, Mediawaves Hungary (2003); and the Romanian National Office of Cinematography Award (2003). Liz Aggiss is currently Professor of Visual Performance at the University of Brighton. www.lizaggiss.com, www.anarchicdance.com.

Ian Bramley is a freelance writer and arts consultant. He is the former Director of Dance UK and was the Editor of *Dance Theatre Journal* and Head of Publications at Laban, London, from 1998 to 2003, where he established the academic dance journal, *Discourses in Dance*. He was the first recipient of the Chris de Marigny Dance Writers' Award in 1995.

Valerie A. Briginshaw Ph.D. is Professor of Dance Studies at University College Chichester. Her book, *Dance, Space and Subjectivity* (2001), which includes an analysis of Aggiss and Cowie's *Grotesque Dancer*, is a collection of readings of postmodern dances informed by poststructuralist theory.

Other publications include chapters in *Analysing Performance* (1996), *Dance in the City* (1997), *Preservation Politics* (2001) and *Performing Nature* (2005). Having just completed research exploring interfaces between writing and performance-making in a three-year AHRB funded project with the choreographer Emilyn Claid, she is currently working on a second book exploring issues of vulnerability and interdependency through ten recent, radically innovative dance works.

Carol Brown Ph.D. is a choreographer, performer and writer. Originally from New Zealand, her company, Carol Brown Dances, is based in London and tours nationally and internationally. Formed in 1996, the company is renowned for its cross-art form collaborations with visual artists, photographers, digital artists, film-makers, architects and sound designers. Carol Brown has received numerous awards including: Jerwood Award for Choreography (1999), an AHRB Research Fellowship in the Creative and Performing Arts (2002–04), the Ludwig Forum International Prize for Innovation (2004) and a NESTA Dream Time (2004–05). She has a doctorate in choreography from the University of Surrey and is a Researcher in the School of Arts, Roehampton University. Her company receives regular support from the Arts Council England and tours with the British Council. www.carolbrowndances.com.

Billy Cowie is a Scottish composer/choreographer/film-maker. He works principally with Liz Aggiss in the area of dance/theatre/live art performance, screen dance and installation. They have made over thirty live performance pieces for their company Divas, have toured Europe extensively and completed five major dance/screen projects (two BBC Dance for Camera commissions and three Arts Council England Capture projects). They have created commissioned work for Extemporary Dance Theatre, Mantis, Transitions, Intoto, Carousel and High Spin.

Billy Cowie has composed music performed by Marie McLaughlin, Nicola Hall, Gerard McChrystal, Daphne Scott-Sawyer, Juliet Russell, Rowan Godel, Parmjit Pammi and Naomi Itami. He has released 12 CDs of his music on the Divas Records label. He has recently composed music for three BBC Radio projects: Shakespeare's *The Tempest*, Philip Pullman's *His Dark Materials* trilogy (both directed by David Hunter) and *Thinking Earth* (directed by Pam Marshall). He has also composed music for film directors Tony Palmer, Chris Rodley, Stephen Frears and Bob Bentley. He is currently a Principal Research Fellow at the University of Brighton. www.billycowie.com, www.anarchicdance.com.

Sherril Dodds Ph.D. is a Senior Lecturer in the Department of Dance Studies at the University of Surrey. She lectures in the areas of dance on screen and popular dance. She is author of *Dance on Screen: Genres and Media from Hollywood to Experimental Art* (2001) and has published chapters on female striptease in *Dance in the City* (1997), on popular culture in the work of Lea Anderson in *Dancing Texts* (1999), on the revolutionary potential of video dance in *Indeterminate Bodies* (2003) and on music video in *Music, Sensation and Sensuality* (2002). She has written articles for *Dancing Times*, *Dance Theatre Journal*, *animated*, *Dance Research Journal* and *Filmwaves*.

Sondra Fraleigh, Professor Emeritus of Dance and Somatic Studies at the State University of New York at Brockport, is the author of *Dancing Identity: Metaphysics in Motion* (2004); *Dancing into Darkness: Butoh, Zen, and Japan* (1999); *Researching Dance: Evolving Modes of Inquiry* (1998); and *Dance and the Lived Body* (1987). She has been Chair of Dance at Brockport and a Faculty Exchange Scholar for the State University of New York. Her innovative choreography has been seen in New York, Germany and Japan, and she is often a guest lecturer in Europe, America and Asia. Fraleigh is the Founding Director of Eastwest Somatics Institute for the study of dance and movement therapy, where she brings her study of Western somatic practices (Feldenkrais, Alexander, Breathwork and CranioSacral Therapy) together with her use of gentle yoga and Japanese Butoh techniques. She teaches her Eastwest Somatics Certification workshops through the International Somatic Education and Therapy Association (ISMETA) in the USA, Japan and the UK. She also continues to write – most recently, a forthcoming book for Routledge on the founders of Japanese Butoh, dancers Hijikata Tatsumi and Ohno Kazuo. For more information on Fraleigh and her work see her website: www.brockport.edu/~dance/somatics.

Donald Hutera has been writing and speaking about dance, theatre and the arts since 1977, first in his native America and latterly in the UK and Europe. Publications include *The Times* of London, the *New York* and *Los Angeles Times*, *Time Out*, *Evening Standard*, *The Scotsman*, *Glasgow Herald*, *Dance Europe*, *Dance Now*, *Dance Theatre Journal*, *Dance Umbrella News*, *The List*, *animated*, *The Doubt Guardian* and many others. He co-authored (with Allen Robertson) *The Dance Handbook* (1988) and has since contributed to the *Chambers Biographical Dictionary* (1997), the *Larousse Encyclopaedia* (Latin American edition), *Fifty Contemporary Choreographers* (1996), the *International Dictionary of Modern Dance* (1998) and *The Rough Guide to Choreography* (2004), of which he was also the editor.

In 2003 Hutera made *Scary Grant*, a choreographic research commission from the presenters' consortium Guardians of Doubt (GoD); worked with Anjali Dance Company's education unit; was artistic consultant for Stacked Wonky's production *401 Pieces*; curated the Jerwood-commissioned Wapping Project, Six White Chairs; and began co-editing the Dance Consortium's worldwidedanceuk.com website. *Choreographus Interruptus*, an audience development project sponsored by

GoD and created with h2dance (Hanna Gillgren and Heidi Rustgaard), was presented at Nottdance 2004 and subsequently toured to Swindon's Taking Risks festival, the Youngblood season at Yorkshire Dance, Leeds and York St John's College.

Marion Kant D.Phil. is a musicologist and dance historian. She earned her Ph.D. in musicology in 1986 at Humboldt University in Berlin on the subject of 'Romantic Ballet: An Inquiry into Gender'. She has taught in Germany (Berlin, Leipzig) and the UK (University of Cambridge, Surrey University) and is presently employed at the University of Pennsylvania, Philadelphia, USA where she teaches courses in dance/theatre history, performance criticism and cultural theory.

She has been a Senior Research Fellow ('Surrey Scholar') in Dance History at the School of Performing Arts, University of Surrey (1998–2000), and a Fellow at the Centre of Advanced Judaic Studies at the University of Pennsylvania (2000/2001).

Her publications, among others, include: *Auf der großen Straße: Jean Weidts Erinnerungen* (1984), *Tanz unterm Hakenkreuz* (1996, second edition 1999), *Hitler's Dancers: German Modern Dance and the Third Reich* (2003) and *Giselle* (2001, commissioned by the State Opera, Berlin).

Her main research and subsequent publications focus on the problems of exile, on dance and music history in the nineteenth and twentieth centuries and on dance aesthetics. Together with musicians Marshall Taylor and Samuel Hsu, she has organized and presented a series of concerts commemorating *Entartete Musik*, music forbidden by the Nazis.

Claudia Kappenberg trained in modern dance, Butoh and movement analysis, and danced professionally in Europe and New Zealand before moving to London in 1991. She studied Fine Art and completed an MA at Central St Martin's School of Art and Design in 1988, teaching on the BA Fine Art until 2002. She is now Lecturer on the Dance and Visual Arts Course at Brighton University.

Claudia worked with the Austrian expressionist dance choreographer, Hilde Holger, for many years and reconstructed and performed a number of her choreographies in London (South Bank Centre, 1996; Riverside Studios, 1998; and Lilian Baylis Theatre, 2000) and the Odeon Theater, Vienna, 1998.

She has exhibited and performed her work internationally, including 'Flush', performance installation, The White Space, London, 2004; *Flush*, as site-specific performance, Centre d'Art en Ile, Switzerland, 2002; *Aeolus*, film/video installation, Aldwych Underground Station, London, 2002; *Umbracadabra*, performance, Hazira Performing Arts, Jerusalem, Israel,

2001; Zim-Zum in *taffeta*, performance and video installation, Gallery Piano Noble, Geneva, Switzerland, 2000.

Commissions include: *Shingle Street*, dance video with Rosemary Lee/ Simon Whitehead, 2003; *Journeys*, video project with members of the deaf community, Camden Arts Centre, London, 2000 and multi-media projects with the Educational Departments of the Royal Opera House and the English National Opera in 1996/1997.

Deborah Levy has always written across the art forms. Her fiction includes *Beautiful Mutants* (1989), *Swallowing Geography* (1993), *The Unloved* (1994), *Billy and Girl* (1996). Her recent collection of short stories, *Pillow Talk In Europe And In Other Places* (2003), is published in the USA by Dalkey Archives Press. Five of these stories were broadcast on BBC Radio 4, as was her ten-part adaptation of Carol Shields' novel *Unless*. Plays written between 1987 and 2000 are published by Methuen in *Levy: Plays 1* (2000). Deborah has written about performance and contemporary culture for a number of anthologies and media, including texts for Forced Entertainment's *Marathon Lexicon of Performance* (2003), texts for *Changing States: Contemporary Art and Ideas in an Era of Globalisation* (2004), *Small Acts: Performance, the Millennium and the Marking of Time* (2000), an essay on the work of Rose English in *A Split Second Of Paradise* (1998) and she edited *Enhanced Performance* by Richard Layzell (1998). She is currently collaborating with German sculptor Asta Groting on a script for a ventriloquist and dummy *The Inner Voice/I am Big* for Theater Der Welt, Stuttgart, and the Museum of Modern Art, Oslo. Deborah is a visiting lecturer in Writing at the Royal College of Art. www.deborahlevy.co.uk.

foreword

donald hutera

Hybrid n. Offspring of two animals or plants of different species or varieties; person of mixed nationality; (fig.) thing, word, composed of incongruous element ~ adj. crossbred, mongrel; heterogeneous.

(*The Reader's Digest Great Encyclopaedic Dictionary* 1964, Volume One: 4)

Using expressionist movement vocabulary, and incorporating elements of cabaret, opera, dance theatre and vaudevillian humour, the work of Liz Aggiss and Billy Cowie is 'cross-genre – integrating film, text and music – and blurs the boundaries between high art and popular culture' (British Council, 2005).

Liz Aggiss and Billy Cowie are creative creatures – artmongers, auteurs, arch entertainers. Billy is the shy-seeming one, the quietly knowing composer-plus, anxious, perhaps, to be understood. Or to go his own way, with Liz prowling beside. She is the public face of Divas, a performer of ravenous and eccentric charm with a long, defiant jaw and a gimlet glint in the eye. Sleek and stealthy as a fox onstage and yet, like her and Billy's work itself, somehow direct, unhidden. Off-stage, Liz exudes a mix of almost maternal warmth and mischief, as if she could happily function as both instigatory colleague and role model/art-auntie to a generation of younger artists. Someone with a ready laugh and, like Billy, an invariably smart slant on a situation and its possibilities.

This is a thumbnail take on the Liz and Billy I have known – not deeply and, largely, if intermittently, through their work – since the mid to late 1980s. They are people about whom I feel I may be permitted to conjecture with first-name familiarity and, as a UK-based dance/performance journalist, about whose work I care.

As the company policy quoted above might suggest, that work can be hard to place. The diversification practised by Divas could be particularly disconcerting for spectators who like their cultural identifiers to be cut and dried, or who prefer the demarcation lines between genres and styles to be drawn in bold. I refer too to tut-tutting purists who are thrown by unpredictability or who wax squeamish at the sight of blood. Not literal gore, but rather the vital metaphorical fluid that may be spilled when the likes of Liz and Billy are operating in full flow.

In an essay in this book, the brainy dancer-choreographer Carol Brown dubs the pair 'smash and grab artists'. The phrase implies a violence born out of creative necessity, and predicated on the notion that you take what you need to make the work, no matter what the source. Yet whatever art forms they pillage, there is never a sense of the arbitrary in Liz and Billy's choices, nor any indiscriminate faffing about. Whether fashioning pieces for stage and screen, eye or ear, they seem to know exactly what they're after and how to go about getting it. That clarity of purpose tends to endow their work with a diamond hard ambiguity.

Take *Grotesque Dancer* (1986), an unforgettable chunk of transcendental Teutonic camp in which the style and atmosphere of the Weimar Republic is turned on its head and tickled. At the same time, its old, cold spirit is sucked up and spat out into the soup of post-feminist aesthetics. Dr Marion Kant examines this solo, and its acutely funny postmodern afterthought, *Hi Jinx* (1995), in a chapter that underlines Divas' status in the lineage of German expressionist Tanztheater. Set up as a mock lecture and featuring film clips, *Hi Jinx* has a built-in appeal for academics. Professor Sondra Fraleigh uses it as a springboard for her own essay, 'Deconstructing Heidi'.

Liz and Billy are as plainly adept at turning their hands to group pieces as they are at tailoring one-person shows to Liz's unique gifts. On the heels of *Grotesque Dancer* came such dazzling, distorted ensemble pieces as *Eleven Executions* (1988) and *Dorothy and Klaus* (1989), a lip-synced and highly gender-conscious dance-opera in which the mechanics of seduction and inspiration, exile and corruption were given the full Divas whack.

I finally caught up with the solo *Absurdities* a decade after its 1994 premiere. Better late than never. Cooing English and barking German in a short, snug silver dress, Liz makes a knowing spectacle of herself on a stage shared with a miniature stuffed monkey and a few phallic baguettes. The magnetic attraction of her precision exhibitionism resides in the contrasts between the naughty but nice, silly yet sophisticated. This book slips Deborah Levy's appreciation of Liz and Billy's exacting yet accommodating art, including *Absurdities*, in amongst the more scholarly musings.

Skipping ahead into another medium, there is the deceptively manic Gothic gorgeousness of the film *Motion Control* (2002). Read about it in Sherril Dodds' chapter 'Screen Divas'. Energetically pitched somewhere between dreams and nightmares, Liz and Billy's film work in general leans towards the weird, wacky and wonderful. Assembled in 2003, *Capture 3* was a touring collection of screen-based installations, more conventional single-screen films and new media works commissioned and funded by Arts Council England. *Men in the Wall* (2003) was one of the hits of the package. 3-D glasses enhanced this four-screen, stereoscopic dance-on-film installation. Situated against various backdrops (day, night, urban, coastal, etc.), each male – a mixed batch of builds, temperaments and nationalities – dwells in his own walled square. They talk, sing, play music and move in a fashion stamped with Liz and Billy's signature blend of quirky-humoured poetry and askew beauty.

Only the most onanistic artists function in a communication-free void. Most want to inspire and/or provoke both audiences and debate. Consider the implications of this publication and the accompanying DVD, a double-barrelled document that signals Liz and Billy's recognition of their place in (British) dance/theatre/performance/live-art history. Together, they proclaim the right of Divas' finely crafted amalgam of what could be called posh and pop culture to be taken seriously, or to be included at all.

The opposite seems to have happened with some regularity to a company that, on home turf, is located not very far south of centre (i.e. London) in Brighton. Yet despite Divas' proximity to the UK's dance capital, Liz and Billy have not always been invited to sit at the table, let alone received sufficient credit for their contribution to the feast. Small but perhaps significant examples of neglect are two Dance Books publications dating from 1992: Judith Mackrell's *Out of Line*, subtitled 'The Story of British New Dance'; and Stephanie Jordan's *Striding Out*, with 'Aspects of Contemporary and New Dance in Britain' as its titular appendage.

Starting in the 1960s, the label 'new dance' gained currency on both sides of the Atlantic, but particularly in Britain, as postmodernism's even more amorphous younger cousin. Unlike the durable if somewhat antiquated modern dance, today it is a term that is all but forgotten. In any case, neither Mackrell's nor Jordan's studies of it mention Aggiss, Cowie or Divas, even in the wake of about a dozen works made up to that time, including the seminal *Grotesque Dancer*. There are further sins of omission. When Debra Craine and Mackrell revamped the *Oxford Dictionary of Dance* for a 2000 publication date, again Aggiss, Cowie and Divas were absent. Not that I mean to point fingers, for they would need to be self-directed: the original edition of *The Dance Handbook*, which I co-authored with Allen Robertson in 1988, is likewise minus any Liz and Billy references.

That some of the freshest, most valuable examples of artistic expression materialize on the socio-cultural fringes is a potentially frustrating truism, because there is always the risk that they may be overlooked by the wider public. While I would hardly characterize Liz and Billy's work as mainstream, neither would I deem it inaccessible. It is simply its own animal, roaming through a territory it has staked out and claimed for itself. Is that why the work of Divas has sometimes fallen through the cracks and been unfairly marginalized, or altogether ignored?

I have no idea how Liz or Billy feel about this state of affairs or, indeed, whether or not they would even agree with my assessment of their situation. To expand on an earlier statement, they appear perfectly willing and able to get on with the business of Divas in their own indefatigable way. But, assuming my words contain even a nugget of truth, this book ought to go some way towards rectifying a sizeable and ongoing oversight. It's not that the depth, breadth and sheer longevity of the work needs to be legitimized. Rather, it is simply the case of giving credit where credit is due.

One of the publication's most salutary aspects is how well Liz and Billy's output stands up to close inspection and step-by-step analysis, without being either robbed of its import or drained of complex or cheeky life. For a dance/theatre hack like me, such reductivity is a primary danger when academia meets art. It has turned out to be eminently readable, whether via Dr Valerie Briginshaw's perspective on spoken and physical language in *Die Orchidee im Plastik Karton* (1989), or co-editor Ian Bramley's self-questioning look at the often divided critical response to the company. Liz herself deals with some of the chequered critique she, Billy and Divas have received in her chapters on reconstruction and what she calls 'Outsider Performance'. The book is further punctuated by her and Billy's methodically detailed thoughts on their own use of time and rhythm, space and visual metaphor.

Move beyond Britain again and even a glance at just a few of the countless possible contemporary artists whose work might be considered hybrid is enough to send me, at any rate, into an associative tail-spin. There's America's Meredith Monk flirting among the worlds of music, dance and film for the past four decades; Spanish-born dance artist La Ribot treating her own body like an installation site; Saburo Teshigawara choreographing, designing and compiling soundtracks for performances by his company Karas; and Israeli duo Inbal Pinto and Avshalom Pollak manipulating dancers and actors almost like puppeteers via live stagings that reference modern, classical, street and show dance, plus acrobatics, theatre, music hall, circus, movies and cartoons. Oh no, another double act. And yet another, José Montalvo and Dominique Hervieu, whose French-based Compagnie is known by their hyphenated surnames. The pair's productions toss together ballet, hip hop, African dance, flamenco and film. The many movement languages they plunder lend their shows a physically polyglot fizz in which everything is up for grabs. It is the skill with which they select and interweave the different styles wherein lies the true art.

Conclusions? I'm not sure I have any, other than the continued value of thinking outside the box, the idea that all good dance is good theatre, and the need for an artistic integrity that is greater than the sum of a work's parts. All of which speaks the word Divas.

acknowledgements

Thanks to: Amino, David Anderson, Lea Anderson, Arts Council England, John Ashford and The Place, Roger Bamber, Ken Bartlett and the Foundation for Community Dance, Jeddi Bassan and the Brighton Natural Health Centre, Jeff Baynes, BBC, Bob Bentley, Norma Binnie and the Gardner Arts Centre, Bonnie Bird, Val Bourne and Dance Umbrella, Anthony Bowne and Laban, Brighton Festival, Val Briginshaw and students from West Sussex Institute of Higher Education (now University College Chichester), the British Council, Neil Butler and The Zap, Rachel Canavan, Carousel, Assis Carrerio, Desi Cherrington, Chisenhale Dance Space, Emilyn Claid and Extemporary Dance Theatre, Anita Corbin, Ginny Farman, Jane Finnis, Caroline Freeman, Richard Gooderick, Portland Green, Liz Hall, Emma Haughton, High Spin, Nigel Hinds, Hilde Holger, Susie Holmes, Peter Hulton and the Live Arts Archive, the Institute of Contemporary Arts, Linda Jasper, Lois Keidan, Janet Lansdale and the University of Surrey, Lighthouse Film and Video, Bob Lockyer, Kay Lynn, Silke Mansholt, Dick Matchett, Jan Matthews and the University of Brighton Media Services, Ross McGibbon, Jennifer McLachlan, Nikki Milican, Ginny Munden, Holly Murray, Joe Murray, Paula Murray, Chris Nash, Sally Owen and Sue Booker and the London Studio Centre, Diane Parker, Sian Prime, Christian Pronay, Franta Provaznik, Simon Richards, Sal Robarts, Talia Rogers, Peter Seddon, Jeanette Siddall, Kathleen M. Smith, South East Dance Agency, Alistair Spalding and the South Bank Centre, Alex Suffolk, Christina Ure, Rodney Wilson, Bruce Brown, Karen Norquay and Jonathan Woodham at the University of Brighton Faculty of Arts and Architecture, and all the various performers in The Wild Wigglers and Divas.

The first draft of chapter 6 was published in *animated* magazine in Spring 2001, as was 'The rough guide to reconstruction' (chapter 14) in Summer 1999. Both essays have been rewritten for this publication and are reproduced by permission of the Foundation for Community Dance (Tel: 0116 251 0516; email: info@communitydance.org.uk).

The films *Beethoven in Love* and *Motion Control* are part of the film collection of Arts Council England and are copyright of Arts Council

England and BBC Television. You are licensed to use them for individual study only. For any other educational use, for example teaching in a classroom, you must obtain a licence from Concord Video, http://www.concordvideo.co.uk.

Extracts from *El Puñal entra en el Corazón*: Music copyright Billy Cowie. Lyrics copyright Herederos de Federico García Lorca. *Solo tu Corazón Caliente* by Federico García Lorca, copyright Herederos de Federico García Lorca. All rights reserved. SGAE. PRCS. All rights reserved.

Further information on Liz Aggiss and Billy Cowie can be found at: http://www.anarchicdance.com; http://www.lizaggiss.com; http://www.billycowie.com.

introduction
navigating the known

liz aggiss and billy cowie

Welcome to our world. We have been creatively joined at the hip since 1980. We met in Brighton on a piano stool, fielding a heated debate with an unwieldy group of visual and performing arts students who wanted to deconstruct 'Funky Town' and give it a 'make-over'. Enough said. After 25 collaborative years, we are still debating what, why, where, when, who-with, what-for, which-way and how. We started to collaborate because we knew no better. We carried on because there was no reason not to. We continue because we have a tried and tested working method that supports our individual strengths. We will continue because we share a common artistic vision with room for debate.

We have been comfortable in being 'maverick hybrids', and have over the years devised dance theatre, cabaret, live art, single and multiple screen dance installation and live performance installation. Our work is presented under our names, Aggiss and Cowie, but also under the umbrella title Divas Dance Theatre. Since one of our primary artistic concerns focuses on the choreographed body, we are most often located within the British dance environment. The shifting hierarchies we employ, whether we use the live or screen space, are as much about being able to work in hybrid practices as they are about being fascinated by the friction between and the reconciliation of distinct aesthetics and disciplines. Our work is driven by content, explores body politics and the performer as subject, and makes commentaries on language, word-play, age, death, love, power, Thatcher, diversity and difference. The physicality of the work is dominated by a trademark grotesque, stylized, dance-performance vocabulary. The choreography is collaged, cut and sited within dramatic visuality. We aim to entertain, provoke, challenge and inspire, and blur the boundaries between high art and popular culture. Our need is not to resist classification but to re(de)fine our own.

Our practice has in no small way been informed by our working as tutors of visual performance within an art school environment at the University of Brighton.[1] There we have attracted those students who fall between the floorboards of dance and art, and have taught them within the 'creative mess' of a visual art environment. The courses we led strove to establish a performance identity informed by appropriate visual media, suitably installed or located, and underpinned by a contextual theoretical research. The student body, at the inception of these particular courses, was a political animal and was instrumental in challenging the prevailing structures and institutional attitudes – in the process spawning some fascinating independent artists.[2] Their insistent creative and energetic ebb and flow provoked discussions that impacted on our own research and development. The question of whether we were being deliberately anarchic was not the issue. We were, and are, artists and, like the students we taught, we are making and defining our world.

In developing the structure of this book, we invited a range of contributors: academics, theoreticians, writers, performers and critics, all of whom were familiar with our work, to hone in on specific pieces from our repertoire. Inasmuch as our practice has been broad, the collection of essays in this book similarly identify 'other' ways of writing about dance, and nestle alongside current debates on what constitutes practice-based research. We invited the contributors to brand their discussions with their various writing expertises – historical, theoretical, academic, critical, analytical, performative – and we gave them carte blanche to maintain their individual voices. In fact we insisted on it. Indeed, we hope you will feel feverishly excited by some of the more maverick texts that punctuate and inform the more academic contributions. In this spirit of difference and diversity we urge you to read the writers' biographies, which go some way towards explaining the diversity of function and form, and the peculiarities and anomalies that jostle for space with each other in this publication. We have also given ourselves a voice by contributing eight essays. The house style of this book is that there is no house style.

Throughout the book there are many instances of cross-referencing and some repetition of facts. This enables the reader to sample any essay independently of the others and saves them from experiencing a sense of inadequacy and failure by not cantering through the whole book in one fell swoop. Additionally, the reader can sometimes experience the same work from a variety of different perspectives (not always in agreement), and be enriched and enchanted by the plethora of methodologies, 'languages' and voices.

Scattered throughout the essays are DVD references. They look like this – (DVD 3:4) – and refer directly to the issues being discussed. This provides an unparalleled opportunity for the reader to match words to movement. Some of the essays have multiple references to different works and consequently each has a page on the DVD that contains all the information for that essay in a numbered sequence.

The filmed documentation of our live works ranges from the non-existent in the early years through to the frankly shabby, adequate and finally brilliant. This is partly due to the increase in availability, and fall in expense, of video equipment over this period, but also due to a change in our perspective. Initially, we were so knackered by producing the work that documentation was the last thing on our minds – years later we would realize that not a scrap of a piece remained, and was in effect lost forever.

So of the early works, *Kakarella Ka Diva* (1986) and *Dva Sa Momimomuvali* (1986), nothing remains. *Grotesque Dancer* (1986) and *Dorothy and Klaus* (1989), on the other hand, were filmed in studios using several cameras, while most of the others are single-camera documentations of live performances. Our dance work made specifically for screen is, of course, not documentation but a genre in its own right, and a whole other marvellous ball game. In compiling the DVD we have been principally concerned with illustrating the essays, so we have on occasion included work that is not of the highest quality in filmic terms. We hope that as you look through the haze of second-generation VHS copies you will be so intrigued by the content that you will forgive us.

As for the 'who did what' question, we should say that, from the outset, all our work is truly collaborative, from the ground up. Inhabiting the dance world, however, by default rather than choice, the question of choreographer most often arises in the minds of critics. Aggiss, being the one who physically fronts the outfit, nearly always gets the blame (or sometimes praise) for the movement. However, the fact is that, after the first few productions, whichever of us was feeling most inspired would take up the choreographic baton and run with it until we were floored by the other's barbed, critical and caustic comments. Latterly we prag-matically sliced up the works into manageable chunks and negotiated who would do which aspects of the 'steps' as we like to call them. Strangely the Yin/Yang combination of Aggiss, the 'stand-up dancer' who can actually perform the movements, and Cowie the 'armchair choreographer' who can only dream them, works surprisingly well. Ironically, or is it tragically, both of us could bring dancers to tears by asking them to do things they couldn't do – Cowie by demanding the truly impossible and Aggiss by demanding the possible (but only by herself). Similarly the texts and music, while seeming more Cowie's department, arise organically from the nature and construction of the works and are once again truly collaborative. As an example, when presented with the first two pages of the script of *Absurditties* (1994) which contained only the word 'my' 79 times, Aggiss was heard to sigh, 'Is that it?' To Cowie's challenge, 'It's not what you say, it's the way that you say it', she rose magnificently, though she says it herself (DVD 1:1).

Notes

1   From approximately 1980 to 2000, after which we moved to the relatively calmer waters of research at the same institution.

2   Among the many passing through our sticky fingers were: Anne Seagrave, Fiona Wright, Silke Mansholt, Miriam King, Ian Smith, Michael Pinsky, Louise Rennison, Marisa Carnesky, George Chakravarthi, Magali Charrier and Alison Murray.

the aesthetics of smash and grab

carol brown

Introduction

> She thrusts her limbs like sharp vectors, spiking the space around her; these propulsive displacements are deviated flows and delicate tangles of visual, acoustic and kinetic perceptions. Her movements are swift, sharp, seductive and insistent; *they demand our attention*. She speaks, turning words around with incantatory rhythmic pulsing; how playfully she dismembers texts braiding languages into a polyvocal plait. What a relief to be in a place where daily politeness is superseded by this naked voice, which sweats and sings.[1]

In the theatre with Divas we are in a country of others. Aggiss and Cowie are smash and grab artists, eclectically borrowing from a range of different dance and performance styles and making them into their own inimitable blended form. Quoting ballet, bondage and bolero, and incorporating elements of cabaret, opera and dance theatre, their works are inherently cross-genre. Unclassifiable, dodging categorization and the taxonomies of sameness through their raids on a host of languages and media, their work exists within a range of locations. On stage and on screen they blur genres and the boundaries between high art and popular culture.

In reviving memories of traces of four Divas' works – *Absurdities* (1994), *No Man's Land* (1993), *Falling Apart at the Seams (so it seems)* (1993), and *The Fetching Bride* (1995) – I am going to draw on feminist philosophy to read and interpret the political heart of their contents. Some of this work is based on earlier research undertaken in the early 1990s, for I must confess to my partiality to their work and own up to my attachments.

Without models it is hard to work, without mentors it can be difficult to speak. I came to know Aggiss through our shared heritage. Both of us studied European expressionist dance theatre and met in the classes of Hilde Holger.[2] During a period of doctoral research, I invited Aggiss to be my mentor. Liz Aggiss continues to be an invisible guest in the process of my performance-making. Watching from a distance she is an inimitable arbiter of style, alive to the faithfulness of a work and its capacity to match feeling to content whilst defying the expected, the sane and routinized.

Dancing genealogy

Dancing is an inter-generational process; our bodies are repositories not only of strong memories but also other bodies and other styles of the flesh; as Peggy Phelan states, 'our own body . . . is the one we have and the history of the ones we've lost' (1993: 172). We learn how to dance through the motions of others, and it is their bodies that hold us in sway. In Divas' performance I witness the fleshy materialism of a genealogy of dance culture; a lineage of descent from European expressionism tracked through the work of women performers like Valeska Gert, Mary Wigman and Hilde Holger. The performance mode of Divas is highly stylized and expressionistic. It frequently incorporates parodic measures of excess, irony, the grotesque and caricature, and traces its roots to the expressionist tradition of Tanztheater and cabaret, which flourished in 1920s Germany and Austria. Expressionist dance radically challenged and revolutionized the performance habits of a classical inheritance. Instead of the 'one size fits all' of the classical body, expressionist women breached the borders of 'good' taste with their appropriation of a range of diverse 'others'. Valeska Gert epitomized the work of this generation of innovators:

> I performed theatre, I longed for the dance; I danced, I longed for the theatre. I was in conflict until the idea occurred to me to combine them: I wanted to dance human characters. I invented an intricate fabric, one of whose strands was modern dance-pantomime; another strand was abstract dance; other strands were satiric dances, dances to sounds, expressionistic dances. I exploded a bundle of stimuli on the world; other dances would make a whole programme out of a single strand, but for me they were loud, whizzing little rockets shooting around the world.
>
> (Gert 1995: 33)

Can one body become a shelter for a community of others? In Divas' work, Aggiss's body as host is visited by a variety of performing personas. They make a home for themselves, posturing and speaking through the syntax of a multiplicity of languages: Polish, Spanish and German. As a contortionist, a fabulist and a caricaturist, the agility of Liz Aggiss to inhabit a series of different identities and yet remain inimitably her-self refuses a reductive singular identity. She must be read as mobile and polyvocal, an unpredictability which unsettles, an 'I/eye' which is not one.[3]

For here we have a female performer whose aura continues a lineage of theatre dance that figures the body as a transgressive, subversive site. In particular, she resists the encoding of the female dancer as feminine. She stamps, she thrusts, she ex-poses herself, she does not contain herself, she is sensuous and seductive, she takes her gaze out to meet the gaze of those 'others', her audience. Her work speaks of the forbidden aspects of being in the flesh and is at the same time proud to be flesh. As a performer she meets the gaze of the audience, not with mute blankness, but with an active reciprocating look which invites her audience in to her co-authored space of invention. She is perceived differently not as an object of a desiring gaze but as the subject of invention.

Flesh laid bare

In *Absurdities* (1994) Aggiss, dressed in a silver frock with a baguette as prop, talks, sings and moves around a bare stage. *Absurdities* is about language, about the playfulness of words and their meanings and about juxtapositions or the 'posing of juxtas' between mathematics, animals and food. It comprises 11 short scenes of grammatical curiosities. Dada meets Barthes (DVD 2:1).

She self-instructs: 'Bear left', and she steps deliberately to the left, 'Bare all', and she removes a pair of silver knickers from under her short silver dress.[4] As she bends to pull off these underpants, she holds her hand to her chest, modestly concealing her cleavage as site/sight. The implied striptease in the lower half of her body is paired with a modest gesture of concealment in her upper body. This double gesture, at once revealing and concealing, can be read as an instance of feminine anxiety; that a woman performer is a marked marker, a site rather than subject of desire (DVD 2:2).

Absurdities is a work in which Aggiss as performer exists within a slipstream of roles as singer, stripper, comedienne, parodist and linguist. Aggiss performs multiplicity: she 'bares all' again and again and again, peeling off one layer of knickers after another like so many layers of skin, not to reveal more nakedness but yet more layers. For there is no naked core and no shame, just more costume cut from skin. The French choreographer Jerome Bel, in *Shirtologie* (1998), similarly layers clothing to 'stuff' the body with significance by signalling the costume as a carrier of signs (Ploebst 2001). In this solo performance, Bel peels off T-shirt after T-shirt, each revealing its own message or 'sign' printed on the front of the shirt. This idea of the body as revealing its own significance is explored by Roland Barthes in *The Pleasure of the Text* as 'that moment when my body pursues its own ideas – for my body does not have the same ideas I do' (1975: 17). Both Divas and Jerome Bel produce an intertextuality of theatre through the encoding of the body and the play of cultural signs, 'writing aloud' across its surface (Barthes 1975: 66).

I married a monster

The playfulness of a woman's body simultaneously revealed and concealed within *Absurditties* gives way to images of fetishistic violation in a later work, *The Fetching Bride* (1995). This darkly satirical work is based on the theme of an arranged marriage. If men territorialize women, can women not also territorialize men; what monsters then? In *The Fetching Bride* both roles, the seducer and seduced, are played by women. The Groom[5] is dressed as a man in a black leather suit. The Bride is dressed in an 'exotic black bridal dress' (Figure 2.1). The bending of gender within the performance defies the travesty of female to male cross-dresser by also being a performance of a heterosexual contract as a contract killing. The bride empties herself into the groom. She assumes an imposture, a deliberate fakeness, averting the reductive definitions that congeal around a woman dancing a role as a woman (DVD 2:3).

Figure 2.1 'Wedding March' – Liz Aggiss in *The Fetching Bride*. Photo: *Roger Bamber, 1995.*

But the contradictory impulses of Divas' work remain. In the final scene of this opera dance, the Bride lies on a table, alone and naked. Her arms frame her head; her legs are splayed out as she lies on her back in an exposed position. Trembling, she moves by slowly weaving her legs through a V-shape, opening and closing, containing and expanding the volume of her body. By animating her body in this way she draws attention both to the vaginal void and to the ensnared meanings to which this zone of a woman's anatomy gives birth. Is she complicitous or devious in doing so? The work is shocking in its sensuality and explicitness but it is the music, a lament, which evokes the sense of a sombre sacrifice. The work veers dangerously close towards the Christian imagery of self-flagellation and martyrdom of female flesh but is perhaps redeemed by its sense of irony in self-consciously portraying her body as open and pliable, being literally married to a host of other meanings. Like an operatic diva who must be killed or seduced at the finish of the opera, she is both dead and sexed. Has she sacrificed herself to a love death or is this an attempt by the woman to reclaim her body for her self within the narration of her own desire? The image is unsettling and open-ended (DVD 2:4).

The dilemma for the Bride in Divas' *The Fetching Bride* is that she is in a no-win situation. The death of the marital contract as heterodoxy is signified by a death drive. The performance in this sense is a deliberate travesty on the institution of marriage, a performance meditation on the violations of misogyny.

> Theatre returns us to the living part of death, or the mortal part of life. I go to the Theatre because I need to understand or at least to contemplate the act of death, or at least to accept it, to meditate on it. And also because I need to cry.
>
> (Cixous 1995: 342)

When the Groom harnesses the Bride, the reins on her body and her brain are ideological as much as physical. She is held in a vice grip of sexual submission. Yet she strains, pulling against the holding reins, and stamps her feet. What resists? What are the possibilities of overcoming her passionate attachment to these rites of subjection (DVD 2:5)?

Twentieth-century feminism sought to bring women 'into the light', to give them visibility through access to representation and confer on them the status of subject. But, as the work of writers such as Judith Butler (1993) make clear, this 'becoming subject' is at the same time also radically subjected. She is both produced and regulated, subject and object. In this sense, the contract between man and woman in the marriage of relations might also be read as the contract between spectator and performer in the empire of the gaze.

Minefields

As feminist performance theorists have revealed, for a woman dancing, the stage is jammed with prior constructs – dances, choreographies, spectacles, performances, displays – that implicate her body as an idealized sign and object par excellence. As a woman dancing it is impossible to discount this past. I can no more install the primacy of my experience as a 'woman' without also addressing the social and cultural embeddedness of gendered markings on my body than explore how these markings are implicated in the apparatus of representation. In other words, the apparatus of representation is a minefield for a woman's body.

According to de Lauretis, for a woman to represent herself without relying on the existing narratives of gender does not mean a search for a utopian she-space, but a working in the margins of hegemonic discourses, in the gaps in existing institutional spaces. As she states:

> The movement in and out of gender as ideological representation . . . is a movement back and forth between the representation of gender (in its male-centered frame of reference) and what that representation leaves out, or, more pointedly makes unrepresentable.
>
> (De Lauretis 1987: 26)

A Divas production, which appeared to directly interrogate this space outside the malestream, was No Man's Land (1993). The work was performed by 18 women, whose ages ranged from 9 to 60. Comprising 12 short dances, the performance presented a series of vignettes of personal experiences shared between women. The women's movements were simple gestures and interactions involving group ensemble work, solos and duets. Crossing race, class, age and sexualities, their dances opened the performance space to often unrecognized and denied facets of experience whilst negotiating dominant images of the female sex through assertions of women's agency.

The presence of live music and voice – four women cellists and three female singers performing in Polish – reinforced the sense of a diverse community of women articulating the fullness of bodily experience. In one dance, 'Egg Dance', the two older women of the group slowly step forward from the main body of dancers arranged in a semicircle on chairs facing the audience. A red cushion lies on the floor and they arrange themselves around this; one kneels and the other stands behind her holding an egg in each hand. A slow, dignified dance involving the passing of these eggs between the women, and their touching, of looks and hands, emerges in the shared space. Affirming the presence of older women's sexualities and physicalities, this dance spoke of loss, the maturation process and fecundity (DVD 2:6).

In the 'Kissing Dance' two young women engage in an extended kiss. Touching lips but not torsos, the space and air between them remains a current of energy and potential becomings. In this image there is a sense of both interconnection and autonomy. The dancers are immersed and yet separated. The sustained kiss in its discreteness exceeds our expect-ations. In reading this dance through the writings of French feminist philosopher Luce Irigaray, in particular her symbolization of the 'two lips' and the mucosity of feminine exchanges, it is possible to delve deeper into the potential meanings embedded within the work (DVD 2:7).

Irigaray proposes a new representation of female sexuality from the perspective of women's *jouissance*, or pleasure in autoeroticism. According to her, woman touches herself all the time, for her labia are always caressing: 'I would like us to play together at being the same and different. You/I exchanging selves endlessly and each staying herself. Living mirrors' (Irigaray 1981b: 61).

Irigaray challenges the ocularcentrism of Western culture through privileging touch, in auto-affection and in an economy of exchanges between women. In *No Man's Land*, relations between women were explored through dialogues of touch, voice and vision. Through these interventions the work opened a space and became a proposition for the stage as a scene where a woman's life takes place. In gestures passed on from one woman to another, their outstretched limbs touch and transmit meaning through generations. Their gestures reach beyond the temporal now, unfolding through generations, installing a simultaneity of percep-tions through a matrilineal inheritance between mothers and daughters, grandmothers and grandchildren.

Coming a-cropper: *Falling Apart at the Seams*

The exclusive practices of dance refuse admission to the 'unbound' body. That is the body that exceeds our expectations of a dancerly body: a fleshy body, an ageing body, a chaotic, undisciplined body, an abject body and a body of ambiguous sex. Feminists have demonstrated how dominant constructions of meaning deny visibility to certain kinds of bodies and certain modes of experience. As Elizabeth Grosz (1987)

explains, reconstituting the body in feminist terms entails refuting the
bifurcatedness of the male/female dichotomy by insisting on the multiplicity of many different kinds of bodies. As she claims, we need to
overcome the dominance of certain kinds of bodies and hence subjec-
tivities. Why not the ageing body, the fleshy body, the sweating, helpless
body, the out of control body, the unstable body?

In *Falling Apart at the Seams* (*so it seems*) (1993), Divas produced a satirical
tragic–comic 'rock opera' on abjection, and the sense of 'falling apart'
which can accompany injury, ageing and illness. The work combines the
wit of stand-up comedy, the pleasurable word games of performance
poetry and the hyperbole of operatic arias. It begins with Aggiss in a two-
dimensional cardboard dress performing a two-dimensional dance. As a
flattened out body-without-organs, she details the siting/sighting of her
liver in a butcher's shop. She mimics the response of the butcher to her
questioning of its destiny; he's taking it home for his wife's birthday
dinner, she reveals. Unfazed by the alcohol-soaked liver, he declares it
will be flambéed (DVD 2:8). Elsewhere in the work the standing-on-one-
leg dancer describes lost legs, fingers that drop off and arms that fray and
disintegrate. As a play on the abject horrors of the body it satirizes the
inability of a youth-obsessed culture to represent ageing female bodies.
In contrast to this, it perversely proclaims the ephemerality of the
body through its representation as fragmented, liable to decay and even
death. In one song the dancers sing to all the lost, dead babies buried in a
metaphorical 'underground' (DVD 2:9).

In its original incarnation, the work was a duet for opera singer
Naomi Itami and Liz Aggiss. Co-directed by Divas and British
comedienne Louise Rennison, it became one of the company's most
renowned pieces. The music, composed by Billy Cowie, takes the form of
five songs sung in Italian and accompanied by a contemporary electronic
score. In my view, much of the appeal of this work stemmed from its
blending of songs and antics played out between the two 'divas', whose
hauteur and blending of high and low art forms created a comedic front
for what is essentially quite a serious subject, the physical borders of a
human being. The 'falling' of the title can be read through the process of
ageing tissues that over time lose resistance to gravity and sag. It also
relates to the suggestion of corpses or cadaver from the Latin *cadere*,
meaning to fall. In making sport of the borders of flesh, there is a perverse play at work here. The concept of the abject is closely related to
perversion. As Julia Kristeva states, 'The abject is perverse because it
neither gives up nor assumes a prohibition, a rule, or a law, but turns
them aside, misleads, corrupts, uses them, takes advantage of them'

(Kelly 2002: 241). A dance culture that prefers exaltation to degradation is troubled by the appearance of visceral excess and makes a taboo of certain subjects and zones of flesh. But the feminine perversity at work here is a writing out loud of that which is disavowed within the mainstream.

Conclusion: Cut-ups and take-outs

Divas' performances are short, sharp ruptures in the social fabric.[6] They delve into the sufferings, pleasures and playfulness of being human through a performance style which is engaging and entertaining. Their method draws on techniques of montage and collage, layering body narratives and pin-pointing these in often extreme and exaggerated ways through movement, gesture, speech, song and design. This metaphorical cutting up of texts and body parts, through display, examination and revelation, creates a split, a cleavage in the social fabric, and an opening for the spectator to enter the work in a state of disbelief.

The use of a collage structure for combining fragments and short-cuts denies any sense of an internal coherence and what Lyotard calls 'the solace of good forms' (1984: 81). Collage techniques are favoured within postmodernism for their ability to destabilize the closure of the artefact around linear structures. The images of Divas thus have an unsettling power in their often contradictory impulses. Yet at the same time, Aggiss, in dancing her mobile identities, is also inimitably her own visceral signature. It is her face that flinches, grimaces and mocks. Dexterous hands and agile facial expressions are essential elements of the microphysics of her style. Hands and face are also the most personalized zones of our bodies. It is the handprint that informs our biological and cultural identity, and the face that is our mark in the world. We feel we know her but then she goes and surprises us, unexpectedly.

Through their performances, Divas explore deviant as well as marginalized images of sexuality and stylizations of gender-as-performance, in defiance of normative images of particularly female bodies. These gestures can be seen to reach toward the representation of the something 'other' in the realm of the unrepresentable. And, from a feminist perspective, to represent a politics in the flesh.

In watching these incursions into the unrepresentable, I am conscious of a continuum of embodied knowledge from the grotesque and parodic dancers of the expressionist era. In this way Divas' performances can be said to communicate a coexistence of differences in a continuity between past and present, night and day, eroticism and memory, male and female.

Notes

1   Text written by the author as part of a pre-show discussion introducing the work of Divas at the University of Surrey Guildford, Performing Arts Studio, 30 November 1994.
2   Holger was an early pupil of Gertrud Bodenwieser, a leading exponent of Ausdruckstanz in Central Europe, 1920–38.
3   See Irigaray (1985).
4   Costume design by Tig Evans.
5   In the original version, commissioned for the University of Surrey Guildford for the Dance and Discourse Conference, the opera singer Chloe Wright performed the role of the Groom, and the Bride was Liz Aggiss. In a later version performed at the South Bank Centre, London, the role of the Groom was performed by Liz Aggiss and the Bride was Colette Sadler. The singer, whilst on stage, is separated from the role of the Groom.
6   All work is written, choreographed and constructed jointly by Liz Aggiss and Billy Cowie.

writing dance

deborah levy

When Liz Aggiss was 17 years old, she had a profound realization while watching the smash hit TV series, *The Good Old Days*. This famous family show was filmed at The City Varieties in Leeds. Britain's longest running music hall, it featured a programme of Victorian acts performed in full costume to a live audience. On this occasion a mezzo soprano made her way onto the stage, opened her arms, sang a fulsome C so powerfully the floorboards trembled and then shouted to the audience: 'All together now!' Aggiss thought, 'Well YES, why not?' The moment in which a skill was delivered with a sliver of self-mockery stuck with her forever. In a few years' time, she would train with Hanya Holm in Colorado and then Hilde Holger in the UK — but that chance TV moment would become a major ingredient in the aesthetic of what later became Divas. Liz Aggiss was going to have to find a collaborator who would savour that moment in the same way she did and have a grip on how to translate it in performance; someone who would share her love affair with German expressionism, her admiration for Max Wall (glimpsed by Aggiss at a gig actually dressed as a wall), the grotesque and startling dances of Valeska Gert, the sexiness of Weimar cabaret, the spectacle of Marlene Dietrich maliciously seducing her way through the *Blue Angel* — all somehow wrapped up in that 'All together now!' atmosphere of British music hall.

This person would turn out to be a pale Scottish classical musician who practised his cello for hours a day and probably never watched *The Good Old Days*. Billy Cowie, a dazzlingly talented wunderkind, went on to study music and composition at Edinburgh University and there began to feel a pang for a life outside the constraints of the classical repertoire. Awarded a first class honours degree, he won a scholarship to study composition and electronic music in Milan and Liège, and then made his way to Cologne to train with Stockhausen. Cowie also wrote poems and texts on the sly, read voraciously, possessed a dark laconic humour and formed a band called Birds with Ears.

Fast forward a few years. Aggiss and Cowie, who at this point don't know each other, land in Brighton where they start teaching dance and music at what used to be the College of Arts, now Brighton University where Aggiss is Professor of Visual Performance. One day they wanted the student dancers to collaborate with the musicians, and when the dancers didn't know how to, Liz got up and showed them. Billy directed from the sidelines. An artistic collaboration that would still be going from strength to strength 20 years later had begun.

I mention these beginnings because, although interdisciplinarity has now become a key word in education and contemporary culture, there was a time when the term 'interdisciplinary artist' provoked real confusion, if not derision. How artists are formed, and how they come to make the art they do, is often a series of pleasurable accidents. But, as Simone de Beauvoir might have said after she had drunk a bottle of Bacardi and found herself sitting naked on Jean Paul Sartre's lap: 'We're not born interdisciplinary artists, we become one.'

We become interdisciplinary artists because there is a language we want to make. All serious, shining artists make new language, a language that has references and cross overs to other languages, but whose own innovations extend, change and add dissonance to the vocabularies of the established language. It's what James Joyce did with *Ulysses*, what Pina Bausch did with her ensemble of women dancers in high heels, what John Lydon did in a string vest, what Picasso did with paint and bicycle saddles, what Vivienne Westwood did with the way she cut material, what Forced Entertainment did with words scrawled on pieces of cardboard, what Duchamp did with sugar lumps and a birdcage, what Alison Goldfrapp did when her voice shivered its way onto the CD that became *Felt Mountain*, and what Aggiss and Cowie did when their synthesis of movement, music and text gave us an unexpected view of what dance was supposed to be.

Cowie's text for Divas can broadly be described as performative writing and on the page they look like poems. His texts are formal, rhythmic, pared, written for Aggiss's inflections and (with the exceptions of *Absurditties*, 1994) spoken on microphone. Much theory has been written about performative writing and it has subsequently become a rather mysterious term in which its heavy-hearted practitioners mutter, 'no metaphor, just metonymy' or 'our task is to create new ontologies and epistemologies'. A raspberry ripple of critical theory runs through a whole generation's texts for performance and, ironically, deforms its performativity. These leaden reflexive texts have been quite pervasive in much postmodern dance and performance: a fug of semiotics, psychoanalysis, biography, art history and critical theory which, strange to relate, its practitioners must believe – as they move through space glumly incanting this stuff – is a better night out than listening to the shipping forecast at home. To be kinder, this writing is probably something we grow out of when we are less depressed or when we find ourselves a girlfriend or boyfriend, or, even, as our skills as artists develop and we no longer feel we have to prove to our peers that we read difficult, complex and fascinating books.

Nevertheless, it is really to Divas' credit that they have never lost sight of working an audience whilst at the same time creating dark and unsettling performances. Their visual, physical and musical vocabularies are startling and odd, but they don't tell us why this is so; they forge an imaginative contract with the audience from the start. Neither do they drone on about 'desire' or instruct us how to think or tell us what Walter Benjamin thinks. For these small mercies we must be grateful and perhaps even forgive them the terrible jokes between scenes.

Cowie's texts are site-specific because they are written for Aggiss's voice and body and for Divas' many collaborators, taking into account their linguistic quirks or the way they walk or the faces they can pull. Likewise, Divas' shows often include professional singers which means Aggiss/Cowie will choreograph around the singers' physical abilities, creating a kinetic relationship between everyone on stage with her (Aggiss keeping the best frock for herself, of course). Cowie's texts leave space for the performer to interpret, invent, enact and rewrite. *Falling Apart at the Seams (so it seems)* (1993) was commissioned by the Gardner Arts Centre and performed at the Spring Loaded festival at The Place, London, and at the Purcell Room at London's South Bank Centre. It has echoes of a Dadaesque mini-variety show – I'm thinking here of Hugo Ball reading his abstract phonetic poems in a cardboard costume – 'gadji beri bimba glandridi laula lonni cadori' – to a baffled audience of minor aristocrats and army generals. Not the usual Spring Loaded audience these days, but had the army and aristocracy come to the show, they would have twigged that *Falling Apart at the Seams* was also a showcase for Cowie's sensational and electrifying music, sung by Naomi Itami, with monologues written for Aggiss, delivered at the microphone wearing a sculptural cardboard dress (Figure 3.1, DVD 3:1).

> I'm falling apart at the seams so it seems
> My arms are all frayed I'm afraid
> My insides are out and they're lying about
> I'm falling apart at the seams

Primarily, Cowie's words are written to create an event, that is to say text is completed in action. Part of this action is movement, music and

Figure 3.1 'Falling Apart' – Liz Aggiss in *Falling Apart at the Seams*. *Photo: Roger Bamber, 1993.*

the composition of objects and images – the task being to get all the languages at play to speak to each other. At times his texts and lyrics have something of the atmosphere of Paul Eluard's poetry crossed with a rock song (DVD 3:2).

> Fright Fright
> jostling near the edge
> Dark night
> Way down there below
> Hold me tight
> Is it time to go now
> Might might
> think that I was rather scared
>
> Left right
> marching on to glory
> Bite Bite
> the bullet so they say
> Don't fight
> No matter how they cry
> quite quite
> sad to say goodbye

A device Cowie often uses is to have two very different experiences of the same text running parallel to each other. In *Falling Apart at the Seams*, Aggiss's text about losing parts of her body in shops and on park benches is spoken in a pool of light, while her legs appear to go one way, her arms the other. Meanwhile, in a parallel spotlight, Itami sings a classical aria, 'La Mia giunture'. We watch her take the breath she needs to get to certain notes, hands clasped to the heart, adding another layer to what Aggiss has just spoken, creating in her stillness and with the force of her voice an atmosphere of controlled panic. Later, when Naomi and Liz crawl on the floor under green light, looking for 'the dead' (DVD 3:3), Aggiss dances with a black hood over her head while Naomi sings 'Qualche nostro amici' like any diva on an opera stage. It is this juxta-position of the surreal and the classical that is most distinctive about the Divas language. There is never any pretence that this is not a live show or that the audience does not exist. While a prop is being brought on stage or a mike adjusted, Cowie scripts banter between the performers: a mixture of deadpan everyday anecdotes and absurd word play – its subject matter ranging from when Liz injured her Achilles tendon to Naomi accusing Liz of being morbidly preoccupied with death.

Another distinguishing feature of the Divas œuvre is that Cowie often uses an irreverent splattering of European languages, presumably because he likes how they sound and Aggiss enjoys shouting (especially in German), but also to change the pace, focus and rhythm of a sequence or scene. Divas use spoken text to create a very direct relationship with the audience, more often a live voice than a voice-over. This relationship is most developed in *Absurditties*, described by Aggiss as 'stand-up dance'. A solo performance with no music and very few props (a toy monkey, two hoops and a baguette), Cowie's extremely skilled text works with Aggiss's dynamic performing presence and expressionist vocabulary with complete synergy; in fact, *Absurditties* is a small masterpiece that resonates long after the show has finished.

Dressed in a small mini sliver of a silver dress, with matching shoes and pants, Aggiss, muscular with flame coloured hair, struts around the stage declaiming Cowie's text in a spectrum of inflections (DVD 3:4):

My my my
My my my
My my my
My my my
My my my
My my my

My my my
My my my
My mother said
I never should
Talk to the animals
In the
'Would that I were in England
Now that Spring is'
Here's a funny thing
As I was walking down the road
I met a man
Whose insincerity showed
I could see it in his eyes – everything he said
He was lying

Aggiss points to the parts of her body she feels to be imperfect as she mutters 'My my my', often leaving a long gap between one line and another. This is not naturalistic speech and it enables her to be very free on stage, despite its formal metre, rhythmic oddness and word play. Some of the inflections resemble Tommy Cooper at his best. (I'm thinking of how Cooper walked on stage dressed as Hamlet, holding a skull in his hand, and muttered: 'To be or not to be. I've had a terrible day.') Because Cowie feels free to introduce an entirely new subject or association in the middle of a line, in some ways Aggiss is really giving expression to a text that resembles a musical score. Absurd, eccentric, amusing, *Absurditties* is also at times strangely melancholy and always beautiful. This is largely to do with the intelligence with which Aggiss moves through space and how she punctuates the text. Her body is strong, disciplined, uninhibited; she never has the 'neutral' or expressionless face that is often the case in much modern dance. In fact, in this particular show, with the help of Cowie's text, Aggiss shows herself to be one of the great female performers of her generation. When she puns on the words 'bear' and 'bare' (DVD 3:5):

Bear left step step step
bear right step step
Bear up stamp stamp stamp
Bear the pants off

and in vaudeville fashion takes off her knickers (she has about ten pairs on), she examines the gaze of the audience on a female dancer, both self-mocking and mocking of the history of how a dancer is supposed to behave and what she is supposed to look like. She is certainly not supposed to bend her knees, take a deep breath and utter a long, loud impersonation of a monkey (DVD 3:6):

> Don't you make a monkey out of Gus
> because he never got eleven plus
> you see the poor thing thinks
> comparison all stinks
> and underneath that fur he's just like
> u u u us.

Cue for Aggiss to deliver the 'u u u us' with an alarming simian cry to 'Gus', a small toy monkey sat on the empty floor, grinning. What Cowie knows is that this moment will translate from the page to the stage in a way that is oddly moving and very, very funny. The diva who stood up all those years ago on the dusty proscenium stage and shouted 'All together now!' would probably have enjoyed it too.

liz aggiss and 'authentick' grotesque expressionism

marion kant

I

I first saw Liz Aggiss when she was invited to appear at the University of Surrey. The programme consisted of one piece only, called *Grotesque Dancer* (1986). After the first few minutes I was captivated by the performance. More, I was amazed and startled too, as I had not expected to encounter the very essence of the culture of the Weimar Republic on a small stage in Guildford. The students, on the other hand, reacted to her choreographies with surprising unease and felt very unsettled.

Weimar's grotesque dance, a satirical, perversely entertaining and subversive view of the world, had been part of a peculiar legacy of the 1920s and early 1930s. Grotesque dance and those who made and performed it never belonged to the canon of German dance in those years; neither the genre nor the performers were ever accepted as part of the tradition on which much of our current notion of modernity depends. Neither then, in the 1920s, nor now were the grotesque performers included in wholesome historical narratives or the prevailing aesthetic categories. They operated beyond the boundaries of acceptable art and hence were labelled strange or bizarre, very much in the way the students in Guildford perceived the piece by Liz Aggiss and Billy Cowie as out of time and place.

Liz Aggiss' performance startled me all the more, because so little work has been done to recover grotesque dances and dancers. Most research in the field of German modern dance has been devoted to mainstream German expressionism and to the history and aesthetics of the Laban and Wigman schools and their disciples. Hardly anybody knows the names of the people, let alone tries to understand the genres, outside of this canon. For a very long time, the dancers of the grotesque type simply disappeared. They were forgotten and their art, or more precisely their anti-art, had also vanished. Yet suddenly there it was, there she was, Liz Aggiss dancing grotesque; dancing Weimar Germany; impersonating Weimar cabaret; turning herself into one of those unforgettable, striking images; sharp and penetrating, affronting the senses, full of sentimentality, hatred, vulnerability, sensitivity, anxiety, aggression; making fun of what people love and hold sacred, mocking bourgeois values, beauty, femininity and reasonableness; in short, full of the contradictions of the Weimar years. There she was as a grotesque dancer reincarnated, offering an eccentric mixture of offence and non-sense. Many, many layers of a complex historical development were caught in her dance performance. I was stunned by it.

II

In an interview, Liz Aggiss (2002b) said that she had been inspired to make *Grotesque Dancer* after she read an article on Valeska Gert written by fellow artist Anne Teresa De Keersmaker that appeared in the autumn of 1981. In other words, Aggiss had no direct contact with the tradition, which makes her achievement even more remarkable.

Valeska Gert was one of those mythical figures that attracted as many performers as she repelled others. Aggiss had a tenuous connection to Gert through her teachers Hanya Holm and Hilde Holger. Holm, a pupil of Mary Wigman, had built and headed in the early 1930s the first Wigman School in New York, and Holger was also an expressionist dancer, an Austrian Jewess who fled from the Nazi regime in the late 1930s. Both women represented different, not entirely compatible, strands of modern Germanic dance traditions but had nothing, so far as I know, to do with Gert.

The shrill, unsettled, neurotic Valeska Gert was quite another matter. Her heritage is of a peculiar kind; she was a woman who was said to consist of nothing but abysses (Niehoff 1962: 122). While Holm opened her studio in New York and spread the principles of Mary Wigman, her mistress and the high priestess of German modern dance, and Holger danced in fellow Austrian Gertrud Bodenwieser's modernist–expressionist group, Gert followed none of the accepted paths and rejected all dogmas and doctrines. She was a woman who taught her audience a new sensibility by scaring it, by confronting it with the unbearable, telling it some horrific 'truth' (Hildenbrandt 1928: 81). Her ghostly and nightmarish characters and the presentation of her own time through dance were unique (Prinz 1930: 21). She was considered the only dancer in 1932 who, as a contemporary critic put it, could create 'the spectre of the disintegration of an entire cultural system, our previous intellectual and spiritual world order' on stage (Lewitan 1932: 4). With her 'spiritual sensitivity [she] grasped and reflected . . . the discrepancies of life, its antinomies and the contradictions of today, from which no principle of salvation can be drawn. She, the one really modern dancer, offers us the dance shred of our shredded lives, but even she cannot really create a dance for our times' (Lewitan 1932: 4). Thus she represented the collapse of a world, her own world, and offered no hope for her characters or survival strategies for herself. Gert danced on her own; she showed no interest in dance groups, dance schools or any form of institution. She was unconcerned with creating any kind of following or gathering disciples. If she entered any work relationships at all, then she did so only temporarily by joining theatre ensembles or film crews. It is therefore no coincidence that more or less all remaining film footage shows her in non-dance films – those by Hans Neumann,[1] Georg Wilhelm Pabst,[2] Henrik Galeen,[3] Robert Siodmak,[4] Jean Renoir,[5] Alberto Cavalcanti,[6] Federico Fellini,[7] Pierre Philipe,[8] Werner Maria Fassbinder,[9] Ulrike Ottinger/Tabea Blumenschein[10] and Volker Schlöndorff[11] (to name a few).

For Gert, Wigman's 'absolute dance' and Nietzschean philosophy smelt of sweat and earnestness; she hated Wigman intensely.[12] Wigman ignored her as she ignored anything that might disturb her high art and high ambitions. Gert's answer to modern German dance, and particularly that of the Wigman circle, was to satirize its Germanic values. She mocked what she disliked; she ridiculed the sanctification of dance; she made fun of its religious aspirations and its conceptual phoniness. Gert attacked all pretensions, not just Wigman's. As soon as any idea became acceptable to the public, she mocked it and replaced it with an outrageous, crazy alternative. The perpetual search for something beyond the tolerable led her, together with her characters, to the margins of society and the brink of morality; it also took her to the edge of the performable, if not beyond it. As a consequence of her extreme visions, she questioned the current principles of political involvement and ethical beliefs. And she questioned what the stage was about.

Valeska Gert, who was Jewish, left Nazi Germany for Paris; from there she sailed to the United States. In late December 1938 she arrived in New York. But in the modern dance world of the United States there was no place for her. She remained less than marginal, because she had lost the society that had provided her with a basis for her critique, with reasons to attack it. The New World ignored her. As one of hundreds of thousands of refugees she had to survive, somehow. She opened the Beggar's Bar in New York's Bowery and insulted anyone who came near her. The 'beast', the strange animal, found no place for herself after she had to emigrate; nor was she welcomed back in Germany in 1945, after the end of World War II.

In her four books on herself, she skilfully turned herself into a legend. That is where later performers took her up. The engagement with Valeska Gert today can be less with a person than with the principles she represented. And they are not easy to discern. She has been described as the first grotesque dancer, the first dancer of expressionism as scream, the first dancer embracing surrealism, the first dancing social critic, the first realist dancer – in fact she believed herself to be the only dancer (Peter 1987: 45). As she escapes any precise categorization, her work and ideas have to be rethought completely if they are to be incorporated into contemporary dance aesthetics. To simply re-create her characters, the ghosts of the underworld, the outcasts and social figures of 1920s Berlin, would make little sense.

Besides, there exists no body of choreographies that can be resurrected, no dance technique that can be recovered, no schooling system that can be restored. Hence her dances have not been reconstructed nor have the film scenes been pieced together and re-animated. What then remains to be discovered?

There is the historically interesting fact of Valeska Gert's existence together with various historical sources and documents. But how can her dances be re-examined, not for historical research but for performances? Can an assessment of her philosophical and aesthetic beliefs initiate a new art, a new grotesque genre, a new outlook on dance as performance?

Several important principles and elements of composition stand out: the invention of characters out of the ordinary, making them extra-ordinary by re-contextualizing them; the introduction of collage[13] techniques that assemble fragments and effectively estrange them from their environment or, to use the Brechtian term, alienate (*verfremden*) them from their original background; her sardonic laughter at serious and generally accepted matters, which turns certainty of values and earnestness into caricature, into its grotesque opposite. This is, I suppose, where Liz Aggiss begins to operate.

As mentioned above, Liz Aggiss was exposed to several distinct artistic philosophies in her dance education; two of them were connected to what is usually referred to as German expressionism. This background provided her with several cultural tropes of twentieth-century modernity in dance.

Grotesque Dancer catches the atmosphere of Weimar Germany; it catches the cutting edge and subversive quality of a certain kind of critique by playing with the principles and motives Valeska Gert established. Liz Aggiss manages the uncanny personification of a historical period and style. At the same time she is not the imitation of the period and its style

but a continuation of modernist critique with the tools modernism itself
– that of the early nineteenth as well as that of the early twentieth century
– had developed.

Grotesque Dancer should be seen in connection to Hi Jinx (1995),
another collaborative piece, in which Liz Aggiss portrays a lecturer whose
teacher was, we learn, a modern dancer and choreographer, through four
short films. The pupil demonstrates her teacher's training principles
and analyses the constituents of her work. It is the loving portrait of a
great figure by a devoted student. The intelligent audience has to consider whether the artist is pure fiction, whether the films are historical
documents or not, though the title indicates that the whole enterprise is
high jinks, a spirited game of mockery. At the same time Liz Aggiss is the
jinx to the believers of modern dance; she plays a nasty trick on them and
their revered notions of art. But it is a puzzle to piece together; it is an
intellectual game to discriminate the real between the un-real, the true
between the un-true pieces, to distinguish fiction from non-fiction.

III

Grotesque Dancer is a carefully crafted piece; music, dance, mime, sung and
spoken passages enter a complicated relationship in which they refer to
each other and act as prompts and allusions; they pick up ideas, carry
them on and pass them along throughout the show, like a ball game. It
was conceived by Liz Aggiss and Billy Cowie for Divas, their joint company, and first performed in Brighton in 1986. The piece does not rely
on spontaneous insights. Improvisational urges are neither the driving
force nor are they played out.

Grotesque Dancer begins with a melancholy overture that sets the tone,
musically and emotionally (DVD 4:1).[14] A sweet and sad melody, the
basis for future variations, is played by a soprano saxophone, accompanied by a piano. The musical composition opens the scene, leads
through the entire piece and ends it. In the turbulent sections to come it
soothes emotions and modifies the outrageousness of the danced and
mimed parts. It connects the various sections and often prompts Liz
Aggiss into performing. The instrumental passages quote or imitate
musical genres and personal composition styles just as much as the
physical performance cites historically preserved images and copies
dance styles.

During the overture a spotlight shines on a face. The light provides a
frame, we look at the face, an image fashioned to resemble a 1920s
woman, and the face looks back at the audience (Figure 4.1). The face is

Figure 4.1 'Overture' – Liz Aggiss in *Grotesque Dancer. Photo: Billy Cowie, 1986.*

still, motionless, staring out at the people, watching. Short black hair, cut to what is known in German as *Bubikopf*, black rimmed eyes, bright red mouth. Is this a heroine from one of the silent movies? Is it Asta Nielsen perhaps, or the nightclub dancer Anita Berber? Or is it some figure out of a George Grosz painting? Is it Valeska Gert? It could be any one of them. We are gazing at a generic invention of Berlin in the 1920s. Then gradually the mouth breaks into a coquettish smile and the rest of the body is revealed. Dressed in a white T-shirt, black shorts, white knee socks and black gym shoes the figure is ready for physical exercise. This is the uniform of German *Turnen*, a particular style of gymnastics that Turnvater Jahn[15] in the early nineteenth century declared vital to the health of the national body. Before the warm-up begins, accompanied by the second half of the introductory saxophone melody, the figure turns and offers views from the side and front. Thus the body is introduced to the audience, which can inspect it like a doctor inspects a patient. Then the right arm is extended, perhaps to shake hands and say hello. With the arm moves one leg, as though connected by string. It is a puppet-like movement, repeated several times over and also quoted later in the piece, towards its end. A photograph of Valeska Gert's *Clown* (1930) comes to mind, hand and leg extended while her unforgettable face stares into the lens. The photograph gives the impression of a marionette clown, a Pierrot figure out of the arsenal of street puppet theatres.

More stretches are carried out. Every slowly developed movement ends in a frozen position as though inspired by a photograph that is briefly animated and then dies down again. Together they produce a series of motions ending in stillness, again comparable to a series of photographs. The movement sequels also resemble the emphatic gestures of the heroines in silent movies; black-and-white silhouettes, like wood-cuts, have to make themselves understood through movement as they have no words. The strength of this kind of movement lies in its stylistic simplicity, its rigorous stripping down to the bare essentials. And very gradually, in a process that lasts the entire piece, these movement sequences are transformed into ingenious reminders of other film idols, idols with whom Valeska Gert appeared on screen, from Greta Garbo and Louise Brooks to Lotte Lenya and Hanna Schygulla.

The next cabaret 'number', a bounce dance, begins (DVD 4:2). Knee bends, making the body bounce up and down, are a kind of movement *cantus firmus*. They continue even though the upper body is more and more contorted, contradicting the meaning of any healthy exercise. Liz Aggiss's face, though, never loses its serious concentration. Her body twists and turns, hopping and bouncing and nevertheless aiming at keeping its balance. Finally, after several uncomfortable manipulations, she manages to entangle herself so thoroughly that she has to sit, then lie on the floor. Legs and knees are now unable to bounce and bend, but the feet are still tapping the rhythm on the floor. The body cannot come to any rest and is only released from this absurd situation through a new musical theme.

The melody of 'Lied an meinen Sohn', text by Richard Dehmel, raises Liz Aggiss from the ground. She walks to the musicians, greets them cordially and delivers the song; speaking, screaming, whispering the words (DVD 4:3). The intense act again points to one of Valeska Gert's cabaret sketches, *Diseuse* (1931). A critic wrote of her that she 'destroys all erotic and sentimental swindle. She is of elemental lasciviousness demolishing all Tillery[16] and allures of chanson singers in dimensions worthy of a Daumier' (Hermann-Neisse 1926: 66). The words were originally set to music by Richard Strauss. In his adaptation of the poem, Billy Cowie mocks the serious tone of the German *Lied* while Liz Aggiss crushes the allure of the *Lieder* singer.

In between the verses, little pantomime acts are carried out. The rendition, beginning as a melodrama, turns more and more aggressive. Suddenly we look down into an abyss, that of the German militant tradition, where physical activity, here *Turnen* as seemingly harmless gymnastics, inevitably turns into marching and violence, into the movement of a war machine.

The song has exhausted Liz Aggiss and she wipes the sweat from her brow.

The fourth section is a 'wall dance' in which Aggiss moves with and against a wall hidden by black backdrops. The scene consists of sliding down, standing up, slithering down again, writhing her body around and around, wriggling in and out of the most awkward positions, some repeated, quoted, from the first section. At the end, Aggiss finds herself on the floor once more. Rather embarrassed, she begins to crawl on all fours, forwards, to the left, then the right, uncertain of where to go. And again it is the music that rescues her from the muddle and prompts the next, fifth section. It is called 'Mengenlehre, Set Theory' (DVD 4:4). It is a nonsense poem (written by Billy Cowie) that leaves Aggiss heartbroken and lonely. With the help of two hoops she explains the logical concept of set theory. When she arrives at the definition of the intersection, the hoops nearly throttle her and she has to realize that her love for either or both is unrequited. The two hoops, representing sets, have each other; they form a union and there is no need nor place for a third set or person. We have witnessed a love triangle, a tragicomedy in which the third is excluded from entering a closed relationship and therefore pushed into existential crisis.

The sixth section uses one of the gems of German poetry and music, 'Heidenröslein', text by Goethe and music by Billy Cowie. The song is so well known that it has reached the status of a folk song. To foreigners it is the quintessential German cultural expression, the essence of German

Kultur. As in all other numbers, the grotesque perspective casts a new light on this old favourite. Aggiss presents it as a tragic, sung love story. The boy breaks the rose and the rose, made to speak directly through its petals (with a little help from Aggiss's hands), pricks the boy. The text, breathlessly yelled and barked at the audience, turns into an adventure story or action thriller with a count down. 'Brach', the threatening break-ing of the rose, is shouted and sharply articulated, like a shot from a gun. Little pantomimic acts are interspersed between the verses. Aggiss steps away from the microphone and executes grand all-encompassing move-ments with extensive, large, sweeping arm gestures. This is unanswered love of a different nature.

The next section is once more determined by the music, which quotes earlier phrases and themes. Liz Aggiss begins to undress; she takes her socks and shoes off (DVD 4:5). But instead of continuing the strip-tease, as one might expect at this point, she puts a black satin frock over her gym clothes. She slips into high heels and then proceeds to take off her wig. Her own long red hair falls over her shoulders; suddenly she has transformed herself. From an androgynous figure she has converted her-self into an elegant-looking woman. She enters a balancing act through-out which the female image clashes with the grotesque movement sequences. When her hands touch down and Aggiss, the new woman, begins to walk on all four extremities, bottom up in the air, legs and arms rigid and clumsy, the hem of the skirt clenched between her teeth, the self-conscious female (on stage and in the audience) thinks she has reached the climax of discomfort, embarrassment and unease. But it gets worse. The woman on the floor, now turned over like a beetle on its back, helplessly struggling, tries to cover up her knees and legs with the skirt as though it were indecent to bare that much flesh. But her activity fails; all is in vain and the skirt slips back up, revealing what she cannot help but show. Eventually she gives up; the body collapses in a heap.

The music begins to play, leading into a new theme, and she heaves herself off the floor. Now we are presented with a different type of singer/chansonette/diseuse, the one who hardly moves, creeps up to the microphone and parades her 'beautiful' hands. 'Oh lieb', so lang du lieben kannst . . .' – 'love as long as you are alive, soon the ones you love or you yourself will be lying in a cold grave' – symbolizes another song much loved in bourgeois Germany of the nineteenth and early twentieth century. With text by Ferdinand Freiligrath,[17] an intense national revo-lutionary and radical democrat, it is a perfect example of the sentimental side of the German national character. Aggiss sings in a soft, husky and quivering voice (DVD 4:6). She is very quickly overwhelmed by the feelings she expresses through the words of the song and the emotions she has stirred up. She wipes away a few tears, standing motionless. This kind of caricature of holy art and its elevating effect on the human spirit provoked Nazi critics in Berlin in 1932 to cry out in rage: 'Valeska Gert, the ugliest woman in the whole world ... spews out her Galician[18] hatred against everything German' (Stein 1932: 230). Another, third, take on sentimentality, false feelings and pretentiousness, the scene carries a double analysis of vocal and movement clichés and, once more, rips apart any hope of intactness or wholeness through art.

The next pantomime scene pokes fun at grand gestures and grandiose movement styles and anticipates the nonsense of the song that is to follow. Christian Morgenstern (DVD 4:7),[19] the author of 'Das Perlhuhn', a poem from his series on animals, was one of the very few German nonsense writers, comparable to Edward Lear. This kind of teasing word play and light-hearted intellectual humour cannot often be found in German culture. Aggiss does not use it as a base to flirt with the humour nor add another layer of satire. Instead she dismantles this harmless folly (as well as the idea of a genre full of fun) by bawling the words out at the audience and marching up and down like a sergeant major. The only thing missing is a little whip with which she can intimidate the audience.

The last section offers another song, 'Heimat' by Richard Dehmel.[20] This time we are introduced to an opera singer who intones the music (the introductory clarinet theme) with such a strong vibrato that not a single word can be understood. The mega-vibrato is achieved by manipulating the throat, the vocal chords and larynx, with the hands. The concept of *Heimat*, of a home and a mother at the stove, waiting and providing shelter, is made completely ridiculous. Going full circle, the music takes us back to the beginning (DVD 4:8).

In the epilogue, Aggiss repeats the movement sequence from the beginning, the side and front view of the performer, now resembling the positions for a 'wanted' photograph, the outstretched arm and leg moving in puppet-like manner.

She removes her frock. In between various stages of undress we see movements freezing into still images. Finally she has taken her dress off and is back in gym garb. One high heel off and one shoe on she limps to the back of the stage. The spotlight focuses on her face once more; the light dims; the music ends. After 40 minutes (according to the rules of the imaginary Heidi Dzinkowska in *Hi Jinx*, a piece must never exceed 42 minutes) the grotesque Weimar cabaret evening is over.

The notion of art as a shield that protects from and enhances life is so thoroughly smashed in the entire piece that nothing remains intact. Every sketch deeply doubts the meaning of art and human existence. Though the angles from which it happens differ, the removal of moral and aesthetic certainties unites the piece. All those little niches in which people take refuge, all those soothing ideas that they use to indulge themselves, all the wholesome notions of goodness, decency and integrity through art are wrecked. A pile of shattered hopes remains; hopes in the form of shards, cultural and artistic, that have extremely sharp edges.

IV

Liz Aggiss balances along the edges of a peculiar genre and it is not clear whether she maintains – or even intends to maintain – her equilibrium. She pulls a Valeska Gert-like grotesque attitude out of the past. She uses it as a magnifying glass that cannot, does not, convey the whole picture. Instead we see deformed and distorted segments, broken pieces from the past. Her talent lies in assembling these fragments, weaving them into a new structure. Her historical material – photographs, cartoons, painted or drawn pictures, graphic art – is strongly visual and *Grotesque Dancer* creates an equally strong visual impact. Because it is conceived fundamentally not from kinetic memory or through kinetic forces, it achieves a peculiar effect. Not unlike Valeska Gert, Aggiss explodes the familiar genres. Her movement registers, which are on a tremendously large scale, yet at the same time meticulously executed, hover just above the understandable, doable and acceptable. They depend entirely on her personality that does not seem to know any fear or modesty.

Hi Jinx, created more than a decade later, complements *Grotesque Dancer* by providing a different side and different characteristics of expressionist dance. If *Grotesque Dancer* is about tearing down all assumptions about common moral and artistic understanding and the acceptability of images, then Hi Jinx creates the – ridiculous – rules and borders which dance is supposed to obey and within which it is supposed to flourish. Both pieces share a particular and peculiar way of dealing with the past and the means by which they convert and transform our knowledge and our assumptions about knowing the past.

Whereas *Grotesque Dancer* uses the grotesque as a bizarre and overstated message, and binds and organizes the various sketches in a collage as an internal technique, Hi Jinx uses an ironic structure. At first, it seems that it rests on a similar, external use of collage. But the film and media parts are not assembled as a collage. They have a different function; they do not displace the idea of modernism but enforce and bolster it. In Hi Jinx, the audience has to recognize that the film clips and the texts are not the historical documents they pretend to be but inventions that have been collated, assembled to give the impression of an artist who has been rescued from historical oblivion (DVD 4:9). They are props in a cunning plot. In the end history, the process of historical research, is imitated and discarded as resting on false premises. But not only the historical approach, also its subject, that with which history is concerned, is mocked and proven wrong. The critique in Hi Jinx aims at the idea of modernity in dance; its claim is made to look absurd. Aggiss and Cowie achieve this in a very different way from Grotesque Dancer. They do not apply the grotesque device to unmask the false or hollow assertions; instead they use the principle of 'dramatic irony' which determines the structure of a work more than the actual meaning of the words spoken. In 'dramatic irony' the audience's knowledge is greater than that of the characters on stage and the events in which they are involved. Hence the actions and words take on a different meaning for the audience than they have for the characters themselves. In Hi Jinx the audience knows (or should be able to know) that Heidi Dzinkowska is not a historical figure but an invention, an imaginary figure, claiming historical importance. What she says turns into the opposite: it does not confirm her claim to fame but dismantles it; it does not strengthen the modernist argument but takes it apart. Whereas Aggiss, who performs the role of the devoted student/academic, does not know and cannot reveal to the audience that Heidi, her teacher, is unreal, and that the student has been misled, the audience knows (or should know) it. Modern dance hence becomes a highly dubious affair. But, as Aggiss/Cowie cannot rely on the audience being aware of the ironic dramatic construction, they create another layer of irony. With Aristotelian word play the meaning of the spoken text is ridiculed. As Aristotle explained, 'you should kill your opponents' earnestness with jesting and their jesting with earnestness' (Aristotle 2005). And that is what they do. Within the ironic dramatic structure of the entire piece, they juggle the words until word irony and dramatic irony are intertwined and it is unclear who can know what and how. Fragments of book titles, portions of quotations, parts of teaching systems are cleverly woven into the fabric of quasi history. Laban's Life for Dance (1975) turns into a life in dance, Wigman's composition principles emerge as commandments, Graham's or Humphrey's techniques show up as teaching conventions. The whole range of modern heritage passes by and is de-constructed. Hi Jinx is the most fundamental questioning of modernism imaginable without outright rejection (DVD 4:10).

The critique in *Grotesque Dancer* seems more obvious and lighter but is, in fact, just as substantial. Through the sieve of aesthetic memory, knowledge itself is questioned. In this sense both pieces seem to me in the true sense 'postmodernist'. Both pieces enter a complicated relationship to the historical phenomena on which they rest. References, quotations and layers of meaning form a thick mesh of intellectual and movement material through which the spectator has to navigate. Not much help is offered and hence orientation is not easy. Aggiss and Cowie cut and paste catchwords and musical/movement phrases that float around until they have created a wonderfully ironic collage. History is not divided into desirable and undesirable developments; the undesirable is not eliminated. It is incorporated to reflect on the complexity of the past as well as on contemporary customs and rituals, above all, on the contemporary selection of dance aesthetics. Conflicting ideas and practices are confronted, made to confront each other; they are mixed and shuffled until they produce a distorted image of their historical sources. The selective memory that shifts through data and is always at work is mocked and used to create utter confusion and disillusionment. The sentimental desire for harmony is abused and cleverly turned into a device to make the audience think about the rearranged past. Nothing is certain and nothing is whole. Instead, the fragments of historical reality become disturbing elements of our present time.

This process of re-cognition forces the viewer to realize that something is not what it seems to be, but entirely different. It shows either the hidden faces or unexpected sides of events, figures or situations. The grotesque genre turns the world upside down. It rejects the categories of orientation, which bourgeois society has established. No longer are there safe guides through reality; the theatrical performance becomes a disturbing journey into an alienated place and strange world, a nightmare, a shocking adventure. Hence the grotesque dancer creates through a negative process – inverting, reversing, distorting and mixing. The grotesque takes meaning away before it permits the estranged or alienated substitute to take its place. The ironic structures deeply question any meaning at all. And yet, paradoxically, the more the observers know the original, and the original historical context, the more they will enjoy (if that is an appropriate word) the performances.

The fundamental difference between Liz Aggiss and Valeska Gert lies in their respective relationship to social reality. Valeska Gert's anger at Weimar Germany was tremendous and it was directed at her world. She became the shocking clown of contempt out of hatred as well as frustration. Such a position is liberating, but also limiting. Liz Aggiss uses

Gert's anger as a foil to satirize history. Her manoeuvres imitate the anger and the frustration; if they are anger and frustration themselves, then they come in disguise. The fragments she finds are remnants of the past, not the present, and she drains them of their original meaning without directly referring to contemporary issues.

As a technique developed in the early twentieth century, the collage was a fresh and relatively unspoilt medium for Valeska Gert. Though Aggiss and Cowie do not have the advantage of the novelty of the medium, they can instead rely on the audience knowing how to decode collages. Therefore their collages can combine disparate elements from different cultural spheres and different periods. It is not necessary for them to identify all elements. Besides, many of the cultural anxieties of the 1920s still exist in our society. Hence they can play with old ambiguities and add new ones. The final structural element that acts as binding agent and relates all materials that have been thrown together, sorted and undone again, is laughter. It is, of course, an ambivalent laughter, a grotesque laughter, dreaded by those to whom it is addressed. It is also a macabre laughter, related to the death of a comfortable arrangement with the past. It frightened the Surrey students and makes other people take refuge in the idea that this is not dance. But dance it is, a most powerful form of dance and performance, of drama and music.

> No matter how many times you see this woman on stage, each time you are astonished, captivated and shaken; astonished by her sovereign mastery, the routine by which she controls all the techniques of theater; captivated by the originality of her conception and presentation; shaken by the truly dramatic power of her performance, which perhaps gets closer to the principle of drama than our entire modern theater.
>
> (Prinz 1930: 21)

The above paragraph was written by Harry Prinz in March 1930 about Valeska Gert. It could be used to describe the art of Liz Aggiss. And there can be no higher compliment to her use of the past than to be congratulated by one of its ghosts.

Notes

1   Ein Sommernachtstraum (*A Midsummer Night's Dream*) (1924).
2   Die Freudlose Gasse (*The Joyless Street* in the UK, *The Street of Sorrow* and *Streets of Sorrow* in the USA) (1925); Das Tagebuch einer Verlorenen (*The Diary of a Lost One, The Diary of a Lost Girl* in the USA, *Le Journal d'une fille perdue* in France) (1929); *The Threepenny Opera* (1931).

 3 *Alraune* (1928).
 4 *Menschen am Sonntag* (*People on Sunday*) (1929).
 5 *Nana* (1926).
 6 *Pett and Pott* (1934).
 7 *Giuletta degli spiriti* (1965).
 8 *La Bonne dame* (1968).
 9 *Acht Stunden sind kein Tag* (1972).
10 *Die Betörung der Blauen Matrosen* (1975).
11 *Coup de grace* (1978); *Nur zum Spass, nur zum Spiel. Kaleidoskop Valeska Gert* (1977).
12 Cf. Gert (1926), Gert (1931a), Gert (1931b) and Gert (1979).
13 See Poggi (1992).
14 This essay refers to the reconstruction of *Grotesque Dancer* from 1999. Where available, DVD references are made to the reconstruction; where not available, the references are made to the original 1986 version. The principal differences between the two versions are that Aggiss has a shaved head in the original version and uses recorded rather than live music.
15 Friedrich Ludwig Jahn (1778–1852). The ancient phrase 'mens sana incorpore sano' meant that you had to keep your body healthy to keep the mind functioning. In the nineteenth century, the sentence was transformed under the influence of racial and eugenic theories into a doctrine that advocated the necessity of a racial body, which later became the right racial community body of a nation that determined healthy thinking as such. Jahn was one of the main supporters of achieving national health through physical activity.
16 Refers to the Tiller Girls.
17 Ferdinand Freiligrath (1810–1876). The poet was known as the 'trumpeter of the revolution' and belongs to the so-called Vormärz, a radical political and literary movement in Germany.
18 Galician was a synonym for Jewish.
19 Christian Morgenstern (1871–1914). Morgenstern wrote satirical prose for Max Reinhardt's cabaret 'Schall und Rauch' and edited theatre journals. Best known for his nonsense poems.
20 Richard Dehmel (1863–1920). The poet Frank Wedekind regarded him as one of the most important German writers of his time.

choreographic vocabulary 1
visual metaphor

billy cowie

The choreographic vocabulary of Liz Aggiss and Billy Cowie is informed by a mixture of multiple dance styles, with one of the most important being German expressionist dance. The vocabulary, however, also includes a wide range of influences from outside the dance world, in particular from the areas of film and visual art. In this essay I propose to concentrate on only one aspect of their choreographic question, i.e. the way Aggiss/Cowie use visual metaphor, especially in its relationship to abstract and non-abstract movement.

Abstract v. non-abstract movement

It is possible to imagine the different contemporary choreographic styles of the last 50 years as a kind of spectrum with at one extreme an emphasis on stylized form – movement for movement's sake, abstraction – and at the other an emphasis on the projection of character, narrative, ideas and personality through movement. As a broad generalization the former is sometimes seen as more American, the latter more European.[1] However, most choreographers from both continents would seem to sit at different points along the line, each with varying emphasis on these different aspects. Perhaps Merce Cunningham is to the left (Atlantic-wise) of, say, Lea Anderson who is to the left of, say, Pina Bausch?

Where then would Aggiss/Cowie's choreographic style fit on such a line? One answer would seem to be to take the line and bend it into a circle. We might then find Aggiss/Cowie sitting on the join, a fusion of the two extremes, without compromising or diluting either in the process.

In order to demonstrate how this unusual synthesis shows itself in the context of visual metaphor I propose to examine in some detail some key segments from the Aggiss/Cowie repertoire – *Dorothy and Klaus* (1989), *La Soupe* (1990) and *El Puñal entra en el Corazón* (1992).

*

Dorothy and Klaus was first performed in 1989 and toured Europe during 1990. It tells the story of Klaus, the experimental German composer who invents electronic music (and who bears absolutely no relationship to any German composer alive or dead), his wife Dorothy, and a group of other composers who are his dearest friends – Johnny, Pascal and Harry. The solos of the two main characters sum up many of Aggiss/Cowie's concerns.

The whole ballet commences with 'Klaus' Solo' (DVD 5:1) in which, after a short speech (performed in lip-sync) extolling the virtues of Amerika (sic), Klaus shows us (choreographically) what he is really made of.

First he reaches below the table and fetches up – his leg. He cradles it like a baby before dropping it onto the table, like a piece of meat or dough. He tries to lift the leg again, but it has suddenly and inexplicably become extremely heavy. Paradoxically, the knee then becomes so light it inadvertently floats away and Klaus must push it back down repeatedly. The leg seems to move on its own and Klaus can only control it by holding it with his forehead in a peculiarly pensive fashion (as often in Aggiss/Cowie's work everything is interchangeable, the leg is an arm, the knee a hand). The leg carries on moving – in a vaguely sexual manner?

In the second section of this solo, Klaus grabs the leg with his mouth and lifts it to turn it as a cat would a kitten.[2] He then leans over the table and now the leg tries to sneak away. Klaus notices and pulls it back as one would a typewriter carriage. Now the leg and arm are standing on the table; the leg hooks the arm and pulls it away, symmetrically the arm hooks the leg; they are interchangeable; they are duetting by themselves as Klaus looks on. Klaus grabs the leg to his chest and it starts to rise – the phallic nature of the movement dispels any previous doubts as to the sexual nature of some of the earlier movements.[3]

One must first ask what makes this sequence any more than a series of commonplace, if rather inventive, mime-tricks[4] and illusions? And second, how does it tie in with the concept of a choreographic spectrum?

Referring back to the fantasized choreographic line we started with – on one, the abstract end, the movements are constructed and developed in related patterns closely linked to the music. The movements are full of symmetries, repetitions, minor variations, and the whole sequence is structured into formal sections. There is also an almost abstract analysis of the way the body works, how the muscles and joints function, the use of tension and release – the final image before Johnny, Pascal and Harry enter shows Klaus' leg jumping as if it was spring loaded.

At the other end of this imaginary choreographic line, however, the movements are intensely character driven. What do they all tell us about Klaus?

He is unpredictable?
He is a father-to-be (firstly of electronic music and then in reality)?
He is obstinate?
He is a craftsman?
He is obsessive?
He is a bit of an animal?
He is not completely in control?
He is not all there?
He is a *man*?

At the end of the scene Klaus' three composer friends enter while Klaus, despite being, one would think, caught in a rather embarrassing set-up, continues with his leg work. We learn that Klaus' friends know him only too well, and that Klaus knows that they know him only too well.

Due to the quixotic, fleeting speed of the metaphorical references, it may seem that the audience on the whole will miss many of them.[5] Hopefully, however, even if not registering consciously, they may make their mark subconsciously, or on repeated viewing, or maybe to just a fraction of the audience? It is of course difficult to second-guess an audience's reaction; for example, the costumes in the two halves of *Dorothy and Klaus* are identical except for the major difference that in the first half they are in black, white and grey only and in the second half they are brightly coloured (cloth patterns and cut remain the same). This change was meant to relate to the fact that five years had passed in the interlude between the sections and the world had moved from black and white into Technicolor – with a little nod in the direction of Dorothy in the *Wizard of Oz*.[6] However, in multiple performances across Europe no member of the audience ever even with prompting could recall the change! Despite this, Aggiss/Cowie remain convinced that the change gave a palpable lift into the second half of the piece. Or so we told the performers who unfortunately had to cart double the number of costumes round half of Europe.[7]

'Dorothy's Solo' (DVD 5:3) is the other side of the coin to Klaus' and occurs at the end of the first half of *Dorothy and Klaus*. Dorothy has just handed Klaus his soprano saxophone. 'Look vot I found ven I vos kleenink, your olt saxophone, remember how you uset to play ven ve first met.' Klaus begins to play it and Dorothy dances to his playing.

The leitmotif of this solo is Dorothy's clenched hand with thumb sticking up. Once again the symbolism of this switches rapidly from moment to moment. Dorothy puts the thumb in her mouth, obviously representing the saxophone itself, then she seems like a child biting its nails, suddenly she looks like a baby sucking its thumb or dummy. Then with suggestive in and out movements the extended thumb starts to symbolize oral sex and the whole saxophone speech suddenly seems to refer to their earlier love life. The visual metaphors continue – the thumb seems to be measuring space, surveying the distance or performing some benediction on the forehead. At times it is suggestive of an ironic thumb's up gesture, at times a hitch-hiking movement, at one of the climaxes Dorothy flicks both her thumbs from under her teeth in an oddly Italianate aggressive movement.

Once again we learn a lot about Dorothy's character.

She is a child (in relation to Klaus)?
She is nervous?
She is a lover?
She is a victim?
She is going somewhere?
She has a certain Latin quality?
She is pissed off?
She is planning something?
She is aware?

These are the simple implications of each individual reference, but by cramming so many into such a short space, the audience is given the opportunity to connect them up in a matrix-like fashion.

Thumb as saxophone + oral sex =
Thumb as child + measuring space =
Thumb as child + hitch-hiking + Italian aggression =
Etc.

As well as being a demonstration and illustration of Dorothy's character and the impulses that are going to form the upcoming drama, the choreography once again is as much about abstract shapes, angles and counterpoint of different body parts. Of particular note is the way that at times, instead of putting her thumb into her mouth by moving the hand, she moves the head (and sometimes the whole body).[8] Another favourite Aggiss/Cowie device is to give the illusion that different body parts are joined by invisible rods or strings.[9] It seems at times as if the body has a kind of internal wiring – as Dorothy walks forward her arms contract, as she reverses they release. Dorothy's facial expressions also seem to be linked to this internal wiring (as well as obviously contributing to the expression of character and mood in the piece as a whole).

In a similar way to Klaus' solo, the final incident sums up the preceding character demonstration – Dorothy has just danced her heart out for her Klaus; however, he thrusts the saxophone back into her hands and is immediately much more concerned with his new project: 'Look, I've got the parts for my new electronic machine, I must start work.' Dorothy has been dancing with Klaus, but Klaus has simply been remembering some previous sax prowess. Whatever they had before is not there now.

Dorothy's final meaningful look directly at the audience is another hallmark of Aggiss/Cowie's technique. This breaking of the audience/performer barrier occurs throughout *Dorothy and Klaus*[10] (as through all Aggiss/Cowie's work) and is used for both comic and tragic effect. Klaus looks into the audience's eyes in his solo because he is so innocently confident, he has nothing to hide. Dorothy, on the other hand, looks because she knows what is going on – she knows we know too (Figure 5.1).

The two solos on a larger scale once again represent a certain dualism between abstraction and narrative. The polar position in the first act of the two solos (and their fundamental duality) is almost a parody of classical structures (for example sonata form). On the other hand, the two main characters have set out their emotional stalls (in the presence of their little Greek chorus) and we can but await their inevitable interaction in the second act.

Figure 5.1 'Dorothy sabotages the Electronic Music Machine' – Maria Burton in *Dorothy and Klaus*. *Photo: Billy Cowie, 1989.*

Rude to Point

In Dorothy's solo the visual hand metaphors are used to drive the story
and character. In another work we see a superficially rather similar use
of hand gesture – this time using an extended index finger rather than
a thumb.[11] But in this case the metaphors are used for rather more
symbolic purposes than character or narrative. This is the 'Rude to
Point' dance from La Soupe, a work that was commissioned by Carousel
for their company which includes performers with learning difficulties
(DVD 5:6). For La Soupe, Aggiss/Cowie decided to amalgamate the
Carousel Company of 15 performers, the four Divas performers and the
Bangra singer Parmjit Pammi. The piece later toured in a cut-down
version as La Petite Soupe with only two members of the Carousel
Company.

The 'Rude to Point' section, as all of La Soupe, took as its starting point
taped conversations with the performers from Carousel about things
that had happened to them – in this case the unpleasant (and apparently
not uncommon) experience of being pointed at. The recorded text (by
Debbie Hartin) was embedded in music and also translated into Punjabi
and sung as part of the piece.

> It's rude to point
> It is
> It's rude
> Rude to point
> 'Cos it's not very nice
> People don't like it
> 'Cos they're getting annoyed at it
> Yeh
> Tell them to get off me
> I do agree about it.

The piece is performed by the four Divas dancers in tight unison and
focuses as mentioned before on the motif of a closed hand with the
exception of the extended index finger – this time, however, frequently
in both hands. As in the previous examples, there is almost an overload of
metaphors conjured up by this finger formation:

1   A call to attention, a listen-to-me gesture.
2   With the arms tucked behind the body and only the hands and finger
    showing, the hands and fingers rise up the torso, giving a strange
    suggestion of meters, as if the body is filling up (with anger?).
3   The two index fingers are brought together and the straight line

between them is then broken suddenly, like a twig (or a neck?) being snapped.

4   The index finger rotates and suddenly appears to be like a clock hand.

5   The finger points at the performers themselves (obviously!).

6   The pointing finger in its up and down movements is also strangely suggestive of a snake and its victim.

7   When the index finger enters the mouth, it is simultaneously reminiscent on the one hand of a desire to make yourself sick and on the other a kind of fuck off gesture (these should strictly be the middle finger, but who is counting?).

8   Pointing to the head in a 'you are crazy' gesture.

9   A vaguely Indian benediction with a feminine shifting of weight onto one hip and the joining of thumb and middle finger.

Here again, the metaphors can either be seen singly as purely illustrative of the text or can be taken in groups to form more complex meanings. On the abstract side, the hand motif provides a unifying link for the section, holding it together rather as a musical motif might hold a composition together. The pointing finger at the end of the arm also emphasizes the arm's linear definition and highlights the almost geometric obsession in the piece with the creation of abstract shapes – arcs, curves, triangles and lines in this case. This shape abstraction is further emphasized by the repetition of the patterns across the four dancers and the mesmeric pace of the piece; the movements unhurriedly fill their allotted times.

Solo tu Corazón Caliente

As well as using parts of the body as visual metaphors, Aggiss/Cowie's choreography frequently extends this process into the use of props. This can be seen very clearly in the work El Puñal entra en el Corazón from 1992, based loosely round a set of Lorca texts set to music (Figure 5.2, DVD 5:7). Here Aggiss represents a solo male dancer whose sparring partner is the (female) vocalist who gradually upturns the conventional male/female dominance between them. At the beginning of the work, Aggiss is a cocky (in both senses of the word), macho figure who is slowly transformed by love and mortality into a tragic, crushed hero, who is eventually led to 'his' death by the singer – crowned with withered orange blossoms.

By the sixth section of the work, Aggiss is already on the way down. She begins the choreography with two roses 'planted' by the singer

Figure 5.2 'Narciso' – Liz Aggiss in *El Puñal entra en el Corazón*. *Photo: Roger Bamber, 1992.*

between her toes. During the beginning of the dance she tries to grasp them but they always move just a little further out of reach. Eventually she manages to capture them. What seems like a triumph, however, quickly turns sour. The roses thrash her back, slash her across the face and finally metamorphose into a knife with which the performer cuts her own throat. In the concluding part of this section, the two roses become arrows fired into her eyes, the red rosebuds becoming her blood-soaked eyeballs.

Once again we have the duality of extremes. On the abstract level, the roses are used to trace out spatial patterns (as visual markers), in particular a twisting spiral that dominates the first section, and in the second section a series of parallel lines and shapes (using the stems). The rose stems also help to highlight the rotation of both the leg and arms – movements that are easily lost. On the dramatic side, the roses represent love out of reach (paradoxically kept out of reach by the performer himself?). When finally attained the roses/love inflict pain and finally blind the performer. At the end of the piece, the singer places two little rivulets of blood under the dancer's eyes before leading him to the next song.

A further counterpoint to the visual metaphors of this section is the Lorca text that accompanies it – 'Solo tu Corazón Caliente' ('Only your warm heart'). The choreography and visual imagery not so much illustrate the texts as provide a parallel commentary. This can be seen by the way that the following section, 'Los Saeteros' (the archers, like love, are blind), takes forward the theme of the roses as arrows as the protagonist makes a final but futile attempt to reassert himself.

Rice Rain

My final example shows once again the use of props as a visual device, but this time standing alone without textual references. This is the 'Ice Rain Solo' (performed by Ben Pierre) from the High Spin commission *Rice Rain* (2001). Although there is a text to the piece – the song 'Ice Rain' – this is sung in Japanese and the predominantly non-Japanese speaking audience is given no clue as to the meaning of the words; the choreography and visual metaphors are therefore functioning in isolation.

The solo performer stands in the middle of the stage dressed in a long black dress that is spread across the stage, giving the impression that he is rooted, growing out of the earth.[12] The performer holds two black umbrellas which, as in the previous example, serve a dual function. On the one hand they act as extensions of the arms (in Schlemmer-like fashion) and as markers and indicators of arm rotations. On the other hand, on a metaphorical plane, they flip from bird wings (or even bat wings) to wheels to parachutes (especially the type used to slow down planes) to the sides of a shell. They are also of course literally umbrellas with all their implications of shelter. What rainstorm is so severe that one needs two umbrellas (DVD 5:8)?

Both of the dual functions seem to merge to produce a kind of heroic resistance to extremely challenging if unspecified circumstances. At the end of the dance a thin stream of lit rice rains down from the sky on the umbrellas.

Conclusion

I would maintain that all of the extracts above could be viewed satisfactorily with one eye as purely abstract dance pieces, or with the other as entirely non-abstract works – the particular fascination of them for me is watching with both eyes. The strange separation of the abstract and the non-abstract into their own bubbles seems to give much of Aggiss/ Cowie's work a dual personality, as if the work is proceeding in two parallel universes at the same time. I would even go so far as to maintain that paradoxically this very separation allows these two areas to have a unique interaction with one another![13]

This dualistic combination of visual metaphor, driving character, but also forming part of an abstract choreographic structure, can be found throughout the Aggiss/Cowie canon, from the early bouncing leg of *Grotesque Dancer* (1986) through to the collapsing man walk of *Divagate* (1997), sometimes to tragic and sometimes to comic effect (and sometimes to both). There is a famous William Morris (1882) edict: 'Have nothing in your houses that you do not know to be useful, or believe to be beautiful.' Perhaps in Aggiss/Cowie's work the beautiful (in the widest sense of the word, which also paradoxically incorporates the ugly) may be represented by the abstract, the useful by the non-abstract. Sometimes Aggiss/Cowie's work attains both together.

Notes

1   This is obviously a very Western-biased statement that begs the discussion of non-Western, particularly Indian dance styles. It is surely no coincidence that one of the pieces used as illustration in this essay is the Indian-inspired *La Soupe* (1990).

2   This animalistic use of the mouth as a substitute hand occurs frequently in Aggiss/Cowie's work. See the end of *Beethoven in Love* (1994) or sections of *Grotesque Dancer* (1986) (DVD 5:2).

3   Of course all the characters in *Dorothy and Klaus* are played by female performers, with a certain relish it must be said for the parodying of male behaviour. See Aggiss' (as Johnny) crutch-grabbing entrance at the end of 'Klaus' Solo'.

4   Aggiss/Cowie's aversion to the world of mime is best seen in the monkey's comments in *Absurditties* (1994): 'Augustus hates all mimes.'

5   Strangely in *Divagate* (1997), Lorca asks Neil the poignant question, 'Is metaphor ever or just a temporary thing?'

6   Aggiss/Cowie's work also starts off in the early days of *Grotesque Dancer*, *Dead Steps* (1988) and *Eleven Executions* (1988) with no colour and over the years, with *Dorothy and Klaus* pivotal, becomes more colourful!

7   Similarly, in *Divagate*, in the boys' duet, Neil is standing at the back of the stage, Lorca at the front; Lorca punches the air and Neil's head flies back. It was pointed out to me that only a tenth of the audience were seated in such a position to make sense of the connected movements, but for those tenth, what a joy to see!

8   Although here related to a certain sexual symbolism, this abstract concept of what exactly is moving and what is still finds further exploration in the middle section of the film *Anarchic Variations* (2002), and its ultimate in *Scripted to Within an Inch of Her Life* (2002) where Aggiss demonstrates how easily she can move the whole earth thousands of miles in an instant (DVD 5:4).

9   The first instance of this in their work would seem to be the introduction to *Grotesque Dancer* (DVD 5:5), where Aggiss stands sideways and as she raises and lowers her arm, her leg correspondingly moves. The device gives the performer a certain puppet-like quality and one is also reminded of those

little toys where the limbs are connected by string and you can manipulate them by pushing a disc under their plinths.

10 Interestingly, in the documentation of the work, as well as looking directly into camera Dorothy also looks at the audience, even when being filmed from the side.

11 One might be tempted to think there might be another three pieces in this series; who knows?

12 This image has its ultimate expression in the final section of Motion Control (2002).

13 For example, the formal, calm geometries of 'Rude to Point' seem to suggest a rising above the trials of everyday life in an almost spiritual sense.

outsider performance
a raw vision: dance and learning difficulties

liz aggiss

Consider, if you will, legends and labels, just for a second. For example, consider the annotations 'dance with learning difficulties' or 'a dance company both with and without learning difficulties' and 'an integrated performance company'. For the purposes of this essay, I would like to redefine 'performance with learning difficulties' as Outsider Performance, and performers with learning difficulties as Outsider Performers. Apart from tripping easily off the tongue this new title embraces speciality, difference and importance with the added bonus of capital letters.

Outsider Performers like Outsider Artists share a common thread. Outsider Art is increasingly recognized as a representation of the purest and most direct form of artistic creation.[1] By determination and foresight patrons have bequeathed a legacy to ensure that Outsider Art is supported and that this impulsive creativity is recognized and can be enjoyed by a wider public. Additionally the terminology and theoretical discourse on the subject of Outsider traditions, from Naive and Primitive Art to Art Brut, ensures Outsider Art can flourish and be part of a broader critical debate.

The relationship between Outsider Artists and Outsider Performers could be argued as parallel. Whilst Outsider Artists are not necessarily categorized as having learning difficulties, with the notable exception of Dutch artist Appie Prinssen who has Down's Syndrome, and Stephen Wiltshire who has Autistic Spectrum Disorder, some Outsider Artists do have psychiatric disorders. However, what Outsider Artists and Outsider Performers share is an unconventional aesthetic and desire to make ritual-istic patterns, often marked by unguarded exuberance, self-containment and simplicity.

The difference is that for the Outsider Artist it is the work and not the person that is contextualized, championed and patronized, whereas for the Outsider Performer the audience must first focus on the body, irregular physicality, the varying forms of learning difficulties and special needs, guaranteed idiosyncratic behaviour, and unconventional performance language and skill base. Like the Outsider Artist, the Outsider Performer has no notion of a right or wrong way, no regular or irregular aesthetic, but is simply engaged in the act of performing to the best of his or her ability, revelling in opportunity, creativity and visibility. Outsider Art, though appealing to a small and enthusiastic audience, has found its niche and clientele. Outsider Performance struggles, often being lumped within community work, which is another contender for marginal work. Outsider Performance can simply get 'lost'.

Working in collaboration with Outsider Performers since 1989, Billy Cowie and I identified an artistic approach and choreographic method that we share with our work and company, Divas. Personalities and strengths are forefronted through a working process that identifies and locates a relevant platform and visibility for the individual, whatever his/her experiences, physicality, expression and sexuality. And as with all Divas work, there is always a theme, a content of social and political significance that is supported by visual integrity.

Interestingly, in 1987 Divas achieved their own Outsider notoriety with the performance *Torei en Veran Veta Arnold!* (1986, Figure 6.1) during the Spring Loaded festival at The Place in London. The programme notes identified personal information on the performers rather than noting the usual training. We wanted to identify difference as a way to underscore

Figure 6.1 'Kakarella Ka Diva!' – Rachel Chaplin, Ellie Curtis, Virginia Farman, Kay Lynn, Louise Rennison and Amanda Tuke in *Torei en Veran Veta Arnold! Photo: Billy Cowie, 1986.*

artistic direction: Amanda Tuke, 21, film-maker; Ginny Farman, 21, cleaner; Ellie Curtis, 19, cognitive scientist; Kay Lynn, 42, lesbian mother; Rachel Chaplin, 25, researcher; Kim Glass, 26, expectant mother; Baby Glass, minus four months, gender unknown. As unknowns, we did not expect to unleash such a knee-jerk response from the critical establishment:

> Sometimes it is possible to derive more from a group after the experience. For example while I did not actually enjoy watching Divas, the images have remained. The six women with rigid expression and forceful marching suggested a repositioning of values. They seemed to want to make us think again about the content of dance, pointing out that it did not require specifics of build or regimented finesse.
>
> (Nugent 1987a: 20)

The programme information and the performance were ferociously criticized in the national newspapers, and identified as a wilful act to undermine the 'dance establishment':

> Liz Aggiss, together with two of her colleagues, has thought up a perfectly ripping wheeze of getting five of her chums (a cleaner, a cognitive scientist, a film maker, a mother and a researcher) to perform in a group named Divas. They have already mastered – no that is too sexist a word for a group of young ladies – they have acquired such advanced performance skills as walking on and off stage.
>
> (Percival 1987: 42)

Boy was he cross. But not half as miffed as Mary Clarke, who used the programme notes to savage Divas in a superfluous half nelson – 'untrained as they are unattractive' (1987: 21).

Divas were thus identified as Outsiders within a dance world and unwittingly achieved instant attention. As Ann Nugent pointed out in The Stage:

> Before dealing with the merits or otherwise, there are two points worth noting in the women's [Divas] favour, first they are trying to develop a style of their own and second they raise questions about accepted values that in turn make an audience stop and think.
>
> (Nugent 1987b: 17)

Banda Banda: A celebration of opportunity and visibility

It seems entirely appropriate therefore that Cowie and I should form a relationship with an Outsider Performance company. In 1989, we initiated a relationship with Carousel, a creative arts organization that works with people with learning difficulties, based in Brighton, and subsequently made the award winning *Banda Banda* (1989). Despite lacking previous experience of working with Outsider Performers, we approached the collaboration in much the same way as we would have done with Divas: working with the total performer, finding relevant, pertinent and personal material to reveal his or her best qualities and individuality.

We gave the performers their voice, inviting each performer to talk about aspects of their lives. In one section, a sparse gestural piece arose from Outsider Performer Eric Grantham's visit to Brighton's Booth Bird Museum and his subsequent interest in flying. In another section, the six Outsider women performers traced their body contour, continuously carving and re-carving each movement shift as if reinterpreting their image as women. In another section, an absurd and grotesque chorus line, which consisted mainly of movement going nowhere, was punctuated by Outsider Performer Debbie Hartin's bawdy voice belting out, 'Right here we go.' As Annette Stapleton said:

> *Banda Banda* is not token participation and I'm glad I didn't need to suspend any criticism. It's a challenging, lively, original and entertaining performance. Two images stay with me; armfuls of white paper thrown into the air with total abandon and the assertion of Carousel performer Margaret Stamp that she likes people watching her.
>
> (Stapleton 1989: 6)

The work itself was as much about the performers and issues of performance, bound by the theme of visibility, as it was a celebration in opportunity and communication. *Banda Banda* was performed at the Institute of Contemporary Arts (ICA) in December 1989 as part of The Ripple Effect series for new performance. It was selected because 'it is a stunning work that defies its received boundaries' (Lois Keidan, Theatre Co-ordinator, ICA, 1990), and ironically was the first Outsider Performance to be shown at this venue. The few reviews that were written were neither guarded nor apologetic, and found a positive critical language. *Banda Banda* went on to win the very visible 1990 Time Out Dance Umbrella Award.

Banda Banda shatters the comfortable illusion that art is to be revered as the special preserve of the gifted few. The performance stresses that the arts are an invaluable means of self expression and that creativity is latent in, and essential to, everyone, whether they are labelled as amateur, professional, disabled or not.

(Clements 1989: 72)

From *La Soupe* to *La Petite Soupe*: The mundane and extraordinary

A year later, coincidentally inspired by the Outsider Art collection at La Fabuloserie, Dicy, France, we made *La Soupe* (1990), a collaboration between Carousel and Divas. *La Soupe* was made for The Music Room in The Royal Pavilion, Brighton. Gaining permission to use this venue for Outsider Performance was in itself a powerful statement about privilege, exclusion and the appropriation of culture.

Again the performers were invited to share aspects of their lives. Their conversations were recorded, sampled, carved and embedded into a score set by Cowie and sung live in Punjabi by Bangra singer Parmjit Pammi (awarded the 1986/1987 Asian Pop Award and Asian Bangra award). The piece went on to win the Alliance and Leicester Award 1990 for the most innovative theatre work in the Brighton Festival.

The research process used was revealing and surprising. Often the diction, when sampled, was unclear and the words did not immediately make sense. But sometimes, just sometimes, it was pure poetry, an insight to a wonderful world of an unselfconscious imagination. Put into the context of the performance it became a poignant reminder to the audience of the place of the individual and the importance of opportunity. Often the autobiographical material was raw and painfully sensitive.

> It's rude to point
> It is
> It's rude
> Rude to point
> 'Cos it's not very nice
> People don't like it
> 'Cos they're getting annoyed at it
> Yeh
> Tell them to get off me
> I do agree about it.
> (Lyrics from *La Soupe* by Outsider Performer Debbie Hartin)

'Rude to Point' was interpreted by a gestural choreography and performed by Divas surrounded by Outsider Performers. As each convoluted rendering of the pointed finger progressed, further emotional and physical complication was implied until the initial gesture became a threatening distortion (DVD 6:1).

Maintaining the purest and simplest forms plucked from workshop material, we worked against cluttering choreographic form:

> The most powerful image of the evening however came from a section called 'Spider'. It could easily have come straight out of a piece by Pina Bausch. A woman stands in the centre of the stage, her shoulders hunched, her hands clasped together. Another woman runs her hands up and down this person's arms and back and body and all we hear against the music are the words 'spider'. She stops doing this and moves away. The woman is left standing and slowly opens her hands to reveal the fact that she has been holding a huge spider between them all this time. In thinking about the beautiful simplicity of this I wondered if this had been flawed since each section was already minimal in movement terms.
>
> (Hamilton 1990a: 12)

It has often been a criticism of our work, and our work with Outsider Performers, that there should be more movement, more choreography, more development, more, more and more. I prefer to interpret this as a backhanded compliment. There are few enough dance performances, or any performances, where I would want to shout for more. I am prone to forming unnatural fixations with glowing exit signs and consider 'sortie' a most excellent choreographer. I am also now reminded of Joseph II, Emperor of Austria, who in the film *Amadeus* cuttingly remarked to Mozart, 'Nice, but too many notes.'

Outsider Artists construct their monuments of self-belief, and ensure they are testaments to the idea that the ordinary can be made extraordinary, that the discarded 'rubbish' of life has value and a potential for a different aesthetic. Outsider Artist Nek Chand created *The Rock Garden* in Chandigarh, India, resourcefully salvaging, processing and reconstituting natural materials and industrial waste, in the pursuit of creativity. In Nek Chand's own words it is 'nature that has created the form, not me. Unlike the "trained" fine artist who is fussy about anatomical and technical details, I make a quick job of the thing' (Bhatti 1989: 25).

Similarly, we processed all the ordinary simple obvious mundane questions, the normally throw-away discarded remarks in order to create an extraordinary product. In fact we asked the rather portentous and stately Outsider Performer Colin Richardson, 'If you could make a dance, any dance on any subject, what kind of dance would it be?' His slow and thoughtful manner was a testament to his creativity and clarity, and related unselfconsciously to his portly but elegant physicality:

> Thinking Dance
> Sitting there thinking
> Sitting down dance
> Sit down
> Smoking dance
> Smoke a cigarette
> That's it
> Thinking dance
> (Lyrics from La Soupe by Outsider Performer Colin Richardson)

Colin Richardson's response revealed an exciting take on the world, exposed an irony which floated in like magic, a creativity which left us at times gobsmacked and prompted further questions: 'If you made soup, what would it be?' After a brief pause he said: 'Dog soup, rat soup, dog soup, rat soup, dog, dog dog soup, dog soup, magic soup.' Genius!

The sumptuous setting of the Royal Pavilion, offset by the magnitude of Outsiders performing in such a monumentally exclusive arena, the gilt chandeliers, the prohibitively expensive 'do not walk on the' carpets, the privilege of palace and place, proved irresistible:

> In the opening introduction they beat out a rhythm with soup spoons . . . in a scene reminiscent of one from Oliver! . . . some find they are being fed rat soup not the leek soup implied by the original ingredients. In a subtle way this seemed to be one of the many political comments underlying the work.
>
> (Hamilton 1990b: 18)

Making work with Outsider Performers is one thing, finding venues and an audience is quite another. Because of the recognition we enjoyed with Divas we were fairly well placed to achieve this almost impossible task and helped secure mainstream professional touring opportunities with Banda Banda. Our continued desire to break boundaries led to the creation of a touring version of La Soupe called La Petite Soupe (1990). Made for The Place's Spring Loaded season it included two Outsider Performers within Divas. We resisted the temptation to promote the work within the accepted annotation 'integrating learning difficulties' since we had carefully selected all the performers for the project based on relevant and related skills.

Using their words as kind of narrative, Aggiss and Cowie somehow dodged a minefield of mawkish sentimentality, littered with suspect devices labelled 'patronising' and 'exploitative', to create a dance experience that communicates such warmth and sincere humanity it managed to both amuse and move without ever resorting to an appeal for pity . . . It could have been all too right-on, too hand on heart sincere, but never once were the special performers at the heart of the piece treated as anything less than fellow human beings. That shouldn't need pointing out, but this isn't a perfect world now, is it?

(Watson 1991: 22)

French Songs and *Beethoven in Love*

The organic integration of La Petite Soupe inspired us to create French Songs (1991) for Divas, featuring the extraordinary Outsider Performer Tommy Bayley. We spotted Tommy clubbing at The Zap, Brighton and his free form, passion, skill and performance presence was mesmeric. He was at the time incongruously dancing an empassioned bullfight with a red hankie surrounded by ravers with whistles.

There is charm by the bucketful in French Songs, but the point though not stated is plainly apparent. One of the performers has learning difficulties but his contribution though central to the work is neither tokenism nor patronising. He is simply there, dancing with the group in a playful, moving and entertaining interpretation of eleven songs.

(Bowen 1991: 11)

There is always a reason, an unseen narrative that charts our artistic endeavours. Having 'found' Tommy, we applied to the Arts Council of England/BBC Dance for Camera Award scheme. Directed by Bob Bentley, Beethoven in Love (1994) featured Outsider Performer Tommy Bayley in a duet with Aggiss (DVD 6:2). His role was Beethoven, one of the world's most illustrious musicians, and himself considered an Outsider. Ironically (or is it tragically?), it was suggested, briefly, that a warning preceded the television screening of Beethoven in Love, clarifying that one of the performers had special needs, a suggestion firmly vetoed by Aggiss/ Cowie. Presumably with a warning firmly in place, an unsuspecting audience need not run to the dressing-up box and put on their sympathy hat. Forewarned would be forearmed; they would already be wearing it! Or perhaps the 'warning' would acceptably censor, pre-empt any potential criticism that 'Outsiders' should be firmly kept in their marginal place as they might be disturbing to a television audience.

Interestingly, in 2003, *AfterLife*, a movie that celebrates being 'differently abled' puts a young woman with Down's Syndrome centre stage. More radical still, the character is played by an actress with Down's. The screen writer Andrea Gibb was asked by a funding executive, 'Don't you think it would be better to make Roberta autistic?' The implication was this would be more camera-friendly and Peebles (the Director) would then have to bring in an established actor to play the part (Hoggard 2003: 5).

The Surgeon's Waltz and *Rice Rain*

In resuming our collaboration with Carousel and their renamed company 'High Spin' in 2000 we made *The Surgeon's Waltz* (DVD 6:3). Local press were enthusiastic: 'The show will make you laugh, cry and clap furiously for more' (Phillips 2000: 23).

Emerging from a series of workshops on the theme of the body and how each part serves a whole, the heart was a focus and resulted in the memorable 'I Give you my Heart': 'An incredibly moving piece sung by Andy Saunders and performed by the troupe was powerful in its simple choreography yet captivated the entire audience with its beauty and emotion' (Hull-Malham 2000: 10).

Our task, as choreographer/directors of this project, is to locate material and choreographic structures that work to the best advantage for a very mixed group of performers. 'The performers all gave stunning performances while still being able to portray the beauty and diversity of being an individual' (Hull-Malham 2000: 10).

Sustaining interest through choreography for choreography's sake is not an option for the tenor of this work nor for the personnel involved. Understanding shortfalls in skills but recognizing potential in expression and performance comes within the remit of this collaboration. *The Surgeon's Waltz* was a cumulative collage of 23 sections hilariously titled by the artists: 'Skeleton Baby', 'Half Monty', 'Rib Dance', 'Coughing Ballerina', 'Bum Bum Bum', 'Winterface', 'Don't Touch my Lemons'. The spatial complexities of recalling 23 diverse sections tested memory, performance skill and creative ingenuity:

> The opening routine had the stage full of crazy surgeons in full operating costume, culminating in the Half Monty, and this Half Monty is the much funnier cousin of The Full Monty. Rubber operating gloves were peeled off, face masks were spun teasingly around the performers' heads, and gowns were tantalisingly

removed as the entire cast became a sassy, brassy, hilarious 'strip' review.

(Hull-Malham 2000: 10)

Without negating these comments, critical reviews for Outsider Performances are usually covered by local press or specialist disability magazines. The Surgeon's Waltz, however, received a number of reviews in the form of Arts Council Show Reports. What is disturbing was that the annotations dwelt on the audience, which was repeatedly identified as being not mainstream and being predominantly disabled. This was clearly perceived as a production failure. Some of the 'unnamed' authors also suggested that performing in mainstream venues should attract mainstream audiences. This implication that a disabled audience is somehow less valuable, and that not having a recognizable mainstream audience somehow negates the work, quite frankly drives me up the wall. 'Mainstream' contemporary dance audiences are notoriously made up of a dance clique of friends, family, students and people 'in the know'. Strangely, some annotations also dwelt negatively on the difficulties the authors had in distinguishing between those performers with disability and those without. These show reports also recommended more complicated choreography. Why? Does complication mean better? Admittedly these are only opinions, and I know you cannot have it both ways, but they get lodged and clog the bowels of a company's archive, and too often fiction becomes fact, and anecdotal evidence becomes statistical information.

And finally to Rice Rain, a collaboration with High Spin, made in 2001 (DVD 6:4). Images of Japanese life and culture were used as inspiration and divided the performance into two parts: sea and ceremony, city life and Karaoke. Using the collage structure and responding to some criticism about the brevity of former 'sketches', we strove to develop more meat on the bones. However, it is a lottery. Either (a) develop complex choreographic structures and in doing so struggle against chaos and 'bending to' the inevitable follow-my-leader syndrome that pervades much 'integrated dance', or (b) forget about the audience and follow the advice of show reports and fall into line with mainstream dance, or (c) use the opportunity to unleash unguarded exuberance, add a morsel of unconventional aesthetics, chuck in camp for good measure, break the rules and keep the show moving. I know what I prefer.

A touching journey by a woman whose shiny black hat masked her face as she threw down her handkerchief and retrieved it over and over again as if reciting a litany . . . The first half closed impressively with Ben Pierre in a long black robe holding aloft an umbrella while rice rain literally hailed down on him . . . Andy Saunders has natural comic timing and the ability to work an audience.

(Dandeker 2001: 28)

Conclusion

Bill Harpe, in writing about *Banda Banda*, preceded his review with some prophetic and defining words:

> There's no shortage of advice available if you want to become a dancer. But there's a definite shortage of such advice if you want to become a choreographer. There is however one piece of excellent direction to would-be choreographers provided by American choreographer Paul Taylor in 12 succinct words – Give yourself a few limitations, and then do the best you can.

(Harpe 1991: 36)

He went on to say in reviewing *Banda Banda*:

> The fact that the audience can understand the ideas and the limitations imposed by the ideas, means that they can appreciate the efforts of the performers. The appreciation on this occasion becomes something special since the performers are accepting not only the limitations which they have chosen, but also additional limitations imposed upon them by nature – and they are building bridges between the two. Paul Taylor himself would surely have joined in the applause.

(Harpe 1991: 36)

You rarely get chances to have organized instant creative access to Outsider Performers so why waste time forcing square pegs into round holes? Thus it is a rare treat to work with High Spin: kindred spirits, extraordinarily interesting, often hilarious and always surprising.

Billy and I owe our lineage to early experimentation in the world of alternative performance and cult cabaret and have focused over the years on an uncompromising and cutting edge choreographic and performance style. This, together with a stylistic and economic use of space and choreographic language, remains at the forefront of our work and indirectly placed us in the position of Outsiders within the dance world for many years. The press we have received over the years has been mixed, we are either loved or loathed. Better that than indifference. But it has raised issues and debates about the role of dance as an art form and hopefully broadened a view of what dance is or could be. Oddly, being cast in the role of Outsider has not been to our disadvantage; we have after all had 23 years of continuous bookings and commissions.

Looking back on the trajectory of working with Outsider Performers, it is transparent that we rattled many cages along the way, challenging and carving into bastions of establishment; venues such as the ICA and the Queen Elizabeth Hall, major funding bodies and schemes. We were driven by an unswerving confidence, demanding a place, not as an inclusion within the establishment, but as an equal and justifiable artistic right to be there.

In each collaborative venture with Outsider Performers, Billy and I have received uncluttered and honest responses from the workshop material. We have always entered the process with a sense of purpose and framework that could reap enough varied and potentially fascinating material. We have never tried to shy away from the difficult, the uncomfortable or politically challenging material. Our job has been to refine and order the information. Our job is to ensure the event is enjoyable rather than worthy, humorous without being patronizing, literate without a dominating and smothering aesthetic, and to allow performance visibility with personalities and individuality that breathe and live.

Outsider vision is raw but nonetheless important. I asked Outsider Performer Joyce Francis what was important to her. Happily she remained true to herself unloading her wash-bag as she danced on to her own voice track:

> I got a big bag,
> My wash-bag
> Does hold a lot
> Bathcubes, mousse, talcum powder, hair lacquer
> Put on yer 'ead
> My wash-bag, my wash-bag
> (Joyce Francis, Outsider Performer – La Soupe)

For some dancers the inspiration is love, relationships and death. For Outsiders it is all of the above but likely to include wash-bags, hats, hankies and shoes. Strangely, audience members who saw these collaborations often quote from these texts which celebrate the uniqueness of the ordinary. Ask any one of them about leek soup, and they will say, intoning the pride in Outsider Performer Veronica Lee's voice, 'Leek soup, I made it, onions and potatoes, you put it in the pot, if it's done, it smells nice.' Call me old fashioned, but I'd say that leaving a visual and aural imprint in the artistic ether long after a transitory event was well worth it.

Acknowledgement

This essay in its first draft was first published in the Spring 2001 edition of *animated* magazine and is reproduced by permission of the Foundation for Community Dance. The essay has been rewritten for this publication.

Note

1   The term 'Outsider Art' was coined by Roger Cardinal in 1972, derived
     from Jean Dubuffet's' 'Art Brut' – literally 'raw art' uncooked by culture,
     unaffected by fashion, unmoved by 'artistic standards'. See Cardinal (1972)
     and Rhodes (2000).

deconstruction in *die orchidee*

mischievous plays in the spaces between language and meanings

valerie a. briginshaw

Introduction

Die Orchidee im Plastik Karton ist Die Blumen für Die Damen, made by Liz Aggiss and Billy Cowie in 1988 for 13 women students (with subsequent versions in 1989 and 1999 for Aggiss/Cowie's company Divas), uses a German/English language tape as the basis for its soundtrack and choreography. Aggiss, having trained with the ex-Wigman dancer Hanya Holm and the Austrian dancer Hilde Holger, is known for her fascination with German subject matter. This is evident in works such as *Grotesque Dancer* (1986),[1] *Eleven Executions* (1988),[2] *Dead Steps Die* (1988)[3] and *Dorothy and Klaus* (1989),[4] where aspects of German cabaret, theatre and movies are explored. *Die Orchidee* plays mischievously with the German phrases on the language tape deliberately chosen to reflect and educate about elements of German culture. Through its choreography and soundtrack the piece exposes the gaps between language and meanings in a deconstructive manner, revealing the undecidability of meaning. By humorously troubling and disrupting conventional closures of meaning, *Die Orchidee* reveals sexism in the language and the patriarchal nature of the culture. This gives it a political edge typical of Aggiss and Cowie's work.

Eleven phrases from the language tape act as starting points for the piece, which consists of eleven sections, each of which exploits the comic potential of one of the phrases on the tape. The soundtrack for each section plays with the German phrase repeating, re-ordering and distorting the words, often rhythmically driven by the accompanying music. This powerful, playful *sprech-gesung* style soundtrack provides a strong rhythmic, semantic and visual basis for the choreography. Just as we read strings of words in a phrase book in lines from left to right, so the choreography is structured horizontally – each section has performers variously arranged in lines and groups moving across the performance space. They mainly travel in unison, often in a jerky and undignified – although precise – manner, sometimes assuming contorted postures, for example with inturned feet, or bodies concertinaed with bent knees, flat backs and heads protruding forward. Groups of performers incessantly repeat phrases of weird, almost sub-human, sometimes insect-like movements looking like animated Escher drawings. Gestures are often naughty, such as fingers tickling under chins, or clawing and scratching the air, and they become more mischievous when accompanied by grotesque grimaces. The play between the formal patterning of the movement phrases and the formal manipulation of the language phrases through fragmentation, repetition, disruption and distortion, and the biting satire of the choreography, is what unsettles the meanings.

The reiteration of the choreography and soundtrack is reinforced by the look of the piece. The performers are all dressed identically, in the original student version, in what looks like regulation school uniform underwear worn for gym classes: white vests and black knickers with white ankle socks and black pumps (Figure 7.1). These identical uniform-like costumes, combined with precisely drilled, rhythmic, repetitive, often unison movement, make the performers appear at times automaton-like. They often mouth the words on the soundtrack, sometimes with partners behind them, looking as if they are operating them like ventriloquists' dummies.

Each section begins with a blackout; as the lights come up, lines or groups of dancers appear in position or edging across the space. They are

Figure 7.1 'Die Orchidee' – students of the University College, Chichester in *Die Orchidee im Plastik Karton*. *Photo reproduced with permission of the University College, Chichester, 1988.*

sparsely lit, mainly from the floor and sides. The effect is of a small German cabaret or club; in the two later versions, the performers are strikingly made-up with red lips and shadowed dark eyes, and they wear red lederhosen-style shorts. Their drilled performance is exaggeratedly 'over-the-top'; they are clearly ridiculing those acts in the Berlin cabarets of the early years of the twentieth century that themselves parodied the *wandervogel* 'back to nature' culture of the period. *Die Orchidee* is, then, a double parody, but at the centre of this parody is the language tape.

Language, deconstruction and translation

Aggiss and Cowie cleverly manage to exploit the gaps that exist in language, and herein lies *Die Orchidee's* intrigue and its political clout. Jacques Derrida, the French poststructuralist theorist and philosopher, renowned for his ideas about deconstruction and language, has said that deconstruction is concerned with 'the destabilization of the stability of the dominant interpretation' of a text (1988: 147). Aggiss and Cowie employ a range of devices in *Die Orchidee* to destabilize and defamiliarize the meanings and interpretations associated with the various words and phrases on the tape. They illustrate, through sound and movement, the openness of language and the free play of meanings that Derrida also reveals through his writings.

By using text from a language tape, Aggiss and Cowie are taking us, in some senses, back to the beginnings of how we learn a second language. Issues about what words, phrases and sentences mean become a key focus. When we are presented with translations of words and phrases, as in a dictionary, then because words can only be explained in terms of other words, there are inevitable gaps in meaning, which often arise from the idiomatic uses of words. This is particularly evident when we translate from one language to another, since translations often do not match word for word. For example, the first phrase in *Die Orchidee* is *Intercity ist Der Zug Der Männer* – *Naturlich* – *Hin und Zuruck* – 'InterCity is the train for the men – there and back' (DVD 7:1). The English has not included a translation of *Naturlich*, which would be 'of course'. Yet the soundtrack, and hence the piece, begins with the word *Naturlich* repeated twelve times before the phrase about the InterCity train is heard followed by several groups of repeated *Hin und Zurucks* ('there and back'). Beginning the soundtrack by reinserting the word that is missing from the translation and ironically means 'of course', as if meanings and translations were straightforward or natural – *Naturlich* – and as if cultural assumptions were also natural, such as the InterCity train *being* the train for the

men, sets the scene for the numerous ironic doublings and deconstructive plays with meanings, translation and language that follow.

The choreography for this section begins with a line of performers,
one behind the other, shunting gradually across the performance space,
precisely in time with each other, with knees slightly bent, to the sound
of the word *Naturlich* repeated again and again. Both the repetition of the
word, as if the tape has got stuck, and the shuffling, shunting line of
performers, disrupt the innocent connection between the word *Naturlich*
and its meaning. Although we hear the word *Naturlich*, what we see is
unnatural. The mischievous play between sound and movement is wittily
subverting and questioning any transparent connection between word
and meaning. By juxtaposing unnatural movement with the sound of
the word *Naturlich*, it is as if Aggiss and Cowie are putting the word
in inverted commas and revealing its constructed and artificial nature.
In this deconstructive manner they show how words no longer have a
simple innocent meaning but mean much more (and much less).

During the course of each step the performers jiggle their pelvises
rapidly back and forth several times to the underlying beats of the music.
This choreography, with the accompanying text of *Hin und Zuruck* ('there
and back') and the InterCity being 'the train for *the men*', suggests sexual
and penetrative activity, as the dancers' pelvises actually go — 'there and
back'. This is a typical example of how the choreography humorously
prises open and plays with and in the gaps of meaning in the language
tape text, not only revealing the slippages in language that are exposed in
translation, but also the patriarchal nature of it.

Translation and transportation

The InterCity train transports us there and back — on a journey. Derrida
suggests that translation is also transportation, taking us on a journey —
the word *translatir* in French means both 'to translate' *and* 'to transport'. To
illustrate this, Derrida often makes the same statement in two languages
(French and English), like the language tape in *Die Orchidee*, demonstrating
the 'slippage between tongues' (Wolfreys 1998: 22). 'There is, as
Derrida's . . . paragraphs indicate and consider, the double question of
translation and transport, translation *as* transport and vice versa'
(Wolfreys 1998: 22). Derrida is suggesting that translation also transports us somewhere else in terms of meaning, which is what language
does all the time. We are often taken somewhere else in terms of meaning
in *Die Orchidee*. The sections of the piece that centre around the phrases
Tango Connie? and *Oh Rosen* are examples. In both, ideas from physical

culture are suggested by some of the movements performed – ostensibly these have nothing to do with tango dancing or roses, but there are, to use Derrida's terms, 'chains of signifiers' that connect them.

To a continuous ostinato of *Tango Connie?*, overlaid with various other rhythmic patterns, pairs of dancers, standing behind each other in profile, with one leg slightly in front of the other and with bent knees, shift their weight back and forth on the spot (DVD 7:2). They then turn and stand in lines with their backs to the audience and bend over forward, with their legs astride, reaching down towards the floor. Turning sideways again, they stretch one leg out behind, keeping the front leg bent. In their vests and pants they, like the models who assume athletic postures in Eadweard Muybridge's black and white photographs, capture motion. It is as if these physical culture fanatics are training for their tango dancing, which is never enacted, only hinted at by the partnerships, where dancers, separated by a tantalizing 6 to 12 inch gap, in stark contrast to the close physical contact of the dance itself, never face each other. The chain of signifiers has transported us somewhere else.

In 'Oh Rosen', the lights go up on a line of dancers, standing legs astride, bent over behind each other, grasping the hips of the performers in front of them (DVD 7:3). The dancers' flat backs provide a long, narrow pathway along which the last of them crawls precariously on her hands and knees with a single red rose clasped between her teeth. On reaching the end, she climbs down and hands the rose to the first in line, who passes it between her legs to the performer behind her. All the dancers swing their rigidly straight arms back and forth between their legs, robotically in time to the beat, like mechanical toy soldiers. The rose is relayed down the line and back as its original carrier tries to keep track of it at leg level. Given the drill dress costumes, this performance looks like one of those team games practised with a ball or bean bag in place of the flower, yet the rose that is being passed began the performance clasped suggestively between a woman's teeth. It has certainly travelled in the course of the performance.

The signifier of the rose in the text (*Oh Rosen*) and the signified actual rose in performance have, in translation, transported us and been transported. Starting as the subject of the phrase – *Oh Rosen* – spoken out of the mouth, the rose then travelled in performance, back into the mouth clasped between the teeth as an object teasingly signifying invitation, and via a precarious route along a line of women's backs, it became, by being passed between their legs, the object of a game. In the original language phrase the rose was simply a rose, but in the course of performance it is revealed as gendered and sexualized by entering and moving between two of the most intimate parts of women's bodies, between two pairs of lips.[5]

The journey of the rose in translation takes us to another cultural idiom – in English, a 'rose' also means a woman. To the accompaniment of *Oh Rosen* – one reviewer commented that the cries of *Oh Rosen* sounded like a woman reaching orgasm (Sacks 1999: 55) – we see a line of women/roses opening their legs, but all in the guise of a team game associated with health, exercise and physical culture. We have certainly been transported in translation here, and taken for a ride via the gendered and sexual connotations of roses in language, which, when played with, are exposed as sexist by objectifying women. Ultimately, it is unclear whether *Oh Rosen* means flower or woman. This is an example of the way in which the deconstructive choreography of *Die Orchidee* explodes meaning, unfixing it, making it undecidable. It shows that a rose can be two (or more) things at once, like Derrida's example of the Greek word *pharmakon*, which means both poison and cure.

Gender and sexuality as sediments in language

Derrida has talked of investigating 'all the sediments deposited [in language] by the history of metaphysics' (1981: 39–91). I am suggesting that gender and sexuality are sediments of this kind that are played with, exposed and investigated in *Die Orchidee*. In every phrase in the piece there is either an overt mention of gender, as in the title – *Die Orchidee im Plastik Karton ist Die Blumen für Die Damen* – 'the orchid in the plastic carton is the flower for *the ladies*' (my emphasis) or a covert mention in a hint of sexual overtone or innuendo as in *Kaffeetrinken und Flirten* – 'coffee drinking and flirting'. The choreography in turn plays shamelessly with these gendered and sexist associations and sexual overtones, as is evident in the examples discussed so far.

These sediments of gender and sexuality in language work in the way they do in part because of association. For example, the phrase *Dann Geht sie Einkaufen* – *Hausfrau und Mutter* – 'then she goes shopping – housewife and mother' – in *Die Orchidee* is accompanied by lines of performers slowly edging across the space, walking uncomfortably on their hands and feet with upturned bodies (DVD 7:4). They often go two or three steps forward and several more back, and different performers edge into the lead at different times. The immediate impression is of rather odd crab-like creatures advancing doggedly in a bizarre race, not making much progress or getting anywhere because they are weighed down with burdens, presumably shopping or offspring or both. The repetitive drudgery of the roles of housewife and mother is instantly exposed in this feminist statement. By juxtaposing the words *Hausfrau und Mutter* with 'then she goes shopping', the language tape is suggesting associated social and cultural meanings. The words 'housewife' and 'mother' are associated with 'going shopping'. Going shopping determines and is part of what it means to be a housewife and/or mother. The sediment of gender in the words 'housewife and mother' is also revealed in 'going shopping'. In addition, *Die Orchidee* exposes in performance that burdens and drudgery also constitute part of that meaning, contributing to the understanding of *Hausfrau und Mutter*.

Gendered plays with writing and speech in the language lesson

The interpretive possibilities associated with gender and sexuality are also multiplied in the 1989 and 1999 versions of *Die Orchidee*, when the cast has an additional performer in the role of a language teacher – male in 1989, when the other performers are female (DVD 7:5), and female in 1999, when they are male (DVD 7:6). In fact the casts of the two later versions, costumed in lederhosen and heavily made-up, look quite androgynous, further freeing up some of the gendered meanings in the text, revealing the potential fluidity of gender and sexuality. Introducing a language teacher, complete with a pointer and a board displaying the German phrases, their English translations and a visual symbol (such as a train, a rose or a shopping basket) for each phrase, adds further signifying levels to the performance, whilst also multiplying the possibilities for gaps and mistranslations. The inclusion of the language teacher, who addresses the audience, involves us more intimately in the construction of these linguistic and social meanings. We too are implicated, and the political impact is strengthened. The performance becomes much more obviously a language lesson, and a heavily parodied one at that.

Before each episode, the language teacher points to the relevant phrase and translation on the board whilst mouthing the text as it is reiterated by a female voice on the language tape. Here *Die Orchidee* is literally confronting us with the difference/*différance* between written and spoken language, which underpins much of Derrida's theory.[6] 'Writing, for Derrida, is the "free-play" or element of undecidability within every system of communication. Its operations are precisely those which escape the self-consciousness of speech' (Norris 1982: 28). By pointing back to the written text of language, it is as if the 'teacher' in *Die Orchidee* is directing us to where the instabilities of language are located. Pointing to the text and mouthing the speech on the language tape highlights the various layers of language and the gaps between them. When the male 'teacher' is mouthing to the female voice on the tape yet another slippage, this time of gender, is revealed in translation. By prefacing each of the sections in *Die Orchidee* with this ironic language lesson, where the board parallels a page from a dictionary, we are reminded that words depend on other words for their explanation or meaning. However, whereas dictionaries regulate language, *Die Orchidee* deconstructs it, blatantly exposing the way it works as a system of shifting translations.

Mischievous plays in the spaces between language and meaning

Aggiss and Cowie mischievously play with phrases and words to bring out some of the idiosyncrasies of German language in *Die Orchidee*. An example occurs in the final section, which brings together many of the features of the piece as a whole. The text is composed of a surreal juxtaposition of three phrases: *Sie Kommen Auch Mit Sekretarinnen* – 'They come also with female secretaries'; *Dusseldorf Ist Eine Sehr Diskrete Stadt* – 'Dusseldorf is a very discreet town'; and *Ich Esse Schweineleber* – 'I am eating pig's liver' (DVD 7:7). The selection and juxtaposition of the phrases exposes the inherent sexism of the first and by association and innuendo transfers it to the others, whilst also poking fun at German bourgeois culture and custom.

As the lights come up the performers are seen lying in lines on their backs on the floor with their arms stretching up at right-angles and their hands grasping each other in the air. They twist their arms to one side and then the other whilst raising and lowering their pelvises. The accompanying soundtrack simply repeats the word *Ich* ('I') over and over. The incessant repetition of one word has been a recurrent element of *Die Orchidee*. An earlier episode, which centred on the phrase *Und Was Darf Ich Dem Herren Geben* – ('and what can I give the man?') – began with various groupings and patterns of the word *und* ('and') repeated. When a single word is repeated, the sense and meaning of the word tends to get lost as its sound predominates, especially when it is used in rhythmic patterns; it then becomes music. This exercise points to the meaninglessness of words – they are simply sounds – with no direct relation to what they are signifying, to what they mean. Yet their reiteration is not reductive, they do not disappear; they instead become something else (DVD 7:8).

The possibility of repetition or iterability of words is, for Derrida, a key characteristic of language; it is built into words and how they work as signifiers of meaning. It enables language to operate as it does with a semblance of stability, but paradoxically it is also the means of its undoing, or the means by which meaning can be seen to be open-ended and undecidable. Derrida illustrates this by taking the word 'yes', which he argues if it is to have meaning must be able to be repeated. If we say 'yes' to something today, we must be able to say 'yes' to the same thing tomorrow for it to conventionally mean 'yes'. But Derrida also points out that the iterability or repetition of the word 'is also threatening, because the second "yes" may be simply a parody, a record, or a mechanical repetition. You may say "yes, yes" like a parrot. The technical reproduction of the originary "yes" is . . . a threat to the living origin of the "yes" ' (cited in Caputo 1997: 27–28). *Die Orchidee* illustrates this in its repetition of words such as *und* and *ich*: they both reassert or reiterate their meaning but in doing so they also lose their meaning, and become something else – music, for example, or the anticipation of something to come . . .

The repetition also has a delaying or deferring effect. Repeating *und* and *ich* suggests something is about to follow, 'and' 'and' 'and' – 'I' 'I' 'I' – but we are initially prevented from finding out what. When the rest of the phrase does follow – *Und Was Darf Ich Dem Herren Geben?* – 'And what can I give the man?', and *Ich Esse Schweineleber* – 'I am eating pig's liver' – its withholding, and the anticipation that builds with the repetition of *und* and *ich*, has revealed a layer of latent, sexual innuendo. This is further emphasized in the performance when the dancers' erect and taut arms not only twist from side to side but also bend at the elbows, slowly lowering and then raising again – not only do the pelvises thrust but the arms do also. After all this bumping and grinding, when the performers suddenly sit up and turn to the audience and mouth *Ich Esse Schweineleber* – 'I am eating pig's liver' – the result is both bizarre and surreal. The intense seriousness of the performance, which inevitably mischievously suggests the stereotype of a certain teutonic dourness, together with the physical exertion, makes it very funny.

The performers resume their supine positions and the pattern of arm twisting and pelvic thrusts, as the full text of *Sie Kommen Auch Mit Sekretarinnen* – 'They come also with female secretaries' – and *Dusseldorf Ist Eine Sehr Diskrete Stadt* – 'Dusseldorf is a very discreet town' – is heard in the accompaniment. Then the pattern of *ichs* repeats again, and the performers turn over and, lying prone, repeat their arm twists and pelvic thrusts, which begin to look quite tortuous in this undignified position, as they try but fail to achieve a vertical line with their arms. As they arch their torsos, raising their heads and turning to the audience again to mouth the text, with their wrists apparently tied together, they look like they are coming up for air in the midst of a sado-masochistic sexual rite. However, the repeated drilled torsions of the arms, which visibly tense the muscles, remind us again of physical culture, taking us on another journey.

Conclusion

I have argued that by playing within and between translations in *Die Orchidee* Aggiss and Cowie have, in a deconstructive manner, exposed 'the way in which translation exemplifies the "abysmal" slippages and detours of all understanding' (Norris 1982: 115). They have exploited the movements and transportation of meaning, the 'slippage between tongues' of different languages and within language itself, by revealing different layers of both textuality and sexuality. Derrida sees texts as 'layers upon layers of "textuality", multiple stratifications, boxes inside boxes' (Caputo 1997: 88). The language phrases Aggiss and Cowie have selected can be seen as a first layer of textuality; their repetition and distortion in the soundtrack, a second layer; the accompanying music, a third layer; and the choreographed movements expose further layers of textuality.

The movement phrases, although processed with repeats and ruptures like the formal structuring of the sound tape, are largely independent of the meaning of the language phrases. They differ and defer from them creating a space or distance between them, which parallels the gaps or spaces Derrida reveals between words and meanings. In this sense, in *Die Orchidee* Aggiss and Cowie unfold the layers and open the gaps in the text but crucially without using more words. They do this through the witty, subversive performance of dance and music with a caustic critical edge. The expressionism of Wigman, Holm and Holger is also deconstructed in the process. The piece looks expressionist because of the grotesque, psychologically painful movement, but actually it subverts, troubles and mocks Wigman's and Holm's high seriousness and deep metaphysical claims. This is where it parallels Derrida's deconstruction of the meta-physical tradition in Western philosophy, of the orderliness of language. Where Derrida revelled in showing up the disorder within language, Aggiss and Cowie revel in wittily showing up the disorderliness of movement, which in turn exposes the sexism in language, giving the piece its political edge.

Acknowledgements

I should like to acknowledge useful critical feedback from the Federation of International Theatre Research 'Choreography and Corporeality' Working Group, who read an early draft of this paper and Ramsay Burt's comments on a later draft. Responsibility for the end result, however, remains entirely my own.

Notes

1   *Grotesque Dancer* is a solo for Aggiss as a German cabaret performer.
2   *Eleven Executions* was inspired by Wedekind's German expressionist Lulu plays.
3   *Dead Steps* developed ideas from *Grotesque Dancer*.
4   *Dorothy and Klaus* was inspired by German expressionist movies.
5   Luce Irigaray has famously claimed that woman's 'sex is composed of two lips' (1981a: 100). The labia are the origin of this image, which Irigaray uses metonomically to think through the distinctive features of female sexuality.
6   Derrida (1968, transl. 1982) exploits the double meaning in the French verb *différer*, which means both to differ (a spatial difference) and to defer (a postponement or temporal difference). 'The neologism différance refers polysemically to both these meanings' (Critchley 1992: 35).

hilde holger, spirit and maracas

liz aggiss and claudia kappenberg[1]

As artists we often have partners, silent or otherwise, to advise, inform, assist, contextualize and criticize our work. Hilde Holger is a firm favourite, embedded into the practice as an ethereal presence, wholly engaged and interested and ready to offer an astute commentary. This book would not have been complete without reference to her.

Born in Vienna in 1905, Hilde Holger trained at the State Academy before joining the Gertrud Bodenwieser Company. In 1923 she began choreographing and performing her own work and was a guest dancer with the Kurt Joos Company. She fled Austria where the Nazis murdered 14 of her family, and arrived in India in 1939, eventually establishing her own school in Bombay and making her living teaching European expressionist dance (Ausdruckstanz) and performing her choreographies. Following Ghandi's assassination ten years later she moved to London, where she founded her School for Contemporary Dance and the Hilde Holger Dance Group. She pioneered performances involving children and adults with learning difficulties, and taught such renowned students as Litz Pisk, Lindsay Kemp, Carl Campbell and Wolfgang Stange, founder of Amici Dance Theatre.

This is an elegant email conversation between two of her pupils: Liz Aggiss and Claudia Kappenberg:[2]

Liz: So, Claudia, what was a nice girl like you, and me, doing in a small, cold basement at some ungodly hour every Saturday for many years, to be suspended for two hours in a world dominated by one charismatic, physically fragile, elderly woman in possession of an iron will, a youthful free spirit and pair of maracas? And another thing: Why was there a regular group of culturally diverse, predominantly mature, performatively experienced individuals, ready, willing and waiting to submit creatively to a space of no compromise, where opportunism was absent, where individuality was congratulated, where everyone counted, where collective and personal identity was lauded and applauded, where complexity and kitsch was given the finger, and critical discourse and clever words were flushed firmly into the overflow?

Survivor, outsider, displaced; Hilde Holger; dancer, choreographer, teacher; born 18 October 1905, died 22 September 2001.

Claudia: 22 September 2001. Strange to read the date of her death in your email. Seeing it in black and white reminds me again of how recent her death has been. She was such a permanent fixture of Camden Town; it seemed she would never give in.

Survivor, outsider, displaced, you say: yes and no. I am a little weary of this configuration of words as it tends to describe Hilde as a victim and, in spite of her life story, I did not experience her as such. Could we complement this sombre aspect with her early years in Vienna, where she was very much part of an extraordinary, groundbreaking, vibrant and diverse community of artists, and successfully performing her own work? I think this is so important with Hilde as she seemed to bring that time with her wherever she went.

Fiery, obstinate, battle-axe.

In this sense she could be described as a 'culture carrier', a term that was used by Radio 3 in a programme of the same title in May 2002. It explored the wave of immigrants from Eastern Europe during and after the Second World War who were experts in the arts, in science and humanities. Hilde experienced the breakdown of cultural boundaries in the cosmopolitan Vienna in the 1920s and early 1930s, and lived through the rise of Fascism in Central Europe as well as the Indian uprising. She brought with her the breadth and wealth of knowledge and experience of different continents, cultures and religions.

Liz: (*Excellent start I feel, I would hate to get it wrong for Hilde which is why I am so pleased you are here in this with me.*)

> One must want to survive to tell the story, to bear witness; and that to survive we must force ourselves to save at least the skeleton, the scaffolding, the form of civilisation. We are slaves, deprived of every right, exposed to every insult, condemned to certain death, but we still possess one power, and we must defend it with our strength for it is the last – the power to refuse our consent.
>
> (Levi 1958: 47)

Hilde dared to be who she was. She dared to not follow fashion. She dared to solve simple ideas in the purest way. She stuck to her guns.

So, as a start, why not put Hilde alongside other individuals who, according to their time and place, have set about constructing and deconstructing, ordering and reordering? Let's start with Yvonne

Rainer's manifesto from the *Tulane Drama Review* and her strategy of denial, her new dance that would recognize the objective presence of things, movement and the body.

> No to spectacle no to virtuosity no to transformations and magic and make believe no to glamour and transcendence of the star image no to the heroic no to the anti hero no to trash imagery no to involvement of performer or spectator no to style no to camp no to seduction of spectator by the wiles of the performer no to eccentricity no to moving or being moved
>
> (Rainer 1965: 178)

Claudia, I only chose this because it is so *not* Hilde but it could provide a kind of template?

This manifesto speaks of a specific performance/dance agenda within a time and place, supported by a developed critique. There is a notion that these rules might provide a perfect objective dance and when we observe this work today, yes, it is what it is but it looks dated. Contrarily, there is something of a timelessness and universality about Hilde's vision. Her desire to not politicize her art form as a way to explain the world from her perspective is perhaps fundamental to this idea. She, more than most, had an agenda that could provide ideas, issues, source material on which to base a plethora of work, yet she chose absolutely to develop an open, receptive vision. And is this why we were all drawn to her, knowing her past and what was written on her body and soul, yet being compelled by her deliberately radical, obstinate refusal to consent to this?

Claudia: Is this a question, or does it describe your own position? In a recent article of the *Artist's Newsletter* the Irish artist Dorothy Cross writes: 'I feel that being an artist is about faith, you are always delving into the darkness in pursuit of newness' (2003: 27). I had copied this quote into my notebook and I remember it here, because it was the unbending faith that drew me to Hilde. Faith above all in the individual, as you say, and in Art, with a capital A. Art for Hilde was two different bodies moving in harmony or the rhythm of a stick echoed in the rhythm of a movement, or the silent dialogue between a body and a plastic bucket. Rather than with past histories or absent friends, she would engage, and engage totally, with what was in front of her, and demand the same commitment from her dancers.

This intense engagement to the present opened, time and again, space for something new to emerge. In each class she would surprise the

Plate 1 'Solo tu Corazón Caliente' – Liz Aggiss in *El Puñal entra en el Corazón*. Photo: Billy Cowie, 1992.

Plate 2 'Kissing Dance' – Liesje Cole and Nusura Mai-Ngarm in *No Man's Land*. *Photo: Billy Cowie, 1993.*

Plate 3 'Golem' – Liz Aggiss in Hilde Holger's *Vier Tänze* reconstructions. *Photo: Billy Cowie, 1992*.

Plate 4 'Offspring are Sprung' – Liz Aggiss and Naomi Itami in *Falling Apart at the Seams. Photo: Billy Cowie, 1993.*

Plate 5 'Who Wants Soup?' – Divas and Carousel in *La Soupe*, Royal Pavilion, Brighton. *Photo: Anita Corbin, 1990.*

Plate 6 'Period Costume' – Liz Aggiss, Sebastian Gonzalez and Richard Knight in *Divagate. Photo: Billy Cowie, 1997.*

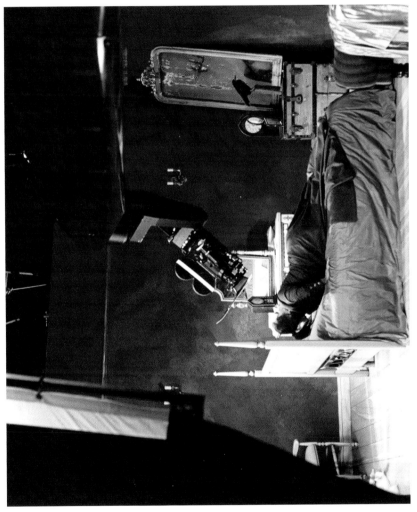

Plate 7 'Film Shoot' – Liz Aggiss in *Motion Control*. Photo: Holly Murray, 2002.

Plate 8 'Solea' – Jeddi Bassan, Sebastian Gonzalez, Scott Smith and Thomas Kampe in *Men in the Wall* installed at the New Art Gallery, Walsall. *Photo: Billy Cowie, 2004.*

dancers with new ideas, and the dancers would be surprised by their own movements. Hilde's manifesto might include: no to pretence, no to absent mindedness, no to mindless repetition. I think this is where Hilde had a timeless quality.

> If we were logical we would resign ourselves to the evidence that our fate is beyond human knowledge, that every conjecture is arbitrary and demonstrably devoid of foundation. But men are rarely logical when their own fate is at stake; on every occasion, they prefer the extreme positions.
>
> (Levi 1958: 38)

Liz: (*I find this 'virtual essaying' so illuminating. I dash in with an extreme demand like, 'Let's write Hilde's manifesto', and you reply with thought and clarity as to why this might be a problem. I like it. And then I plague you some more and say: 'So could we write her manifesto now please? Pretty please?' And you are so delightfully sane and drag me back to reality and why it is not so simple.*)

Your last reference to a potential manifesto made me chuckle, I could almost hear her spitting out the words. My own position as a refusal to consent . . . mmm, I think you have touched a nerve here as to why I felt so drawn to Hilde. She both intimidated and delighted me with her directness and lack of compromise. All of these qualities have been 'directed' at me personally and our work, so this may be part of an intuitive need to be included in her feisty artistic world.

Direct, uncompromising, determined.

I like your description of faith in the context of Hilde. I went with Thomas Kampe to her concert at the Hampstead Theatre in 1988 and saw amongst others her *Dances of Egon Shiele* (1988). Here was simplicity, lack of pretension, commitment to ideas and above all an integrity that paid attention to form and space. Each composition performed, whether group, duet, trio or solo, demonstrated an absolute craft that enabled the audience to see space often aided by small props – little bamboo sticks and hoops. Each movement had a purpose and each dance went on for as long as it needed and no more. Her choreographies were in hindsight a testament to her compositional and pedagogic craft. They affirmed for me a 'European' legacy that I knew through my experience with Hanya Holm, Alwin Nikolais and Murray Louis: compositional nuts and bolts alongside artistic principles; studies in time, space, body within universal ideas; technique embedded into composition; improvisation with clear boundaries; freedom is discipline.

Within the context of Hilde's classes the reference to a contemporary world was ever present. She set group tasks that she manipulated. There was a method to the madness. Our improvisations were crafted towards a choreographic purpose; moving figures of eight were woven into magical duets, patterns were created out of advancing and retreating groups in Picasso Walks (Hilde's answer to a physical manifestation of Cubism), a symmetry created out of a chaotic group. She made things very live. The classroom was like a stage, art and craft together, and she was the director and audience. Here she was timeless and contemporary. Though her hallway was littered with history, it was without indulgence. Everyone who passed through her life could grasp her 'truths' scrawled on post-its and jammed into the wall: 'An all round development of personality is the one thing so essential for the dancer of today.' Am I getting sentimental here?

Would you say Hilde knowingly passed on her legacy, her lineage, so that her artistic history could transcend time and become part of a contemporary reality that would always be present through us as interpretative artists? As her pupil, and with the wherewithal to execute the odd performative act, I indirectly 'quote' Hilde within the substance of my work. Could this be what we mean by her timelessness, a legacy we can develop?

Claudia: (*Our text seems to be finding its own shape, which is what is so wonderful about a conversational piece. It makes me laugh that I have become this voice of mindfulness. But this kind of polarization between you and me works well as a text. It performs, if I may use such a postmodernism, the two sides of the coin of this posthumous writing.*)

I would even go further in that, for Hilde, dance was the absolute cornerstone of education. An article which Hilde wrote in 1947 for the *Evening News*, Bombay could perhaps be read as a manifesto:

> Today creative dance is the essential element of education … Modern dance occupies the first position in the arts. It develops the individual holistically and establishes an intimate relation between the intellect and the emotions. Modern dance is of unique importance in education as it develops the three important aspects of a personality: expression of the body, the spirit and the soul.
>
> (quoted in Hirschbach and Takvorian 1990: 72)

(*Liz, the book translates this from English into German and I am re-translating it into English, but it would take some searching to find the original.*)

Liz: (*Claudia, I think I'll leave this translation as is; it reflects rather well the way Hilde spanned, adopted and embraced so much.*)

I would like you to talk a little about authenticity. These words – authenticity, intuition and instinctive – often get marginalized. Can you speak about this and Hilde if you think it relevant?

Claudia: Authentic? I would hesitate to use this word because I am not sure how we could reclaim a concept, which has been one of the definite casualties of the his- and her-stories and debates of Hilde's century. If the idea of anything being 'truly' original is no more tenable, can anything be authentic? And in what way authentic? In relation to her time or herself or her work? Hilde is very much tied to, and representational of, a particular aspect of history:

> Here I am, then, on the bottom. One learns quickly enough to wipe out the past and the future when one is forced to.
>
> (Levi 1958: 38)

Hilde may have dealt with the past in a way typical to thousands of others who shared her fate; does it make her authentic? Was she authentic Jewish, authentic Viennese, authentic 1920s? At the end of Hilde's century, authenticity was, and still is, if at all, situated within the artificial, the referential and the multicultural. And Hilde's work evolved with time to incorporate, reference and sample a huge number of cultural forms and concepts. In Hilde's book, *Die Kraft des Tanzes* (*The Power of Dance*), the editor Rick Takvorian writes:

> Her art is the aesthetic result of a European dance tradition of the 20's and 30's, without ever becoming frozen in time. Rather her open and positive attitude has always allowed for an integration of her life experiences into her art and led to universal as well as truly individual creations. Her dances are wonderful, exotic miniatures, filigree vignettes, which ban the superfluous with a grace and assurance, which is seldom seen on stage.
>
> (Hirschbach and Takvorian 1990: 9, translation mine)

Hilde was what she came from; she was her time, her century and she was uniquely herself.

I can only speculate, Liz, as to what aspect of Hilde's you feel you are quoting in your work – perhaps you could say some more about this – but this uncompromising, unique, individual quality of Hilde's certainly also pervades your work.

Liz: There are several ways in which I employ the 'quote' as generic form. Hilde is one part of the whole complex sub-strata of contexts in which the 'quote' is a reference to my performance legacy. I can clarify quoting in three ways: mentoring, sampling, referencing. Each has a different property. With Hilde as mentor, I have imaginary conversations. I try to recall what made the movement potent; what made her laugh, excited and engaged; what made me avoid obvious options or make movement for movement's sake. I imagine Hilde mentoring me through this unsightly mess, pushing me on and, because I was a little in awe of her, I try to do my best. For quote-sampling, I recall a movement tic which I borrow, rework, bury as a relevant image within the form, pretty much how current popular music borrows and reworks as a homage or challenge. A good sample example would be Hilde's adaptation of the Nijinsky Walks (Hilde's shorthand for her stylised two-dimensional walk). This is a very visual image which provides sturdy spatial and physically embodied references (L'Après-midi d'un Faune), and we assume Hilde devised this as her own quote-sample. More formally, as in our (Aggiss/Cowie's) work, Hi Jinx (1995), we quote Hilde the person in order to construct the character Heidi Dzinkowska. We are thus enabled to perform pseudo-reconstructions which we identify in the per-formance as from specific dates: 'Joints' (1902), 'Still Born' (1914) and 'My New Family' (1922). In this case the idea of quoting is complex, for without knowledge, physical study and academic understanding of this era I would not have the conceit to perform this role and establish Heidi as reality. As a reference-quote I will be bolder and source relevant visual quotes: a photograph of Valeska Gert, a film still from Nosferatu, a painting by Otto Dix, Nijinska's Les Noces, to inspire the development of a choreo-graphic premise. Like Hanya Holm, Hilde also taught class lessons setting a specific premise or point of view as a way to test evidence and inven-tion. There was no room for indulgence, this was a method to see what physical mannerisms obstructed the movement development. Can you stick to the point? Similarly I test myself with these visual reference quotes, 'reading' them in order to devise and develop a physical premise. I never disguise these quote-references as anything other than what they are and I am rather excited by the possibility of critics or audience members spotting these landmark signs. Ironically, or perhaps tragically, we even 'quote' ourselves in our own choreographies – and rather oddly that is a quote from our solo work Absurditties (1994).

I am now compelled to quote this for no other reason than it seems such a simple idea, and sometimes it is heartening to just be simple:

> The conviction that life has purpose is rooted in every fibre of man, it is a property of human substance. Free men give many names to

Figure 8.1 'Camden Dance Class' – Liz Aggiss and Hilde Holger. *Photo: Jane Finnis, 1992.*

this purpose and think and talk a lot about its nature, but for us the question is simpler. Today, in this place our only purpose is to reach Spring.

(Levi 1958: 77)

Claudia: Reflecting on the question of purpose, I would suggest that the purpose of Hilde was to be present, and to be dancing. One may argue that it was all that was left for her, that it was a means of survival, as Primo Levi suggests. I believe though that for Hilde it was more than survival because there was too much excitement in her, too much pleasure, true satisfaction and commitment to her art, her teaching and her students.

Compared to contemporary thinkers such as Paul Virilio, who discusses the present society in terms of interchangeability and the loss of geographical dimensions, Hilde was deeply rooted in the specific, the individual and the relational. And I mean rooted, like a firm old tree, in spite of all the emigration, immigration, displacements and losses. Starting always with a simple movement or a particular relation between two elements, she would build a choreographic structure without ever losing sight of the notion 'simple is best', or 'less is more'.

What mattered to her was the impact of one body onto another, the sense of weight, the structure of a bamboo stick or the colour of the scarf she was wearing. There was an un-mistaken singularity: 'Front is not side and Andrew's movement is not like that of Thomas.' During improvisation, everybody's variation of a movement was interesting to her and she would make time to watch each person individually.

Liz: True, and reconstructing her work was an act of faith for us 'post-modern dancers' in our ability to translate and embody her material without superfluous embellishment, retain its singular substance and give it individuality. I loved those brief, potent pieces that she choreo-graphed and reconstructed on me. Bill Harpe was accurate in his review in the *Guardian* (1992: 33) when he said 'simple, brief and moving – travelling like the truthful observation of a knowing child directly to the heart of the matter – these solos are more than they seem, poems for the body in motion, clearly and consciously informed by the work of Freud'.

Claudia: Freud, yes; as with all her contemporaries in Vienna, Hilde was deeply influenced by the ideas of Freud. In 1927, Hilde's teacher Gertrud Bodenwieser choreographed a series of dances entitled *Rhythmus des Unbewusste* for a small group of dancers, performed by Hilde, Bodenwieser and other students. In 2000, I was part of a reconstruction of this work when Hilde created a cycle of four dances loosely after Bodenwieser's original as part of a cultural season at the Austrian Institute, London for the centenary of Freud's *Interpretation of Dreams*. It was performed at the Lilian Baylis Theatre. Even if Hilde's memory and eye for detail had somewhat declined by the time of the reconstruction, she still had a very clear vision of the movements that were to convey the sense of the unconscious, of dreaming and desire.

Liz: Going back to your original thought that we should acknowledge the vibrancy of Hilde's formative dance education, Hilde paid detailed attention to the whole production, the music, the costume as if to con-firm her place within a larger entity, a testament to a positive affirmation of the diverse artistic world which influenced her practice: Shiele, Bauhaus, the marionette theatre. Paying tribute to the costume designers, composers and influences was an important part of the reconstruction process. But revivals are tricky and it was important to infuse personal contemporary currency into the performance of her work. I had to find my own story. Sophie Constanti in the *Guardian* (1993: 3) said that they provided 'a fascinating historical insight into the lost Ausdruckstanz of Central Europe'. Since I was performing, my take on this is somewhat different. Can you comment on this? I would prefer to talk of self-expression without sentiment, emotion and wallowing in angst. Yes, a lost history in a broad context of a time, but more timeless than lost history.

Claudia: Indeed you made the pieces yours; you bring together the European tradition of theatre and the grotesque with your British sense of humour and your very own streak of absurdity. When you do the *Mechanisches Ballett* (1926), *Le Martyre de San Sebastien* (1923), *The Golem* (1937) or *The Trout* (1923), I see Hilde's work and I see you, and I have to laugh. Why?

I think we may need to qualify the issue of timelessness. A certain comic element is produced by an encounter of past and present; Hilde's choreographies are extremely bare and direct in their acknowledgement of emotions and conflicts, with a simplicity which appears somewhat at odds with the postmodern emphasis on complexity. Bill Harpe (1992: 33) expressed this very aptly in describing Hilde's choreographic work as 'observations of a knowing child' in the *Guardian* review, which you mention above.

I find that even in writing this essay I can barely say one thing without adding some differentiation. Hilde would simply assert: 'Modern dance occupies the first position in the arts.' Point and finish. This is Hilde in particular, but it is also her time.

Simplicity is itself universal, but choreographically and conceptually it belongs to a certain time. I think my laughter is produced by this wonderful clash between Hilde's simplicity, your own uncompromising presence and the complexity of my contemporary self.

Liz: I admit that performing her work was quite a task. Is this too anecdotal?

Claudia: No no, these details say so much.

Liz: Our work occupies a fine line between tragedy and comedy but maybe it was in my struggle as an interpretative dancer that you saw the cracks. I do not really think I easily perform anything other than my own work since stylistically I use my performing skills to comment on dance and the act of performance by implying questions, giving opinions and possibilities directly to an audience. I recognized that in Hilde's work the necessity is to embody and submit the work to the audience. In fact there is little chance within her choreography to do anything else. Dynamically, Hilde's work is very demanding – like her, either full on or not at all. *The Trout (Die Forelle)* was horribly knackering to perform with its continuous high energy and light convulsive jitterings, which covered the entire stage space. *The Golem* had a densely weighted, solid physicality demanding an enormous presence alongside a refined use of a mask which rendered me blind. *Mechanisches Ballett* had a grounded angularity of flatness and sharpness. Hilde's Picasso Walks was offset by precise gesture while manipulating a complex costume construction. *Le Martyre de San Sebastien* has a feminine purity and delicacy with a high centre, and receptive, open fluidity and expressiveness. This decentralized placement every three minutes was physically confusing and challenging, requiring a fluidity of mind imagery and response. (Alwin Nikolais's philosophy deals with decentralization, a malleable placement and a floating concentration as a practice to gain motional mobility as well as freedom from egocentricity.) With Hilde's work, it really was: 'The king is dead! Long live the king!' These deceptively simple choreographic jewels were driven by clear narratives and accom-panied by powerful music which threatened to overcome the work unless you committed body and soul to the performance. Performing them as a continuous suite of four made me aware of the range of dynamic extremes demanded by each work. The choreographies were more important than 'me' the performer; an exercise in freedom from egocentricity and a complex role to undertake. This is maybe another part of the crack you saw in the interpretations. But how did Hilde ever perform more than four, as in a concert there must have been about ten pieces? Now that is faith!

Total submission, no indulgence, pure concentration, utter commitment.

So anyway, could we write Hilde's manifesto, her strategy of denial or affirmation? What do you think?

Claudia: We can at least speculate. We should try to clarify the term 'expression', which you have used above and which was so often heard in class. It is another one of those historically fixed, old-fashioned terms but it may benefit from a bit of dusting.

Hilde stands clearly within the tradition of Austrian expressionist dance, but I would like to argue that her understanding of expression is perhaps more subtle, and more contemporary than one might think. A key to understanding the notion of expression can be found in a comment by the critic Alfons Torok with regards to the first solo recital by Gertrud Bodenwieser in Vienna in 1919. Torok (1919: 21) finds an 'unconditional rejection of everything handed down and the honest search for new, purely personal expressive values'.

This comment on the work of Hilde's great teacher indicates the value given to difference and individuality and reveals part of the foundation of Hilde Holger's œuvre. Hilde also comments on this herself in her book, *Die Kraft des Tanzes*:

> I had the fortune to have Bodenwieser as my teacher. She was like a volcano, constantly erupting with ideas. She was very inspiring, and she never went against the individual. She was always very appreciative and allowed us to create ourselves.
>
> (Hirschbach and Takvorian 1990: 14, translation mine)

But before I paint a rosy picture I should also add that Hilde struggled immensely with the discipline and style demanded by Bodenwieser, as she had her own ideas even as a young student. Hilde:

> Of course I had to learn a technique, but I always wanted to do things my way. Upon which (Bodenwieser) said: 'No, you must learn what I teach you. Only when you have gone beyond it can you do your own things.' It was very difficult for me to adapt to a style, which was foreign to me. I forced myself.
>
> (Hirschbach and Takvorian 1990: 14, translation mine)

From my everyday experience of Hilde, I am tempted to say that she had an almost blind faith, which kept her going, and which allowed her not to see, or to remember, what could have destroyed her. But this is of course Hilde as she chose to present herself. Recalling her time in India, where she earned a living by performing to the wealthy, she said:

> I had to dance and couldn't reveal my terrible sorrow and pain. I had to hide my tears. They wanted to be entertained and I said to myself: they want to see the dance and not the sadness. But afterwards, behind the stage, I cried.
>
> (Hirschbach and Takvorian 1990: 36, translation mine)

As I wouldn't want to end on that quote, here is another comment, again by Rick Takvorian (Hirschbach and Takvorian 1990: 9). He emphasizes that Hilde's serious lifelong devotion to her art leaves no room for doubt: her *Beruf* (profession) was also a *Berufung*, a calling, a life.

Liz, we have interpreted Hilde's work as both denial and affirmation, and I rather like that contradiction as it describes Hilde quite well.

Mad . . .

Liz: *(I prefer rabid, like a frothing terrier that will not let go!)*

Claudia: . . . kind, loving, unforgiving, demanding, generous.
Can we stop here?

Liz: Yes my friend, but an ending is really another beginning.

Claudia: Can you suggest another beginning?

Acknowledgements

Liz: The process of writing this essay in collaboration with Claudia has
been a joy. It recreates the many happy hours we spent improvising,
batting ideas back and forth, looking at what we had done, considering
alternatives, trying to create the best work that we could whilst being
scrutinized in both body and soul by Hilde.

Claudia: Thank you Liz for inviting me into this process. I have had
moments of sadness and a sense of missed opportunities as well as great
pleasure in remembering the relentless vitality of bossy old *Krüppel* – as she
called herself.

Thanks to Carol Brown for unearthing the Torok (1919) quote during
her research on Gertrud Bodenweiser.

Notes

1   Liz Aggiss performed reconstructions of Hilde Holger's works, *Die Forelle*
     (1923), *Le Martyr de San Sebastien* (1923), *Mechanisches Ballett* (1926) and *The
     Golem* (1937) at Manchester Festival of Expressionism, March 1992,
     Brighton Festival 1992, Institute of Contemporary Arts, June 1993, Bonnie
     Bird Theatre, Laban Centre 1993, Künstlerhaus, Vienna, October 1993, and
     Ballroom Blitz, August 1996.
         Claudia Kappenberg performed reconstructions of *Hoops* (1961),
     Bauhaus (1972), *Orchidee* (1933) and *Indian Impressions*, based on *Rhythm of the
     East* (1954), at the Ballroom Blitz, South Bank Centre, 1996, with Amici
     Dance Company at Riverside Studios, London, and Odeon Theatre, Vienna,
     1998, as well as *Desire*, a new choreography for *Rhythms of The Unconscious Mind*,
     after *Rhythmus des Unbewussten*, a choreography by Gertrud Bodenwieser
     (1927), Lilian Baylis Theatre, 2000.
2   All DVD references for this chapter can be found on the Vier Tänze menu.

choreographic vocabulary 2
time and rhythm

billy cowie

Liz Aggiss and Billy Cowie's work has over the years used a broad diversity of musical and rhythmic styles which would lead one to suspect that their varying choreographies might not have much in common in the context of rhythm. What I would like to argue in this essay, however, is that despite this diversity there exists a certain commonality in their use of rhythm and time, both on the small-scale level (i.e. from moment to moment) and on the large-scale level (sectional, structural) in this body of work.

Here, after a brief discussion about the relationship of music and dance, I am going to examine sections of two of the Aggiss/Cowie commissions for other companies – *The 38 Steps* (1999) for Intoto and *Bird in a Ribcage* (1995) for Transitions[1] – from a rhythmic perspective on the smaller scale and then look at how the exploitation of time and rhythm informs the actual structure of the solo piece *Absurdities* (1994).

Music and dance

The composer Arnold Schönberg was concerned in his atonal works, such as *Pierrot Lunaire*, that having lost the use of tonal constructions he was now using verbal texts as a crutch structurally, emotionally and dramatically for his music. This concerned him to such an extent that he devised his serial system to take the place of tonal structures and free himself from the tyranny of using texts in his music.

There is an obvious parallel possibility that choreographers could fall into a similar dilemma if they use music as a dominant framework (once again structurally, emotionally or dramatically) for their choreography. The choreographer might ask herself how she could avoid this type of subservience of her work to another art form?

One way to avoid this musical dominance would be for the choreo-graphic rhythm and structures to contradict the musical rhythm – *counter-point*.[2] A second way is to create the choreography first and then allow this to form the basis for the musical structures – *dominance*. Another method would be to view the work holistically where musical and choreographic (and also perhaps visual, textual, etc.) elements are all simply one part of an organic whole (a true *Gesamstkunstwerk*) – this rather demands that the elements are created in tandem and are able to influence each other as part of the creative process – *synthesis*. A fourth way is of course not to use music at all and to force the choreography to supply its own structures – *absence*.

On the other hand, one could of course ignore the 'problem' and let the choreography serve the music – after all, Pierrot Lunaire is one of Schönberg's greatest compositions – *subservience*.

The 38 Steps

The 38 Steps was commissioned for Intoto in 1999 and is a 20-minute piece for 19 dancers (hence the title).[3] The piece is based on five pop songs sung by Jennifer Lee from the Divas compact disc entitled *Eatingest*.

The first dance, 'Bed of Nails', has a lengthy, music-free, comic introduction (DVD 9:1) that provides the opening to the piece. This introduction takes the form of three 'false-starts' where a choreography is performed first by two dancers, then by seven and then by the whole company; at the end of each, the performers lose interest and disconsolately leave the stage. The repeated 'entrances' are informed by a sense of panicky lateness, and a certain inter-performer rivalry and struggle for power.

The choreography of the introductions is concerned, among other things, with the contrast between instantaneous movements and those with durations. The movements are controlled by one of the performers making live vocal sounds to literally cue the movements (and importantly their ends) and to suggest the movement quality. The sustained durations and the point movements seem reminiscent of Morse code with its dots and dashes.

An important feature in the sequences is the use of movement gaps, the visual equivalent to rests or silences in music. The use of static pauses can here frame a movement to give it more emphasis, or a group of movements can be isolated to form motifs.[4] This focus on movement silences also helps to define in time the ends of movements. Normally in choreographies the starts of movements are very well defined temporally (for example a jump might commence on the beat) and the endings to some extent left to themselves (the landing will be, temporally, where the landing is).[5] In this piece each movement has a precise duration fixed by its vocal counterpart.[6]

One might wonder just what is going on in these introductions? In fact they are setting up the context for the entire piece with its principal themes of the linked dualities of control/submission, performing/non-performing and individuality/conformity. Structurally the introductions, with their stops and starts, serve as a launch pad for the first song – almost like the cranking of an old-fashioned car starting handle that finally gets the motor running.

With the start of the song, we then enter another rhythmic world entirely. In 'Bed of Nails' (DVD 9:3) many of the same movements from the introductions are used, but here the movements' rhythmical structures are firmly pinned to the song's rhythmic impulses. What is more, the movements unashamedly, and occasionally quite literally, illustrate the sentiments of the song's text, as a sort of choreographic 'word painting'[7] – in Schönberg's eyes the movements might be seen to be hobbling on not one but two crutches!

In 'Bed of Nails', the movements reflect the musical rhythm to a large extent (subservience). However, in the penultimate section of The 38 Steps, 'Love Hurts' (DVD 9:4), the choreography maintains its own independent and complementary line against that of the vocal part (counterpoint). As a simple example of this, if we look at the first line of the song we see that musically the two halves of the phrase 'love hurts' and 'can you feel the pain' start not on the first beats of their respective bars but on the second. This delay runs through the song and imparts a strange quality to the music, which is further enhanced by the placing of the word 'pain'. To fit into a normal eight-beat structure, it should fall directly after 'feel the' and last for one beat. It is, however, delayed by half a beat and elongated into two and a half beats. This hiccup or catch in the music gives a strange, breathy importance to the word and ties in with the whole sentiment of the song. If we now look at the choreographic rhythm, we see that we have two rising movements on the 'love hurts' but then we have a falling back onto an arm on the last half of the first bar (where nothing happens vocally); the exact counterpart of where the 'pain' falls in the second bar. This syncing and then contradiction carries on through the four repetitions of the phrase and becomes even more marked in the 'verse' of the song where long, sustained movements cut across the vocal part and the offbeat punctuations become even more marked.

Basini

A section of choreography where a more subtle control of the dynamics of movement exists is the solo 'Basini' from *Bird in a Ribcage* (DVD 9:5). The piece is a marriage between abstract movement and, in this case, the emotional illustration of the poetic texts.[8]

> You turn your head with your own hand
> You command yourself with your own tongue
> You stop yourself with your own sigh
>
> You beckon to yourself with your own fingers
> You embrace yourself with your own arms in sadness
> You stop yourself with your own sigh[9]

As opposed to the rather crude precision of the previous example, what we are concerned with here is a subtler attention given to the rhythmic control of any movement throughout its duration. Rather than seeing a movement as an impulse which then happens slowly or quickly, the movements are controlled with a certain sustained quality. A musical analogy might be the difference between a note played on the piano and one played on a violin. In the first, after the player has played the note, the only control she has over the dynamic of the sound is when to end it. The violin player is in continuous control of the dynamic of the note; it can get louder, softer, change character, etc. many times in its short existence.

Over the music introduction to 'Basini', the performer raises her arms into an open position – an important concept here and elsewhere in Aggiss/Cowie's work is the idea that there is a difference between actual musically structured movements and what might be termed more pedestrian movement, such as preparations for movements, etc. which I will return to in the next section.

On the first line of the vocal part the performer brings her two hands together in a sustained controlled movement; halfway through the musical phrase the impulse is reversed and the hands come apart again. What is important in the execution of this seemingly simple move is that the illusion must be given that in the change of direction there is no slowing down, in fact there is to be no impression of stillness between the two halves of the move – at one instant they are travelling in one direction, in the next instant the opposite.[10]

In the second phrase of the music/choreography the performer brings the back of her hand toward her forehead. Once again, halfway through the movement, the hand turns and is instantly travelling away again. What was, perhaps, a gesture of despair is transformed into a wave, perhaps even a 'dance movement'.[11]

In the third phrase, the hand and arm surround the head while the mouth opens to a grimace; both actions take the duration of the phrase and appear in an almost cinematic slow motion, as if an accident is being witnessed.

The fourth and fifth phrases show the performer pushing the heel of her other hand forward in three staccato stabs showing the wrist (another Aggiss/Cowie trademark – something to do with the suicidal vulnerability of this part of the body).[12]

The sixth and final phrase of the sequence has the hand over the head 'rescued' by the other hand as if the body splits itself into separate parts, here one hand becoming paralysed (by fear?) and the other helping it recover, as a friend might help another person. Of course, the whole poem is directly about the duality of human nature.

Once again we have on the one hand a physicality which when well performed is breathtaking, and on the other an illustration of the emotional text, here the concept of human volatility, of changeability, the fact that everything can change in an instant. The poem seems to be referring to someone who is controlling herself, but, paradoxically, hints that despite this they are not really in control.

As the introduction plays again, the performer once again moves into a non-performance (whatever that might mean) type of rhythmic movement. To go back to the earlier violin analogy, this whole piece should almost have the effect of the performer playing her body like a musical instrument, with this first pedestrian movement a little like the raising of the bow before the first note, and the instantaneous direction changes a little like the seamless joining of up bows and down bows of a virtuosic string player.[13]

Absurditties

The original premise of *Absurditties* was to create a piece that was entirely stripped down – a single performer (Aggiss) with no set, no lighting changes, no music (Figure 9.1). This absence of music highlights, as already mentioned, the internal rhythms of the choreography. The piece is a set of (deliberately) discontinuous sections,[14] most of them with their own different approach to rhythm and time, almost a catalogue of rhythmical techniques.

'Es Ist Einfach Wundervoll' (DVD 9:6) seems the most straight-forwardly musical of the sections. Aggiss intones the ditty, punctuated

Figure 9.1 'Hoop' – Liz Aggiss in *Absurditties*. *Photo: Billy Cowie, 1994.*

with rhythmic stamping. Each word lasts one beat, two-syllable words being two half-beats and the stamps of the right foot (X) are also each a beat. The first sequence, which is repeated from four to eight times, is:

ES X IST X EIN-FACH X WUN-DER VOLL X X

DASS X MANN X WIE-DER X TAN-ZEN SOLL X X

Two elements conspire first to make this difficult to execute, and second to make it strangely mesmeric to watch, these being the speed of the beats (which is just beyond the threshold where one can mentally disentangle what is going on) and the tripping-up of expectations by the use of twos and threes[15] (if the stamps were alternate beats it would be easy but boring).

ES X IST X EIN-FACH X WUN-DER X VOLL X

DASS X MANN X WIE-DER X TAN-ZEN X SOLL X

At the climax of this section, Aggiss interlaces the English translation of the phrase with the German; what was a rhythmic tongue-twister now becomes a tour de force of concentration.[16]

ES X IT X IST X IS X EIN-FACH X SIM-PLY X WUND-ER VOLL X WON-DER FUL X X

DASS X THAT X MAN X ONE X WIE-DER X STILL X

TAN-ZEN X DANCE X SOLL X CAN X X

Despite its subtlety, this section is undoubtedly a metrical, rhythmic piece. At the other end of the rhythmic spectrum some sections of *Absurditties* could be seen as arrhythmic, such as the opening 'My my' section where Aggiss simply wanders around. (Any succession of events whatever could be said to have a rhythm – what I mean here is the absence of intention by the performer to create any meaningful rhythmic patterns.) This contrast between rhythmically structured and free sections is used to mark a difference between Aggiss the performer and Aggiss the non-performer or audience confidant. Of course the whole piece is obviously a performance, so perhaps the difference is between Aggiss the dancing performer and Aggiss the non-dancing performer.

Most of the work hovers, however, in between these two extremes, and indeed plays on the dividing lines. For example, the 'Bear with Us' (DVD 9:7) section could be performed as rhythmically as the stamping section:

Bear Left
Bear Right
Bear Up
Bear Down
Bear the pants OFF.

However, each line is interspersed with a pedestrian sequence of indeterminate length. The resulting rhythmic structure has a sort of accordion-like form with fixed pairs of points (pants) separated by elastic joins.

Part of the dynamic structure of *Absurdittes* is the jamming together of these different rhythmic approaches with no gaps in between. These immediate changes of mood and pace seem almost reminiscent of film edits in their suddenness – although sometimes it even appears as though a new section has begun before the last is ended and occasionally they seem to coexist. This coexistence can be seen in the 'Baguette Dance' (DVD 9:8) where Aggiss dances a fluid but rhythmically highly structured choreography. However, at the same time, she is eating the half-baguettes that she is holding. This superimposition of non-rhythmic, pedestrian movement and 'dance' movement is strangely unsettling, an effect that is also highlighted by the disparity between the casualness of eating and chewing and the concentrated intent of the choreography. This section culminates in a rhythmically stepped approach to a one-legged cruciform position. Aggiss then remains motionless in this position for a while; she notices a speck of dust, removes it and returns to position, she carries on chewing, looks around, adjusts her leg. Aggiss is at one and the same time, magically, in the dance space and in the non-dance space.

Conclusion

If there is an underlying focus in Aggiss/Cowie's approach to rhythm and time (apart from the paradoxical intention of non-repetition from each piece to the next that runs through all aspects of their work[17]), it is a certain fascination with the paring down of the joins between elements to the point of nothingness, whether it is between two movements or between two sections. This device is used both structurally as a thing in itself and also as means of joining disparate ideas, movements, etc. together to make new ones. As already mentioned, this immediate joining with no temporal gap in between has close links with the practice of film editing, where an audience has learned to make sense of impossible jumps in time and space. This apparently episodic nature of Aggiss/Cowie's work has occasionally led to a certain amount of criticism but, viewed from another angle, this type of structure is very appropriate for the construction of ideas-based works and, paradoxically, can produce work that is more organic and coherent than works with a more outwardly graduated texture.

The other main aspect of rhythm in their work is Aggiss/Cowie's intention to give their choreography an internal musicality. Obviously, all choreography is intrinsically musical – this can perhaps be seen by the number of musical terms used in dance, such as: fugue, canon, counterpoint, motif, etc. However, it is all too easy to allow a choreography simply to hang on a musical framework, merely using the music as a grid in time to fasten movements onto, without investing in its internal musicality. In Aggiss/Cowie's works with music they have tried to tease out the underlying expressiveness inherent in the music (and, in the works without music, tried to shape the choreography in an essentially musical fashion). To return to the 'Schönberg' question from the opening of this essay, a choreography that is determined by a piece of music will not become subservient to it if it actually reinvents the music, i.e. does not passively sit on its structures, but actively seeks to explore new aspects of them and thus enriches it.

Notes

1 The touring companies of the London Studio Centre and Laban, respectively.
2 The most extreme form of this would seem to be some of the Cage/ Cunningham pieces where the music and choreography were created independently and only united at the last moment.
3 Ironically, the only male dancer in the piece had to withdraw due to injury so there were in effect only 18 dancers in the piece.
4 As Heidi Dzinkowska in Hi Jinx (1995) was fond of saying to her agent: 'In this world plenty of people get paid for doing nothing, why shouldn't I?'
5 In 'Hop on Pops' (DVD 9:2), one of the seminal Wild Wigglers dances, it always seemed a little strange that such an inane choreography could be so endlessly fascinating to watch. However, the nature of the piece, involving continuous springing into the air, forced the jumps to end rhythmically as each end was the start of the next leap.
6 The use of singing or vocalizations has proved extremely useful in Aggiss/ Cowie's choreographies over the years and it might be an idea to encourage its use in dance training more, as seems to happen in some non-Western dance techniques, particularly Indian styles.
7 In a musical context word painting is the literal reflection in the music of a word in the song text, for example up, down, sad, river, etc.
8 One would assume the use of poetry in dance pieces to be a fertile area for development, but this seems not to have occurred to any significant extent compared to the overwhelming influence of music in dance.
9 This poem is by Billy Cowie and is translated into Turkish by Mine Kaylan for the song. The English version of the poem was spoken in both the original version and the Hi Jinx filmed presentation.
10 There exists a scientific thought experiment which asks, if a locomotive and

a fly are travelling in opposite directions and collide is there a point in time when the fly actually stops the locomotive?

11   In *Drool and Drivel They Care!* (1990) Aggiss and Cowie gleefully 'quote' the then in vogue dance movement of hitting the forehead with the base of the hand. When performed endlessly by six Margaret Thatchers, however, the move now seems more prescient of Homer Simpson than the refined world of contemporary dance.

12   It should be mentioned that in this piece the performer is standing crane-like on one leg. The sharp movements of the hand make this particularly difficult. While filming the work for Hi Jinx, in the second section the cameraman suggested that, as we were in close-up, perhaps Akiko could put her foot down. However, Aggiss and Cowie heartlessly insisted that the minute fluctuations of the face in the attempt to balance required her to keep it up throughout.

13   The beginner violinist plays with a rigid bow arm and has obvious gaps between the up and down bows. The experienced violinist has a flexible wrist, and as she nears the end of a bow stroke she changes the direction of the arm; the flexible wrist allows the hand and the bow to continue in the same direction. At the end of the stroke, the comparatively more massive arm is already moving back for the next stroke and the wrist can flick imperceptibly to the other direction.

14   Aggiss explains what the piece is about: 'Link three is of course the absurd, i.e. the meaningless aaaaand I mean-ing-less juxtaposition of juxtas in the wrong position.'

15   A similar combination of speed and combinations of simple patterns occur at the end of Stravinsky's *Rite of Spring*, albeit in a much more complex structure. The players count a very fast pulse which they combine in twos, threes and fives – this produces rhythms that sound extremely complex and unpredictable to an audience not able to comprehend their simple basis.

16   The original text is by Franz Wedekind, the translation is wilfully inaccurate and should really read: 'It is simply wonderful that one must dance again.'

17   In the musical sense, Aggiss/Cowie have used a wide range of rhythmical types, which have informed the rhythmic structure of their choreographic vocabulary. These range from the early mechanically accurate music of The Wild Wigglers to the use of looped vocal phrases, entirely live music, mixed live and recorded music. Stylistically the music has ranged from lyrically classical to avant-garde dissonant to popular styles.

the impossibility of the review
in the mind of the critic

ian bramley

In 1995, I first saw Transitions Dance Company perform Liz Aggiss and Billy Cowie's dance work, *Bird in a Ribcage* (Figures 10.1 and 10.2), as part of a mixed bill of short repertory pieces.[1] But despite having seen – and having been incredibly moved by – the performance, I found myself unable to write anything about it. One reason for this was that the piece – a dark, expressionistic look at love and loss danced by a young, all-female

Figure 10.1 'Sea is a Lover 1' – Wei-Ying Hsu and Rachael Read in *Bird in a Ribcage*. *Photo: Chris Nash, 1995.*

Figure 10.2 'Sea is a Lover 2' – Wei-Ying Hsu and Rachael Read in *Bird in a Ribcage*.
Photo: Chris Nash, 1995.

cast – has never really loosened its emotional hold on me. *Bird* was unrelentingly mournful and, at times, uncomfortable to watch. I can still easily summon up the ghosts of the emotions that I felt during that performance; it is the only dance work that has ever made me cry. At the time of viewing, the strength of my emotional response and the completeness of my engagement with its subject matter made it impossible to find the requisite critical distance, the illusory objectivity, that would allow me to step away from myself and apply my intellect consciously to examine my reactions to the work. The directness of the images, the rawness in the emotions presented and elicited, the wholeness of the theatrical conception, all prevented the necessary in-the-moment disassociation separating the 'critic' from the 'viewer' that occurs either during the performance or when reflecting on it later. In addition, I was reluctant to unpick the methods through which Aggiss and Cowie had created their effects; I didn't want to explain the 'trick' to myself.

What follows is the review that I didn't, couldn't, write in 1995. It's still a difficult piece to write; even after seven years, the critical distance between me and the piece is not so wide.

Liz Aggiss and Billy Cowie's *Bird in a Ribcage* is almost unremittingly black in appearance. The lighting of the piece hardly illuminates the action, merely picks out the exposed flesh of the performers from the black background and black costumes. Without reference points, the piece becomes a universal meditation on love and loss and creates a theatrical world whose inhabitants are trapped within the boundaries of grief.

Completing the caged feeling, Billy Cowie's soundscape wraps the piece within a suffocating blanket of intense emotion. The music and the lyrics in both Turkish and English (by Mine Kaylan and Cowie) add to a multi-sensorial experience of suffused misery and anguish.

In the midst of this fully realized presentation of an internal landscape, a group of young women enact choreography that at its core embodies – rather than merely performs – the feelings that Aggiss and Cowie are exploring.

At one point, the cast move in unison, balanced on one leg. Awkward and destabilizing movements are performed slowly for prolonged periods of time. They seem painful to effect, difficult and risky to execute. The whole section is excruciating to watch.

In a duet, a woman seemingly attempts to resurrect her prone, dead lover by gradually bringing her to a sitting position using only one bare foot to kick and push her upright. This is oddly moving in its ungainliness, its tentativeness and its instability, but the unique method of resuscitation is ambiguous in its controlling caresses, reflecting both selfishness and desperation.

Another woman steps forward and contorts her face into distorted portrayals of bleak emotion. These extreme and grotesque facial expressions in another context could seem risible, but in this claustrophobic world they become masks of grief and agony – as unnatural and uncomfortable as the state of mourning itself (DVD 10:1).

When the cast simultaneously raise their shift dresses above their heads to reveal their bare breasts while hiding their faces, the result is a depiction of vulnerability, the obliteration of self-hood in extremes of emotion, rather than an exercise in titillation or objectification.

Throughout, *Bird in a Ribcage* achieves its impact through a limited palette of movement images delivered with complete conviction. It is this simplicity and directness, encapsulated as it is within an inescapably bleak visual and aural landscape, that makes the piece irresistibly moving. I cried.[2]

There were, however, at least two critics who did feel able to write publicly about *Bird in a Ribcage* at the time. Keith Watson, in the *Hampstead and Highgate Express*, and Allen Robertson, in *Time Out*, both seemed surprised that they liked the piece so much. They were, however, very quick to contrast their praise for this particular work with their problems with the rest of Aggiss and Cowie's choreographic output.

Watson (1995: 44) described *Bird in a Ribcage* as 'brief and bittersweet, the surprise was that it was made by Brighton's guru of German Expressionism Liz Aggiss'.[3] If Watson thought that the 'night belonged to *Bird in a Ribcage*' above the other works in the programme, he also was very clear about what he perceived was problematic with Aggiss and Cowie's previous creations: 'the effect often comes across as overwrought, ending up as a parody of Cabaret' and the contrasting merits of this latest piece: 'nothing was spelled out, nothing was overstated'.

Robertson too praised and damned simultaneously:

This is Aggiss at her best. Rather than making concessions to her own highly personal style, Aggiss has instead made adjustments . . . Her obsessions with the line between sexual freedom and sexual domination are here, but are evoked more serenely than usual – perhaps because her cast . . . are simply not worldly enough to achieve the ravaged extremes to which Aggiss pushes her own performance.

(Robertson 1995: 64)

I only came across these reviews when researching this chapter. I was quite surprised when I read them, as they differ markedly from my own response to the piece. While *Bird* takes an elegiac tone rather than the more usual strident, confrontational attitude of Aggiss and Cowie's work, I certainly could determine 'ravaged extremes' within the piece and the performances. To me, the work aligns just as much with Aggiss and Cowie's style as their other works (although it is delivered in a different emotional register) and is just as expressionistic. The clear and simple images of the work contribute to a message that is just as didactic as that of more aggressive Aggiss/Cowie pieces.

Given my own problems in writing about the piece, and the variation between my own responses and those of these other two critics, I became keen to discover more about the critical reaction to Aggiss and Cowie's work and how it related to my own reception of their theatrical dance.

But how do dance critics review a work? What are the underlying mechanisms that allow the responsive and (dare I say it?) creative process of viewing, reflection and written articulation to take place?

What follows is my own viewpoint on what these mechanisms might be. They are not based on any particular theory, but instead on an acknowledgement of my own practice as a sometime dance critic and upon the reading of other critics' reviews in a range of contexts. I believe the illusory objectivity I refer to in the opening paragraph of this chapter pervades the role of the critic. While one person's viewpoint can only ever be subjective and individual – based upon their own unique responses to a dance work, and dependent on their own personality and lived experiences with which they frame their responses – the mechanisms by which a critic is able to review dance creates an illusion of objectivity for the critic, at least temporarily. Complementarily, the public presentation of one person's response to the work (the critic's review) gives it the appearance of an objective report upon which readers can rely.[4]

But what constitutes the critic's mistaken sense of objectivity?

For everyone in a traditional theatre setting, the act of viewing in the dark, in silence, is done in isolation. But in addition, for the critic, the act of writing is a solitary one and this – along with the isolated presentation of a critic's voice in print – creates a slippage between the individual and the universal, the objective and the subjective.

There also needs to be some 'critical distance' between the critic and the work to be reviewed. Joe and Jane Public can happily immerse themselves in a theatrical experience without worrying about what they need to say about it. A critic on the other hand is in the business of describing and analysing a work – or at least his or her responses to it – and therefore any direct reaction to the work is undermined by conscious or subconscious rumblings of the review to be written. Either while watching the work – or while thinking and writing about it at a later time – a critic must disassociate him or herself from his or her responses or the direct effects of the work itself in order to be able to articulate those responses and that work in words. This stepping outside of your own responses can give a sense of viewing those subjective, singular reactions from a distanced, objective viewpoint.

There needs to be a certain confidence and certainty of response on the part of a critic – a definite reaction and appraisal of a work. Critics are expected to be knowledgeable about dance – to bring to their reviews a sense of history and context, as well as an authority based both on experience and upon knowledge gained from other sources that allows the reader to trust their responses. This sense of 'authority' – the critic as a repository of information derived from both their own past exposures to dance and from other people's writing and responses – also has a tendency to erase the difference between subjectivity and objectivity. The danger with this is that everyone's knowledge is finite and selective, and critics may rely upon a certain understanding of aesthetic criteria and a familiarity with a certain kind of work to inform their writing. If what they watch exists beyond this framework, the feeling of objectivity and authority is challenged.

As a way of investigating responses to Aggiss and Cowie's work further, I began to look at critical writing on *Grotesque Dancer* (1986), created for their company, Divas.[5] The main reason for this is that the piece in many ways typifies the works that both Watson and Robertson find so problematic in Aggiss and Cowie's œuvre: it is a solo that concentrates on and relies upon Aggiss' singular performing presence; it is, as the title would suggest, grotesque and challenges received notions of aesthetics and beauty; it explores issues of identity, androgyny and sexuality. Significantly, it also interrogates the expressionist roots of Aggiss's performance, by adopting the idiom of Germanic cabaret performance from the first half of the twentieth century.[6]

As already evidenced within the commentary by Watson and Robertson on *Bird*, there is a difficult relationship between contemporary critics and the expressionistic early modern dance of pre-World War II Germany that often explicitly or implicitly underlies Aggiss and Cowie's works. While Robertson (1995: 64) feels uncomfortable with the 'ravaged extremes' of expressionist emotional intensity, Watson (1995: 44) is more overt in his labelling of the works as coming across as a 'parody of Cabaret'. The capital 'C' is important: Watson is referring to the 1972 film directed by Bob Fosse and the stage musical on which it is based, rather than the historical cabaret of Berlin and elsewhere from which the film takes its basis. One of Watson's strengths as a critic is his utilization of popular culture references to make dance accessible to a wide audience, and his reference to *Cabaret* forms part of this tactic. It does, however, hint at a lack of engagement with the artistic foundations of Aggiss and Cowie's choreography.

Sophie Constanti (1987a: 26), in a positive review of *Grotesque Dancer* in *Dance Theatre Journal*, also refers to *Cabaret* when commenting on the androgyny present in the work: 'Aggiss is part Liza Minnelli in *Cabaret*, part football star'. Constanti then goes on to draw links between the work and that of Grosz and Dix, rather than the dance that is contemporaneous with the work of these visual artists. Indeed, even where the references to the Germanic roots of the work are thoughtful, they rarely link directly with the dance art form. For example, cinema is used by two critics as a way of characterizing the piece: Judith Mackrell (1987: 11) describes the piece as a 'highly cinematic version of German culture . . . flaunting a hard muscular beauty between decadent narcissism and Hitler Youth Fanaticism' (and comparing Aggiss to a 'silent screen villain'); Stephanie Jordan (1987: 2) in the *New Statesman* finds in the work 'the bleak world of Weimar Cinema from Louise Brooks to Nosferatu'. Elsewhere, critical response seems to confuse the genre through which the work is presented with the perceived subject matter and aims of the piece: Jenny Gilbert (1999: 8) in the *Independent on Sunday* opines that as 'a recreation of Third Reich cabaret this is absolute tosh: not dark enough, not vicious enough, not socially pointed enough', while Louise Levene (1999: 8) in the *Sunday Telegraph* suggests that '[e]ven if Divas intended a satire on the British fondness for German-bashing it was insultingly shallow'.

All of the above comments, which come from both positive and negative reactions to *Grotesque Dancer*, suggest to me that at the end of the twentieth century, either Ausdruckstanz was something that critics felt ill-equipped to write about or they suspected that references to this era of dance history would be of little interest to their readership.

I found a parallel to this viewpoint in a *Guardian* article on the German painter Ernst Ludwig Kirschner, in which Sebastian Smee (2003) describes an underlying 'bedrock of embarrassment that today undermines both our ability and willingness to respond to the style of art we call expressionism'. He suggests that this contemporary resistance to expressionist visual art is based upon a discomfort with the insanity and mental breakdown that a number of expressionist artists (for example Van Gogh, Edvard Munch, Kirschner himself) experienced and the now unacceptable idea that 'to be an artist you have to experience madness and psychological breakdown'.

I believe that this is linked to a more general distaste for what Smee (2003) calls the 'emotional self-abandonment' of expressionism on the part of white, middle-class British audiences; an embarrassment at watching artists expose the 'ravaged' extremes of emotion that we culturally expect to be hidden. And it is precisely these ravaged extremes and the unease that they cause that prevent Aggiss and Cowie's work being seen as contained works of art that can be coolly viewed as an aesthetic object. These are works that bleed and attack, not necessarily works to be admired safely from a distance. They are works that reach out and attempt to implicate us in their irrational world.

Half-way through the performance of *Grotesque Dancer* at which I was present,[7] a couple noisily walked out. This is a brave thing to do at the best of times in the Purcell Room at London's South Bank Centre, as the door is at the front of the auditorium and can only be reached by passing very close to the stage and into the audience's field of vision. The desire to leave must have been extreme: stronger, at any rate, than the fear of passing within reach of the terrible and authoritarian presence of Aggiss's stage character. This overt rejection of the work may represent the flip side to my complete surrender to *Bird in a Ribcage*. I allowed myself to be implicated in the emotional world of the piece, but without that surrendering – giving myself permission to participate in the theatrical extremes of emotion – would the response have been disengagement or repulsion? In a number of negative reviews that I read during the course of this research, the tone suggests a distancing from the work, a complete and utter lack of engagement. There is I suspect an all or nothing situation – you either submit yourself to Aggiss in all her terror or misery or you are left out in the cold; either the piece never leaves you or you are compelled to go.

What is interesting is that at least one critic has discerned an equivalent position for Aggiss as a performer. In a review of a previous incarnation of the piece in *New Dance*, Virginia Farman (1987: 20) suggested that Aggiss 'makes no excuses or compromises to her audience . . . In return Aggiss lays herself completely open, making herself vulnerable.'

This contradictory juxtaposition of assertiveness and vulnerability may be exactly what I find so compelling in all of Aggiss and Cowie's work that I have seen. But I suggest that to watch a performance by Aggiss is to strike a deal, one in which you make yourself as vulnerable as she is as a performer. This creates an honest but risky engagement for both parties, and one that is difficult to achieve if you are also trying to maintain enough critical distance to write about the work.

One of the other strong features of Aggiss and Cowie's work is that it dwells in perceived ambiguity and the juxtaposition of opposites. For example, Stephanie Jordan (1987: 2) describes *Grotesque Dancer* as a disturbing 'mixture of humour and horror, dignity and absurdity'. Comments are often made about the androgynous nature of Aggiss's characters, or about the ambivalent portrayal of her personas' sexuality. Tellingly, Judith Mackrell (1987: 11) locates the ambiguity of Aggiss's performance in *Grotesque Dancer* as something that 'hovers brilliantly between invitation and repulsion'. This alludes to something more than ambiguity of content; it suggests the dilemma of the work and the ambivalence of response on the part of the viewer or the critic to Aggiss and Cowie's work. One of the most intriguing things about the writing on *Grotesque Dancer* is that critics often express their own opinion, while at the same time acknowledging that a different viewpoint exists. Occasionally a phantom 'other' is referred to that loves or hates the work in opposition to the critic, as within the Virginia Farman piece (1987: 20) where she talks pejoratively about the 'some' who find the work's 'shocking contrast between aesthetic beauty and unglamorized physicality . . . an unnecessary subversion' (Figure 10.3).

At other times, attempts are made at explaining the divergence of opinion. Julia Pascal (1988: 19) in the *Guardian* locates the division along lines of gender, saying that *Grotesque Dancer* presented 'a scenario which disgusted male critics but was greeted with warmth by women writers'. Ann Nugent (1987b: 17) in *The Stage* divines that genre and art form are the basis for the split: 'The Place's audience . . . was apparently divided in response: those with a theatre background derived something from it. Those with a dance background did not.' Sophie Constanti instead presents aesthetics as the underlying cause during a polemical piece in *Spare Rib*:

> A lot of people hated *Grotesque Dancer*. If that's because [Aggiss] had the guts to be really grotesque in a work where it's demanded shouldn't she be commended instead? It's depressing that dance 'purists' can't cope with a savage truth.
>
> (Constanti 1987b: 33)

Even Robertson's and Watson's reviews of *Bird in a Ribcage* can be seen as presenting opposing viewpoints, though in this instance both perspectives belong to the same writer. This duality both suggests defensiveness arising from the critics' lack of confidence in their own interpretation and a realization that their opinion is neither universal nor necessarily 'correct'. Generally, critics assert their own opinions and interpretations as unchallenged (though implicitly subjective) truths. At times critics will recognize that their own opinion differs either from the general response of the audience or from received opinion, but the acknowledgement of different viewpoints in writing on *Grotesque Dancer* is unusual in its frequency. There seems to be something in Aggiss and Cowie's

Figure 10.3 'Shaved Head' – Liz Aggiss in the original version of *Grotesque Dancer*. *Photo: Billy Cowie, 1986.*

work that undermines the critic's self-assurance. It may be possible that the mutual surrender that I have suggested is required to fully engage with the work undermines the easy assertion of the writer's confidence in their own critical viewpoint by problematizing the simple object/ subject relationship. Alternatively, it may simply be apparent to critics that the audience is divided in its reception of the work, and in seeking explanations for this they come up with a number of different answers that fit within their own political viewpoint, world experience and that of their perceived readership.

In the end, Aggiss and Cowie's work resists becoming a passive object of critical response by undermining the mechanisms through which critics operate. Indeed, my own problems in writing about *Bird in a Ribcage* arise from a difficulty in being able to assert myself as a separate subject in relation to the piece. The emotive words used in the reviews of their work – even if they are presented to be dismissed – 'shock', 'disgust', 'repulsion', 'horror' – demonstrate an unsettled relationship between the reviewer and the piece on stage. This, while it is the power of the work, becomes the source of a body of critical writing that finds it hard to pin down Aggiss and Cowie's output in words.

Notes

1   *Bird in a Ribcage* was first performed publicly by Transitions Dance Company on 9 February 1995 at the Bonnie Bird Theatre in London. The cast was: Becky Brown, Lucy Dundon, Wei-Ying Hsu, Akiko Kajihara, Kathinka Lühr, Rachael Read, Colette Sadler. The lighting design was by Anthony Bowne and costume design by Suzie Holmes. It was later revived by the company, on a new cast, in 1999.

2   Of course, with this review, I am cheating. This cannot be an equivalent of the review I would have written seven years ago. In writing it, I was reminded of Wordsworth's *Tintern Abbey* (1984: 133): 'And now, with gleams of half extinguished thought, / With many recognitions dim and faint / And somewhat of a sad perplexity, / the picture of the mind revives again'. The review, in fact, represents a composite of my recollected feelings to the 1995 theatrical performance and more recent responses to watching an archive video of a 1995 performance by Transitions Dance Company of *Bird in a Ribcage*. Following the writing of this paper, I am now also conscious of what I consider to be the 'pitfalls' into which other critics' writing on Aggiss and Cowie's work has fallen.

3   Many critics – myself included on occasion – restrict Billy Cowie's input to composition. However, Cowie also collaborates with Aggiss on the choreographic content of works created for their company Divas and other commissions. It can be noted in this and a number of the quotations taken from reviews in this chapter that Aggiss is referred to as the sole *auteur* of a piece.

4   This is a simplification and a generalization. Readers of reviews may be highly sophisticated in determining how their own subjective viewpoint matches or otherwise the subjective perspective of the critic. However, the publishing of reviews within newspapers or magazines as a sole report of a dance work within that arena does, at a base level, give a semblance of objective reportage.

5   *Grotesque Dancer* has also been performed on a number of occasions over a number of years and there is a considerable amount of writing relating to this piece.

6   Aggiss's relationship to expressionist early modern dance is a direct one, through her training with Hanya Holm and Hilde Holger.

7   I first saw a late incarnation of *Grotesque Dancer* at the Purcell Room of the South Bank Centre, London, in 1999.

deconstructing heidi

sondra fraleigh

Written in response to a lecture performance by Liz Aggiss of Hi Jinx (1995) at the Centre for Performance Research Grounded in Europe Conference, 1 December 2001, held at the University of Surrey, Roehampton.

I am peering into a time tunnel opening upon a dark stage, waiting for a piece of my own past to appear – I am an American revisiting her experience of German expressionism at the 2001 conference in London, 'Grounded in Europe: German Expressionism and Tanztheater'. The corridor of my imagination extends over a hundred years, encompassing the twentieth century and the new millennium. As I concentrate on the darkness at the other end, I catch flashes of myself through the lens of expressionism: my birth in 1939, at the height of Hitler's maniacal nationalism and six years before the end of World War II; my study with Hanya Holm in 1961, and her encouragement of my journey to Berlin in 1965 to study at the source of expressionist dance with the legendary Mary Wigman. Holm, who exported German expressionism to America, was my first contact with this style. Later, I recognized its influence on American modern dance through my university studies and my classes with Alwin Nikolais. I also watched with admiration the renewal of expressionism in the postmodern work of Suzanne Linke who was a student with me at the Wigman School. We reconnected in 1985, and I began to write about the feminism of her dances.

I am here at the conference to visit my past on other grounds, to speak about the influence of German expressionism on Butoh, a form of dance arising from post-war Japan that has since become international in participation. I hope to turn the tables back to the late nineteenth century with Japan's influence on European impressionism and symbolism, the movements behind expressionism, then move forward to Tatsumi Hijikata's founding of Butoh through the use of surrealist tactics and East–West contradictions. I will detail how I connect to Butoh in its global reach, not simply through Japanese introspection or German expressionism, but existentially through my life story. I will relate how the bombing of Hiroshima and Nagasaki, the subliminal ashes from which Butoh arose, echoes in my own exposure to radiation fall-out during nuclear testing on the Nevada–Utah border throughout my teenage years.

Butoh and the Tanztheater of Pina Bausch both had roots in German expressionism and its acceptance of the grotesque, but they were also responding to the graveyards and ruins of World War II. Each in its own way was anti-authoritarian: Bausch in a sassy way, and Butoh in deviation from aesthetic rules through hanging, awkward postures, beautiful ugliness and painfully twisted faces.

I think how my post-war immersion in modern dance at the Mary Wigman School is such a small slice of the real thing as I see Isa Berghson in the conference audience. She studied with Wigman immediately after the war in bleak, cold studios. Last night she told me of her experiences over dinner. My intersection with expressionism is more distant, but nevertheless founded in what Mathilde Thiele (c. 1988) called 'the original stew' of modern dance. Aside from Wigman herself, Thiele was the principal teacher at the Wigman School in Berlin from the time of its founding just after the war in 1945 until it closed in 1967. She was one of my teachers there, eventually coming to live just 20 minutes away from me in upstate New York where I saw her often and listened to her memories of dance and war. Thiele, one of the original expressionist dancers, was born in 1904 and died very recently in 2002, having lived through a century of modern dance and modern technological warfare, surviving the bombing of Dresden.

Before I left the Wigman School, I made a very amateur film of the goings-on at the school and Wigman's 79th birthday party in 1966 which included our student dances for her. It is a reminder to me of the controversial diva whose reputation is now called into question through her possible connections to the Nazis. Liz Aggiss, a current diva dubbed postmodern punk, performs tonight with a script by Billy Cowie. She also studied with Hanya Holm and with Hilde Holger who kept the spirit of German expressionism alive in London, choreographing works reflecting the flowering of German and Austrian, Jewish and gentile symbiosis almost until she died in 2001 at the age of 95. Marion Kant is in the concert audience. After the performance, she will speak to the silence she feels surrounding the possible Fascist leanings of Wigman and Laban. I think to myself how lives in the past do not reduce easily to historical archaeology, but I also sense the importance of digging.

Here we sit at this end of the time corridor, bathed in the light of hindsight. What would I have done about Fascism had I lived in similar circumstances, I wonder? What am I doing now? Am I willing to take responsibility for the injustices that I see? They, the foreigners at the other end of the tunnel, on the other side of history, are silent. They no longer speak for themselves. Shards – bits and pieces – are what we have left of who they were and how they danced. We know that they danced wildly sometimes and also with tenderness, that they sought a form of human expression free from the strictures of society, dancing nude in nature and building on tribal impulses as they voiced their dance in movement choruses. They also championed the individual: 'I know how I dance', Wigman would say in her classes. 'What is your dance?' was her challenge. The voice from the tunnel of history reminds me that tribal connections are powerful motivators of personality. Shared aims emanate from the root chakra of the body's energy system and are important to a sense of belonging. But choice, the voice says, is clearly a higher state, often the polar opposite of group bonding. Choice originates in the second chakra; it is the creative agency we exercise as we individuate and declare who we will be – how we will dance.

At our end of the corridor, the audience waits without a clue about the upcoming performance. What, beyond Pina Bausch's blending of Teutonic ruins with Brechtian gestures, might anyone make of German expressionism now? I don't expect volcanic Tanztheater from the severe looking woman who walks onto the stage. Now I know I'm in another era because she's not wearing a postmodern T-shirt and sweats. She is wearing a long body-wrap black dress and boots – *wunderbar*! Her exposed arms are muscular and round. This is no skinny dancer. She is self-referentially sturdy, aware of her brawn, and likes herself this way. Her in-your-face hair is dyed a burnished red. I don't know it yet, but I'm about to meet Heidi, the mind child of present day German expressionist Liz Aggiss.

My senses expand to attention. As my body catches up with my mind, it strikes me that dance is not a verbal language, however we may try to make it speak. Dance is extralinguistic; it speaks in tongues and bodily utterance, and we are its sorry interpreters. When I see Liz, my curiosity rises. I can't imagine what she will make of history. She certainly appears 'mod' in a blocky, familiar, yet strangely time-warped fashion. She is definitely not the loosely strung or neutral postmodern of America. She is early modern dance of the past made present and some-what matter-of-fact.

My mind sifts through the metaphysical artifacts of war, and I try to locate Aggiss in the fall-out. I can't figure out exactly from whence she hails, but even before she speaks, there is something of a vaudeville villain about her, an aura of melodrama, and the licence of a cabaret singer. That she is neither here nor there, not post-war, not Weimar, yet somehow both, intrigues me. The stage is set with a small table. There is a book on the table. Aggiss introduces herself. She is going to tell us about Heidi Dzinkowska (known in America as Hi Jinx), a lost figure in the annals of German Ausdruckstanz, and she will also attempt some select reconstructions of Heidi's most important works. Now I see that her performance is also in a time tunnel. It is only in the last two years that Dzinkowska's work has begun to resurface after 20 years lying in obscurity, and her importance in the development of twentieth-century dance is still the subject of fierce debate. Aggiss begins her lecture performance on an inclusive note, and with a German accent:

> Fellow dancers – for as Madame Dzinkowska was so fond of saying, 'Are we not all dancers? Are we not all singers, are we not all philosophers, and under our skin are we not all human?' This is not a lecture but a celebration of Dzinkowska's life. We have films, reconstructions passed to 'moi' and we have Heidi's memoir and what is known as every dancer's bible *A Life in Dance*.

Aggiss picks up the book on the table and reads directly from Heidi's memoir:

> A life in dance is a life well spent; for is not life a dance, from cradle to grave with many a side step along the way, many a battement and many a . . .

As she continues, I lighten up considerably. Dzinkowska comes to life in the lecture demonstration of her work, and I find myself laughing at expressionism, feeling a little guilty and not sure why. The artist as a full human being was emphasized throughout early modern dance; no movement could be truthful without an inner impulse. Movement and meaning were a part of each other. So how about humour? Did it have a place? Yes, I remember gratefully; laughter came unannounced, like a thin spot rubbed bare in dark fabric, a hole with a pathetic finger winking through. Holm became noted for her comedy, and she gave us problems in composition classes to stimulate our funny bone. For all her mystery, Wigman could also smile. 'Surprise me' was one of her improvisation assignments, and, 'Make me laugh.' Creativity could not be complete, nor humanity fully expressed, without comedy.

Aggiss confronts expressionism head on and tongue in cheek as she pursues Heidi's career and dance writings. She introduces a film of Heidi herself dancing *Bateau de Peau (Boat of Skin)* (DVD 11:1):

I am rowing, rowing down the river of blood, and my boat is made of skin stretched tight across a frame of bones, and the current of blood is so strong I shall never return to where I came from, and the people on the sides of the river shout, and they wave at me, but I row on alone in my little boat of skin.

A young Heidi, obviously not Aggiss, appears in the film. She performs (almost mimes) pedestrian tasks, balances the wooden oars, standing them on the floor stoically, while accordion music and a simple French song accompany her gestures of independence.

Technique, of course, is not to be pursued for its own sake in the emerging modern dance of the 1920s and 1930s (as also in the post-modern of the 1960s and 1970s). Heidi (an original modern/postmodern) underplays it. She appears childlike with straight black hair and blunt bangs framing her innocent face, rowing on through the song, sitting on a chair, cycling earnestly with the oars. Toward the end, her legs tread mid-air. Finally she sits very still, balancing the oars in front of her body, holding them by the knees as her dainty arms sweep through the space. The camera catches the essential dance. Heidi's face reflects the matter-of-fact use of oars out of water as she bends forward and back, crossing the oars behind her head, and so on.

'In the original production of that piece Heidi accompanied herself with song,' Aggiss tells us. I laugh at the corny music, the lyric under-reach and triviality, and I remind myself that humour lets us in through the back door, deflating grand designs. Aggiss is not going to let us wallow in the heaviness of expressionist lore. No, she means to deconstruct it, by pushing funny buttons, resisting what could be called with some semiotic importance 'the dominant discourse' of the Grounded in Europe Conference.

Producing a sonic masterpiece, Aggiss performs a bone crunching musical dance, replete with *gestalt in raum*, shaping the space (body-space in relation to surrounding space), cracking fingers, ankles and shoulder joints in Heidi's piece from 1904 – *Joints* (DVD 11:2). Reconstructing Heidi's work, Aggiss strides one leg forward in a jutting pose then holds her finger, pulling it until it pops. Now I see: she will really milk this one. Her body must be wired, I think, or the cracking sounds pre-recorded so she can jerk on cue. The audience drops into the time tunnel cackling, falling into Heidi's trap. In *Joints*, a sober Aggiss pops away unpredictably, assuming wrought expressionist shapes, as I crunch into words:

Angst ridden, the more for ruse
She tenses into shapes,

Wrenches her neck to the side for cracking,
Returns to the finger motif,
Masochism
In her averted face.

Takes off the long skirt
Over the mini-skirt
To show her naked legs,
Fishbelly white above the black boots.
Stands on one leg to lift the other.

Then there is more cracking
With each percussive upward
Elevation of the lifted leg.

She laces her fingers behind her neck
Twisting it abruptly.
The crack
Snakes through her
Rippling retrograde to the beginning stride.

Heidi ends her dance with a rub of the neck
To see if she is still OK.

'1910 saw the birth of Dzinkowska's *Still Born*,' Aggiss tells the audience.
She then goes on to quote portions of Dzinkowska's dance philosophy:

In my work I frequently emphasize stillness and the use of
immobility. With increasing age and memory lapse this can come
in very handy, as the audience never quite knows if the still beating
of their own hearts is part of the piece or just performer's brain
seizure. I often say to my agent: 'In this world there are plenty of
people who get paid for doing nothing; so why shouldn't I?'

Still Born
Taught to Liz
By one of Heidi's most famous pupils Akiko
Begins with a swift lift of the leg,
Places and holds it at various intervals.

Reaching her arms out – one step at a time,
Heidi looks into her hand,
Shaping her hands and arms, feet and legs
Fluttering her fingers.

Two dimensional body torques
Accent her anything-but-free dance.
Lower and lower, gravity weighs her down.
Holding fast, her dance focuses on the floor.
Motifs are repeated, earnestly.

Perpetuity waits as the dancer
Looks away from us.
Reaching,
Then turns away from the gesture
Bending, head to knee, for the end.

The dance progresses as a reconstruction of poses, well focused and held
for a few seconds each. We hear the accordion again – observe Heidi
observing the floor in a two dimensional consciousness, well sculpted
and pliant. We listen and laugh at Heidi's dilemma, each footstep is
so crucial. We focus our eyes with Heidi into the distance, suddenly
changing shapes with her, then morph slowly into another equally tense,
meaningless gesture.

There is more of Heidi's philosophy: 'I often say to my pupils keep
your heads on. This is of course known as hedonism.'

And from her diary we learn about subtle signals in the dance world:
'Today there are different ways of lacing up one's ballet slippers to show
sexual preference.'

Akiko (who was probably one of Heidi's lovers) performs one of
Heidi's works. We see it on the film that Aggiss shows (DVD 11:3):

You embrace yourself
With your arms, stop yourself
With your own sigh.

Akiko balances on one leg
And opens her arms
Along with her mouth,
Then frames her head over the top
With one extended gesture.

The piano plays solo.
Then comes a voice
Just in time for Akiko's
Hand to cover her eyes and face.

Opening her mouth
In a modified Cry from Edvard Munch,

In the shadow of the shape,
A past master disappears.

In the words of Mary Wigman (Synder and MacDonald 1983): 'Every work of art is the result of a unique and unrepeatable process of creation ... It can be effective only at the moment of its living realization.' Or as we like to say in America (and as applies especially to Akiko's interpretation of Heidi's dance): 'You had to be there.'

Here in the corridor of time, we link the past with the present and hear from the conference speakers about cultural identity, dismembered identities, eliminated identities, mistaken identities and rhythmic totalitarianism – so much to identify and everything in pieces, sifting through the dead and the living. Bausch problematizes the nature of community, Meg Mumford says in her paper, 'Performing national identity: From the greater wholes of German Ausdruckstanz to the gaping holes of Bausch's Tanztheater' (2001), Bausch challenges the spectator to imagine forms of identity and history unthreatened by the notion of wholeness. I am reminded through her paper of Michel Foucault, a philosopher-expressionist who was the first to point out the dangers of obedience through 'docile bodies' as he deconstructed sex in his History of Sexuality (1978). He would have a field day with Bausch's work, I think. She accomplishes similar themes and turns them around in dance. Where collective identity is overtly at play, both Bausch and Foucault are lurking. Foucault dramatizes this with his own life, refusing dominant patterns of sexuality. Bausch tests limits of contemporary gender conflicts through dramaturgy and dance with her desire to work from subjectivity rather than fixed technique. (As deconstructive precursor, Dzinkowska anticipates both Bausch and Foucault.)

Anna Sanchez Colberg's lecture (2001) draws parallels between past and present expressionist strategies as she maps patterns of corporeality. The emphasis on emotion seems key: form as emergent, synthetic or 'total' theatre, relationships of self and world, and the anti-mimetic dancer who doesn't represent an absent other. Bausch especially presents a 'desemiotized' chain of events that has layers of interpretive potential.

Underneath these discussions, I try to seize a broad stroke that sweeps through the time corridor. I suspect it is this aspect of emotion, moving bodily from the second chakra up through the third to the fourth, from agency through intuition to emotion, manifesting in the chest through the heart chakra. Melodrama dwells here in this tempest before it rises through the will, the throat chakra, and travels up behind the eyes to be transformed by consciousness and the power of detachment. Melodrama is the very definition of attachment, and it can be used theatrically in a mode of resistance, as Peter Brooks makes clear in *The Melodramatic Imagination* (1976: 41): 'The melodramatic utterance breaks through everything that constitutes the "reality principle", all its censorships, accommodations, tonings-down.'

Wigman's *Hexentanz* (*Witch Dance*, 1926) is an early example of resistive expressionist melodrama. It thrives on intensity and signals to the future through its fugitive spirit. It functions as a form of counter-discourse undermining realism and suggesting a range of fears and desires that dominant social discourses simply cannot account for. It is on the high end of melodrama, since it seeks no particular closure. It dives deep and stirs the passions, lets us probe the dishevelled moment. Wigman's Witch coincides with Richard Murphy's explanation in *Theorizing the Avant-Garde* (1998: 144) of how expressionist melodrama exerts an oppositional power upon repressive discourses, forcing them to reveal their limitations and sites of power.

So how about Heidi? She is also a reformer and innovator who uses melodrama to resist the dumbing-down of the body. Crucial in the development of twentieth-century dance are the seven positions that Heidi Dzinkowska introduced into ballet technique, according to Aggiss (DVD 11:4):

1 The Envelope
2 Harmonielehre
3 The Silent Wife
4 Cross Stitch
5 Hot Tub [I think this comes through the influence of Akiko]
6 Arctic Waste
7 Approaching Dawn

Transformations of Hot Tub, we learn through Aggiss' research, became a classic Japanese dance style, and *My New Family*, the dance that took the world by storm, was based on the seven positions. A soaring soprano accompanies this dance as I distil it here:

Heidi sits on a chair and uses #2 to begin with,
Manipulating her legs with imaginary strings.
Next she leans into the middle of her legs and stands.
Twisting to the side, she paces and twines her arms.

Goes to #1 The Envelope, arms around head.
Goes to #3 Silent Wife, covering her mouth.

Then tiptoes into #7, Approaching Dawn.
Goes down into #6, Arctic Waste.

Kneels on both knees with her arms imploring the heavens,
Drawing essence down into her body
For an Envelope cover #1
Over Arctic Waste #6.

In a short film showing Heidi's three-person dance training, shoes attach to mechanical dummies that the pupils learn to manipulate (DVD 11:5). This device enables her choreography of *Her Him and the Other One*, a trio for one. 'First I turn one way then the other,' she says, making sense of the multiple solo, somehow. Heidi dances this work with herself – *Lei, lui e l'altro* – as though she had never been modern (Figure 11.1). As I see it:

Poles with boots attached,
Extensions with loops,
Circle when the feet move,
And frame her sweet face.

She backs up, then comes forward,
Speaks to the circles.

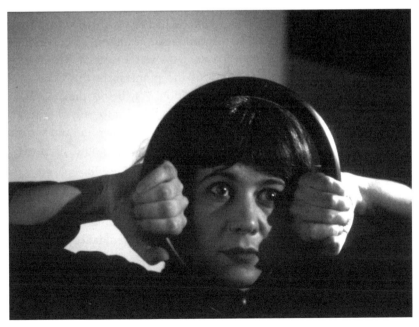

Figure 11.1 'Lei, Lui e L'altro' – Heidi Dzinkowska in *Hi Jinx*. *Photo: Max Wigman, 1911.*

Alwin Nikolais, Oscar Schlemmer,
Eat your heart out,
And Cry Uncle!

So much ahead of its time, the dada-esque *Meet the Neighbours* invited all the neighbours to perform all the parts. ('I am like a club sandwich' best describes this dance.)

Heidi's final piece, *I Forgive You Anthony*, was inspired from real life: her former lover Anthony shot her in the back of the head in a fit of rage (DVD 11:6). Heidi performs this dance sitting, folding a piece of cloth, laying her head, silent as a paper doll, down upon it. Violin and piano catch her sombre mood. She turns and reclines the back of her head upon the cloth. Picks up a cigarette and takes a puff, drops some paint into a bucket of water (or something) and stirs. Toward the end she takes out a huge syringe, fills it, and uses it as an eye dropper. She places the cloth around her neck . . . a precursor to postmodern pedestrian task dance. Serious stuff this being oneself. Woops another puff of the cigarette. And casts a downward glance.

I Forgive You Anthony parallels the plight of women as they come from an older system to a modern state of being. This dance contains (as we like to notice) *all kinds of symbols*: of transgression, destruction and metamorphosis. The moral of this dance is: when someone shoots you in the back of the head you had better wake up, Dzinkowska! Unfortunately like many artists, she was not recognized in her own male-dominated time. Her lover brought about her professional demise, as has often been the end game for women. Dzinkowska was a woman who was to influence so many to come – one of the pioneers in this ecological century with her Arctic Waste dance position. Way before the *Exxon Valdez* catastrophe, where the drunken captain ploughed into one of nature's jewels off the coast of Alaska, Dzinkowska was both a heroine and a tragic figure, her life an inspiration (lesson?) for women to come. *I Forgive You Anthony* represents the core of Dzinkowska's dance training.

We hope Aggiss and Cowie will seek funding to continue their research into the life and works of Heidi Dzinkowska, for she embodies something classic in her iconoclastic timelessness. Dzinkowska certainly deserves our praise if for nothing more than her seven dance commandments, and I quote them here (DVD 11:7):

1   Thou shalt not improvise, keep your improvising for the bathroom.
2   Thou shalt never run around the stage in circles for no apparent reason, no one wishes to see that.

3   Look your audience in the eye, dancers who only look at themselves
     have something to hide.
4   Thou shalt not wear leotards made from green artificial fibres.
5   On no account hurt or damage your dancers with the thrash and
     crash techniques.
6   Say what you have to say then stop. If you have nothing to say don't
     even start.
7   No dance piece shall last longer than 42 minutes. So get on with it.

And I add an eighth especially for Aggiss in her short skirt: Thou shalt
not show the audience your muscular legs, unattractively bared from
mid-calf above your boots to just under your butt, rendering your knees
quite knobbly. No one wishes to see that either.

Melodramatic comedy allows us to escape the ponderousness of history
as we remake ourselves in light of the present. We can revise the past
in the present, not forget it, but 'invert it' as in Foucault's upending of
egocentric anthropology. When we turn history upside down with
Heidi, we deconstruct with humour; like seeing the world for the first
time when you stand on your head. Aggiss is also looking through the
time tunnel. She is Heidi looking back at Heidi – exaggerating, even
underplaying, the expressionist programme to make it more visible.
When we laugh at Heidi, we are laughing at history through fiction and
reinstating zero (or maybe one) as a powerful number. We erase ourselves in absurdity and renew our breath, cracking knuckles for chuckles
to see how our expressionist body births in the dance.

choreographic vocabulary 3
space

billy cowie

From one perspective, Liz Aggiss and Billy Cowie's film projects[1] – *Beethoven in Love* (1994), *Motion Control* (2002), *Anarchic Variations* (2002) and the 3-D, four-screen installation *Men in the Wall* (2003) – can all be seen as explorations of space, and spaces, not just those inhabited by the performers, but also the spaces between the viewer and the performance. I propose to examine them from that perspective in this essay.

Initially, Aggiss and Cowie started out making purely live dance performance and using video merely to document those pieces. Their first specifically 'made for film' dance work was a BBC2/Arts Council of England commission directed by Bob Bentley in 1994 – *Beethoven In Love*. Thereafter, two of Aggiss/Cowie's live works contained film elements: four black and white 16 mm films in *Hi Jinx* (1995) and four videos shot for *Divagate* (1997). Since 2000, Aggiss/Cowie have shifted their practice much more into screen dance and made *Motion Control* (in collaboration with the animator David Anderson), *Anarchic Variations* and *Men in the Wall*.

This move away from live stage work towards film practice can be seen to be driven by three general currents that have flowed through Aggiss/Cowie's work from the start – these being control, visuality and scale – all three of which are intimately connected with the central spatial theme of this essay.

Control

It is often thought of as a limitation of screen dance that the audience is less able to participate in the creative viewing process by directing their gaze where they wish. In a live performance situation, the viewer can choose to look at one performer or another, to focus on certain body parts or movements, in other words to have a unique and personal interpretation of the work. In a filmed dance piece, to some extent those decisions have already been taken by the director, and the audience is in a certain sense disempowered. Everyone must be familiar with viewing screen dance (this is especially true of documentations of live work) where they feel, 'This is not where I want to be looking at this time.'[2] The other side of this coin, however, is that this focused direction of the gaze can become part of the choreographic process itself, especially in made for screen work, and even more so in those cases where the director and choreographer have a close working relationship or are one and the same person.

Visuality

Aggiss and Cowie have always laid strong emphasis on visual aspects in their work. In their early pieces — given the practicalities of live touring on limited budgets (basically any set or props would have to be physically carried from venue to venue by the performers) — visuality was limited to the choreography itself, the costume, the multiple slide projections in *Divagate* (by the visual artist Jane Fox) and a few startling portable props.[3] Film obviously gives huge possibilities for not only embedding the choreography in locations and sets (either real or virtual), but also in controlling the look of the work through framing and editing. Indeed, the regulation black box space of so much live performance — which is necessary to provide the continuity and maintain the integrity of work that is touring — is not only flat in terms of visuality — it is physically flat as well. Sets that may lift the dancers off a single plane of performance require juggernauts for touring and then, because they tend to be fixed, themselves become constraints on the movement. One obvious answer to the ubiquitous black box is the site-specific dance work where the choreographer can indeed use the vertical dimension — stairs, balconies, hills, etc. and where a wealth of visually interesting contexts can inform the work. The obvious drawback of the site-specific work is just that: it is site specific and can't be easily toured. Film, however, lets the choreographer take the site to the audience, wherever they are.

Scale

An important element in Aggiss/Cowie's choreographic technique is the expression, through movement, of character and personality. This is most easily done through smaller movements, gestures and facial expressions, which are necessarily limited in a theatrical context from a purely practical point of view. In order to make them visible the movements have to be scaled up and thus lose their subtlety and intimate character.[4] The medium of film with its infinite possibilities of close-up and editing has no such limitations — it gives the dancers the opportunity to speak choreographically rather than shouting.

Beethoven in Love

Beethoven in Love is a 15-minute dance for camera work commissioned by the BBC/Arts Council of England. Of the four works considered here, this is the only truly site based work and is set in an actual building. The use of a specific site can, as already stated, enhance the visual richness of a scene, contribute to the choreographic content and illustrate the narrative. In the section 'Mailied' (DVD 12:1), the choreographic device most used is a reflection or mirroring of the two dancers. Both perform roughly similar phrases – travelling up and down the balconies, the old 'disappearing behind a wall' joke, scissor gestures, etc. It is, however, the difference between the two performances that is important for the illustration of narrative and character – the playfulness of Tommy Bayley (as Beethoven) and the coolness of Aggiss (as one of the objects of his romantic affection). This choreography could of course have been performed in a black box space, but it is the symmetrical mirroring of the actual space (a small chapel) with its two identical balconies that makes it work – in actuality the whole space is never really seen and it is only deft camerawork, particularly the over-the-performer's-shoulder shots, that 'builds' the scene in the viewer's mind. This mapping of the volume of space between the two protagonists also provides an important metaphor for the psychological 'space' between them. At the end of the scene is the flower cutting section, where the flowerpots are knocked over the edge of the balcony down into the space of the choir below. This introduces a vertical element into the construction – we are able to simultaneously see the join between two worlds, the personal and the professional. Indeed, one of the joys of Beethoven in Love is the exquisitely crafted links between the five sections of the film – which seamlessly and effortlessly take the viewer through five completely different 'worlds'. These joins are a testament to the close working relationship of Aggiss/Cowie with director Bentley and lighting camera Baynes.

Motion Control

Motion Control is an eight-minute dance for camera made in collaboration with director David Anderson – Aggiss/Cowie's second commission for the BBC/Arts Council of England. The principal conceit of Motion Control is the illusion that the camera is an actual presence with intelligence and a certain curiosity. This is created by the practice of moving the camera in a continuous fluid path with great mobility and very few edits.[5] This examination of the space and its inhabitance by the camera, as well as giving the camera an identity, also changes the nature of the performer; the obtrusive observation of her turns her into a kind of specimen. The uncomfortably voyeuristic nature of the camera's behaviour is also turned back on the viewers – after all they are in a way represented by the camera (DVD 12:2).

In most films, the direction (in both senses of the word) of the gaze by the director is normally disguised. It would be disruptive if the viewer were to register each edit or camera movement; we have in effect been trained and conditioned to accept the artifices of film and ignore them. In *Motion Control*, however, the nature of the continuous takes and the sometimes extreme camera positions, for example when the camera first encounters the performer it shoots up 30 feet above her, forefront the camera viewpoint so the viewer is always conscious of what the camera is doing. The piece was filmed with a motion control camera (hence the title), which, while capable of amazing precision and flexibility in the positioning of the camera, proved incapable of faster, rhythmically precise movements that would have allowed the camera to be choreographed to match the performer – the original intention of the film. It is envisaged that in future projects Aggiss/Cowie will use hand held and steadicam cameras to move closer to this goal of the choreographed camera.

In *Motion Control*, the movements of the camera are further signalled by being audible on the soundtrack; the audience can hear the camera move. In the film, Aggiss/Cowie use a heightened form of sound termed hypersound. This could be considered an aural counterpart of the visual close-up – in a live dance piece it is only fairly loud sounds, say leaps or exaggerated breathing, that are normally heard by the audience. In film, it is possible to bring much smaller sounds, for example material moving, a touch, a sigh, etc. into audible range, either through amplification of the original sounds or, more commonly, through producing new equivalents artificially and dubbing them on.[6] In *Motion Control* the hypersound is so extreme that on the one hand it adopts a comical effect and on the other becomes part of the musical score (DVD 12:3).

Anarchic Variations

Anarchic Variations is a seven-and-a-half-minute dance for camera film made in 2002. The title of the film contains the two basic elements that come together to make the film – the idea of a confined space exerting a controlling influence on someone who eventually rebels against it in the *anarchic*, and the formal musical structure of the *variation* with its episodic nature and play on the juxtaposition of change and similarity. The theme of the variations is the nature of space and time, and the variations are the squeezing and manipulating of those elements (the actual music and costume also follow the variation structure).

The first section of the film (DVD 12:5) – the theme – defines the space and plays on the idea of not giving the viewer enough information to establish what is actually happening – for example the opening shot is pure white with no sense of perspective or scale and it is only when the first boot enters the scene that we realize our location and proximity. Similarly, as Aggiss traces round the walls, defining the space, they are so bleached out that is only when she collides with each one that we realize they are there. Only by the end of the section do we realize she is trapped in a white cubic box.

The first variation (DVD 12:6) explores the distortion of scale. The performer appears to be in the same white box but as she moves to one side she enlarges, to the other she shrinks. This effect is achieved by the old 'false perspective trick' where the camera is positioned at such an extreme angle and tilt that the right of the back wall is almost three times as far away as the left. The right side wall is false and not perpendicular but leaning into the space at an angle of roughly 60 degrees.

Variation two (DVD 12:7) plays with the idea of the 'relativity' of movement. If the observer is moving exactly in parallel with the observed, it, the object, appears to be still – we are after all hurtling round the sun at millions of miles an hour but yet feel we can stand still. In this variation, the choreographic technique of freezing a part of the body in space and moving around it is enhanced technically. Aggiss performs such a choreography, holding at one point her arm in stasis and at another her hand. Inevitable tiny movement fluctuations and rotations occur in the hand/arm in such a performance – however, in post production the picture frame was later moved and rotated frame by frame to negate these tiny movements. The hand/arm thus is magically still while their small movement irregularities are transferred to the dancer's body. This is only possible due to the pure white background which has no reference points which would have revealed the frame movements.

In the third variation (DVD 12:8), the performer attempts to escape from the box by running. The nature of the closed space, however, necessitates that she simply runs up the wall, across the roof, falls down the other wall, ending up where she started – in effect her universe is closed. In the fourth variation, order seems to have returned and Aggiss seems to have run out of steam. As she performs a graceful arabesque we, however, realize that the wall is now the floor and the floor the wall. It is as if, after the turbulence of the previous variation, the universe has settled down again, only in the wrong position.

The sum of these various sections is a sense of entrapment and of confusion as to the nature of reality. In the final graffiti variation the dancer attempts to regain some control over the white space by spraying it with colour. Her last action is to paint the front wall of the cube, the one through which we have been observing her (DVD 12:9). The question remains whether her final actions have in some way liberated her or even further enclosed her. As in reality, perhaps all anarchic gestures are doomed to futility but graced with a certain effort of resistance.

Men in the Wall

Men in the Wall, created in 2003, is a four-screen stereoscopic gallery installation that runs continuously on a 25-minute loop. Entering the gallery space we see four life-sized windows/pictures looking onto various backgrounds and in each window is framed both literally and metaphorically a man. Each is in touch vocally with his three fellows, but at the same time isolated from them. They pass time, dance, make some jokes, sing, sleep, waken, repeat, pass more time – endlessly – and then do it all again – and again (DVD 12:10).

The medium of film is often thought of as two-dimensional as opposed to three-dimensional live performance. However, a moment's thought will show that this difference is really an illusion. In the first place the live performance ends up as a two-dimensional image on the back of your eye. Second, a projected film contains a wealth of detail (perspective, relative size, masking of one object by another) that enables your brain to create a solid impression of depth and space and work out how objects and people are moving in it. What then are we to make of three-dimensional stereoscopic films? If normal film is really three-dimensional where does that leave the 3-D film? I would argue that it is in a way even more 'dimensional' than, say, a normal live performance because its nature highlights this 'dimensionality' and provokes questions regarding space. When a live dancer stretches her hand toward you, you don't really think 'that hand is getting closer to me' – when a 3-D film performer does, you do.

The four men are trapped in their existentialist worlds not solely by the frames, but also by the two-dimensional surface of their projections. This two-dimensional skin can be stretched both forward and backward but never broken. The stereoscopic effect, while occasionally used in its conventional dramatic sense (as when the dancers appear to reach out of the screen), is here much more important for the solidity that it imparts to the figures: limbs are rounded, if a leg is behind another then it really seems as if it is (DVD 12:11). This solidity enhances the illusion that these men really are embedded in the wall and also highlights just what three-dimensional creatures we all are and how, particularly in dance, the body is literally exploring space – something that it is easy to take for granted.

Although screen-based, *Men in the Wall* is not the same as *Motion Control* and *Anarchic Variations*. Three important differences change the way the audience views the work: the presence of four screens, the fact that the camera position never moves, and the endless looping of the piece. These first two remove the directorial control of the viewer's gaze – by fixing the camera the directors have abdicated the power to suggest where the audience should focus their attention, and by providing four screens and the freedom to move around the gallery they have reinstated the viewer's ability to choose where to look at any point. In this respect, the piece aligns itself more with live dance performance than film. Paradoxically, the ongoing, endless nature of the piece, while relating to the existential-ist predicament of the protagonists, takes the piece away from the fixed duration/beginning/ending of most live performances, while at the same time yet again increasing the viewer's control of how they will view the piece – they may leave when they wish, remain for several cycles, return at will.

Conclusion

Beethoven in Love can be viewed in a fairly conventional manner but the three later pieces share a certain uneasy connection between the audience and the performers. In *Motion Control*, the observer enters the performer's space and even the performer. In *Men in the Wall*, the performers are somehow attempting to break into the viewer's real space – they even appear to be aware of them. (Warren: 'I saw them again', Holger: 'Who?' Jeddi: 'He means his bloody ghosts', Holger: 'What ghosts?' Warren: 'The ones with the green and red eyes.'[7]) In *Anarchic Variations*, the audience form the final wall of the white cube, looking in through a sort of two-way observation mirror that is finally painted out. Aggiss, however, knows we are there and can see through that mirror. Indeed, Aggiss/Cowie's live work has always strived to avoid the presenting of pictorial work, i.e. where the audience views a scene in a detached manner. This has been done principally through the directing of the performance towards and even into the audience, sometimes in quite a confrontational manner.[8] This is derived from Cowie/Aggiss's backgrounds in cabaret performance and goes right through the live work from *Grotesque Dancer* (1986) to the 'stand-up dance' of *Divagate*. In film, it takes the form of the direct look into camera – a potent way of breaking out of the internal screen world all the way from Oliver Hardy to *Alfie* and *Orlando*.

It might seem strange that in attempting to escape the tyranny of the live performance black box space Aggiss and Cowie have forgotten to get rid of the box itself. I would argue, however, that the boxes and frames that run like a leitmotif through all these films are the opposite of the neutral black box performing space and are dynamic partners in the choreography itself. Aggiss and Cowie's concern with the camera framing the body in *Beethoven in Love* is, in the later films, made literal. As their work, through this interest in framing, is approaching the format of the visual artwork, the shift in their recent pieces towards the gallery as an appropriate space for it is perhaps appropriate.

One of the mantras of the BBC/Arts Council of England dance film commissioning structure was always: 'Thou shalt not make a screen dance work that can be performed live.' This understandable anxiety of those august bodies not to come anywhere near the already mentioned problems of dance performance documentation and their earnest desire to create a new art form was always seriously embraced by Aggiss and Cowie. *Motion Control* was always intended to be a film work that could never be performed live – and yet?

Never say never. *Scripted to Within an Inch of Her Life* (2002) deconstructs, rearranges, and then reconstructs the film *Motion Control* in a live, interdisciplinary, installation context, using four screen projections. This 40-minute piece embeds (in more ways than one) the film in a performance context. The specific film techniques, such as edits, speed changes and hyper-sound, are recreated live. The live work has fed the film; the film now feeds the live work. Interestingly, though, *Scripted* is performed in art galleries. Aggiss and Cowie are out of the black box and they are not going back in.

Notes

1   In this essay I propose to use the word film to cover both video and film, i.e. that which is filmed rather than the medium it is filmed on; apologies to film purists – we like film more as well.

2   In documentations of live dance performances there is a tendency to show everything coupled with an anxiety not to miss anything out. This usually ends up in extensive use of long shots where, ironically, the lack of

choreographic detail ends up in nothing of interest being shown and nearly everything important being missed out.

3   Most notably the hanging, folding babies designed by artist Gary Goodman for *Falling Apart at the Seams* (*so it seems*) (1993) which on many occasions prompted the following exchange: Customs Officer: 'What's in that enormous box?' Aggiss: 'Just three 10-foot high hanging babies, that's all.' Customs Officer [*wearily*]: 'Open the box.'

4   An apocryphal turning point in Aggiss and Cowie's move towards film may have been the performance of *Die Orchidee im Plastik Karton* (1989) at the Bagnolet festival in 1990 in a 4,000 seater Paris auditorium. Merce Cunningham, sitting at the back, was heard to ask Bonnie Bird, 'Are they just standing there doing nothing?' The six Divas performers were actually performing an exquisitely intricate, choreographed blinking sequence, totally invisible to the naked eye a hundred metres away.

5   The initial intention in the piece was to have no edits except between the four sections, i.e. the entire piece made up of only four shots. In the end, the second and fourth sections had some super 8 and animation camera shots inserted for dramatic reasons but, by returning immediately to the continuous shot, the camera identity seems to be preserved and the inserts feel like flashbacks or flashforwards.

6   The use of hypersound in live performance is not impossible, however. An example of this occurs in the section of *Hi Jinx* entitled 'Joints', where Aggiss performs to a tape of joints clicking in a synchronized fashion (DVD 12:4).

7   The audiences are wearing red/green stereoscopic glasses.

8   As Heidi says in *Hi Jinx*, 'A dancer should always look her audience in the eye, one who does not has something to hide.'

chapter 13

screen divas
a filmic expression of the grotesque aesthetic

sherril dodds

With cruel coldness Dix lays stress on the ugliness of bodies and souls, on deformities, misfortunes and meanness, on situations that are grotesque, painful and disgusting.

(Müller 1973: 39)

The pertinence of the above statement to this chapter is that it brings together several ideas that encapsulate the œuvre of performer-choreographer Liz Aggiss and composer-choreographer Billy Cowie, collectively known as Divas. Perhaps the most immediate is the link that critics identify between their stage work and the paintings of visual artist Otto Dix (Constanti 1987a, Phillips 1991), in particular the exploration and representation of human subjectivity at its most extreme. Related to this is the location of Dix within the early twentieth-century expression-ist art movement since it is well documented that Divas' choreography bears the lineage of an expressionist tradition (Constanti 1987a, Briginshaw 1988, Penman 1994, Phillips 1991).[1] Finally there is the reference to the 'grotesque', a concept frequently alluded to as a source of inspiration for, and a stylistic trait of, Divas' work (Constanti 1987a, Briginshaw 1988, Penman 1994, Phillips 1991, Aggiss 2000). With this in mind, I set out to examine how these choreographic characteristics extend to Divas' film work in relation to both subject matter and its formal treatment.

Before addressing the two films under investigation, it would be useful to tease out further ideas concerning the expressionist tradition and grotesque aesthetic evident in Divas' work. Aggiss's own dance training reveals a close alliance with Central European expressionism since she studied with two exponents of Ausdruckstanz, both of whom worked with seminal figures within 'expressionist dance' practice: Hanya Holm, a former dancer with Mary Wigman, and Hilde Holger, who trained under Gertrud Bodenwieser (Briginshaw 1988, Aggiss 2002a). One of the key tenets of expressionist dance is the external expression of personal experience (Müller and Servos 1984, Müller 1985, Scheier 1987, Nugent 1992), an idea that clearly emerges in other branches of expressionist work, such as art and cinema. Müller (1973) describes how expressionist painting is an outward display of inner feeling and is characterized by anxiety, anguish and torment. Likewise, in a discussion of expressionist film, a style of cinema associated with 1920s Weimar Germany, Hayward states, 'expressionism means "squeezing out", thus making the true essence of things and people emerge into a visible form' (2000: 172). Expressionist film similarly contains overtones of death, horror, angst and paranoia (Eisner 1973, Kuhn 1996) with its sharp angles and tilted perspectives (Quaresima 1997, Hayward 2000). The importance of expressionist visual art and cinema to this chapter is that some of the thematic and formal characteristics of these genres are evident in the two works under discussion.

The centrality of the grotesque aesthetic to the work of Divas is recognized both by Aggiss and spectators alike. In 1986, Divas created *Grotesque Dancer*, which has now become a signature piece. Aggiss (2000: 30) comments, 'It broke all the rules. It was like nothing else around at the time. It was solo, female, ugly.' Thematically rooted in 1930s Germany, its punishing movement content clearly challenges accepted images of feminine corporeality, with critics making reference to 'sinister contortions' (Constanti 1987a: 26) and an 'unglamorised physicality' (Farman 1987: 20). The influence of pre-war European modern dance on her choreography per se is acknowledged by Aggiss (2002a), in particular the avant-garde artist, Valeska Gert. Gert's performative exploration of women in the margins, such as prostitutes and vagabonds, prompted critics to characterize her work as grotesque, especially in relation to its exaggerated performance style (Müller 1985, Burt 1998). The interest in a grotesque aesthetic is apparent in Divas' choreography, which often deals with awkward and unflattering movement that is simultaneously comical and disturbing. Notably, the conflict between mirth and disgust is a key feature of the grotesque (Thomson 1973). As a female performer, the use of such 'indelicate' movement pushes Aggiss's work into the arena of sexual politics in its subversion of received notions of feminine behaviour and beauty (Farman 1987). Aggiss is keenly aware of this herself: 'dancers do not generally look like me, big shoulders, hatchety face, large breasts, squat, old' (2000: 30).

In this chapter, I argue that the allusions to European expressionism and the concept of the grotesque that have come to characterize Aggiss' stage performance extend to the screen work of Divas, both in terms of subject matter and its formal treatment through the filmic apparatus. The two films used in this analysis, both of which were created for the

BBC/Arts Council of England Dance for the Camera series, are *Beethoven in Love* (1994) and *Motion Control* (2002).

Beethoven in Love

Beethoven in Love is choreographed by Aggiss and Cowie, directed by Bob Bentley and with music by Cowie. Although loosely based on the celebrated composer Ludwig van Beethoven, it is subtitled 'A Fantasy in Five Songs' to suggest that it is not a realist depiction of his life. The film primarily features Tommy Bayley, a young man with Down's Syndrome, who plays the part of Beethoven and Aggiss, who becomes the object of the composer's affections. It is interesting that Aggiss and Cowie selected a performer with a learning disability for this part. Although they clearly recognized the performance strengths and qualities that he could bring to the role, their interest in people situated on the margins is reflected in Bayley who is automatically placed outside the norms of society through being categorized 'disabled' or 'differently abled'.[2] This is also pertinent to the film's subject matter in that Beethoven too occupied the role of an outsider through a physical disability. Although fêted as a compositional genius, he became profoundly isolated through his gradual loss of hearing (Potter 2001).

The film is structured through five songs and is set in what appears to be an old house with vast rooms and numerous corridors, doorways and levels. The analysis primarily concentrates on the first two songs, with brief references to the remaining three. The film commences with Beethoven pouring himself a glass of beer in contemplative solitude as he hums a few notes (DVD 13:1). His concentration is abruptly shattered by a burst of piano accompanied by a female soprano. Momentarily startled, he drops his glass but then rises to seek out this disturbance. The camera cuts to a medium shot of Aggiss, the source of the dramatic vocals, who is presented in a style that immediately calls attention to an expressionist aesthetic. Wearing a long black dress, with her flame red hair scraped back in a French twist, she cuts an austere figure. The insistent piano and shrill vocal style, which play between a clipped delivery and long, soaring notes, create a sense of anxiety and torment typical of an expressionist tradition. This is heightened by the extreme contrasts of lighting, a feature that is notable throughout the film. While half the screen is bathed in the warm yellow glow of the walls, the other half is cast in dark shadows that partially obscure the image. This chiaroscuro lighting style, which radically contrasts light and shade, is a key stylistic feature of expressionist film (Kuhn 1996, Quaresima 1997, Hayward 2000).

A close-up of Beethoven reveals that he is no longer vexed but is beguiled by this woman, and this is echoed in the following few shots; wherever he goes, she appears. First she is seen through a door frame, then through a cellar door and, later, down a long corridor. Of particular interest in this series of shots is the manner in which Aggiss is filmed and the poses that she holds. In each instance, she is enclosed in a door or entrance way which acts as a framing device. Further references are made to visual art through her static positions which are two-dimensional in style. She is often posed in profile with her arms flexed at an acute angle so that, in combination with her sharp jaw line and pointed nose, her appearance is menacing and extreme. Her severe features in relation to the tight framing not only conjure up the expressionist images of a Dix portrait, but also allude to expressionist film in which the formal organization of the actor's body is integrated with the stylized and two-dimensional mise-en-scène (Kuhn 1996, Hayward 2000) (DVD 13:2).[3]

At one point, the spectator witnesses an extreme close-up of Aggiss as she lip syncs directly towards the camera and this is of interest on several counts. The close-up device automatically magnifies her face so that the screen is dominated by the brilliant whites of her eyes, her ruby-painted lips that reveal a cavernous mouth when she holds a note and her snapping teeth which flash as she executes a line of the song. This visual excess produced through the close range camera work is a key feature of the grotesque, which is known for extravagance and exaggeration (Thomson 1973, Bakhtin 1984). While her wild eyes hint at notions of madness, a subject close to the expressionist aesthetic, it is the mouth which throws open a host of meanings. The gaping mouth is both a significant feature of the grotesque (Bakhtin 1984) and of expressionist film (Eisner 1973). Bakhtin (1984) describes how the grotesque is characterized by excess and indulgence and the mouth is the region whereby pleasures, such as gluttonous feasting, drinking and foul language, take place. Aggiss's exposed orifice is a startling reference to the grotesque. The importance of the mouth to expressionism is perhaps definitively realized in Edvard Munch's painting *The Scream*, which depicts an angst-ridden image of a solitary figure with a wide-open mouth who emits a scream that resonates through the formal design of the work. A similar anxiety is apparent in this close-up shot since Aggiss's mouth is the tool by which the drama and urgency of the music is expressed. It is as if she shrieks out her innermost thoughts and this externalization of the internal is key to the expressionist ethos.

Another area of significance lies in her direct address to the camera. Whereas traditionally the female is positioned as the object of the camera's patriarchal gaze (Mulvey 1989), Aggiss looks back with a defiant glare. It is well documented in feminist film theory that, within dominant film-making practices, women are presented as a site of passive erotic spectacle (Mulvey 1989, Kuhn 1992). In a direct challenge to this paradigm of pleasure, Aggiss presents a grotesque image of woman with her geometric visage, internal fury and icy stare. This shift in power relations is reflected in two consecutive close-ups: in the first Beethoven's face evokes intimidation; in the second Aggiss towers over him. As the song comes to an end, however, Beethoven smiles and presents her with a pot of red primulas.

The second song is far more tranquil in character and romantic in style. The action takes place on a square balcony, with Aggiss on one side and Beethoven on the other (DVD 13:3). The spatial organization of this scene implies an emotional as well as a physical distance and, as the camera cross-cuts between the two performers, a filmic dialogue emerges between them. The image is marked by brilliant and contrasting colours. The vivid yellow walls, Aggiss's deep gold dress, and the bright red petals and green leaves of the primulas, which are placed on the balcony hand rail, all contribute to a bold aesthetic design. Significantly, expressionist art is characterized by vibrant colours (Hayward 2000) and hues that do not conform to a realist aesthetic (Vogt 1980). The camera follows Aggiss as she slowly walks along the balcony in profile and Beethoven attempts to win her attention. Her refusal to take notice creates an alienating effect and, when she does stop to look at him, she stares with a supercilious air. Beethoven gives a brief wave, but Aggiss shows her contempt by continuing to walk. Beethoven increases his efforts to charm her with progressively comical methods: he waves, blows a kiss, catches it with a handkerchief and gives her the thumbs up. All the while, Aggiss remains unmoved. The scene is one of grotesque paradox: his desperate antics are laughable while her apparent contempt is painful to witness. This scenario of unrequited love indeed parallels Beethoven's own life in his failure to achieve sustained happiness with a woman (Potter 2001).

Eventually, Aggiss concedes a glimmer of interest through a provocative raise of the eyebrows and Beethoven pulls a face of delighted surprise. Yet as she walks back along the balcony, Aggiss mischievously sinks below the handrail, as if descending a flight of stairs, only for a pair of gardening shears to rise up from where she disappeared. The narrative tension continues as she brandishes the shears and holds them wide open, while emphasizing their form through v-shaped hand gestures and extended arm lines. Beethoven naively mirrors her movement, apparently unaware of any threat to either himself or the flowers. As Aggiss walks towards the camera, her menacing eyes hint at madness and the flowers come into view. With a single chop she decapitates the plant and knocks the pot over the balcony.

The scene is ripe with symbolic meanings in its references to expressionism, film noir and Freud. To commence, the air of lunacy and destruction that surrounds Aggiss is typical of an expressionist film tradition. Hayward (2000) suggests that expressionist cinema often deals with a character's subjective and mad existence while Kuhn (1996) describes how the genre creates a self-contained fantasy world separate from the everyday. Of particular significance is that the perpetrator is female, as this alludes to the film noir genre. Several commentators identify formal and thematic links between film noir and expressionist film, with their high contrast lighting, dark shadows, extreme camera angles and themes of fear and anxiety (Gledhill 1996, Hayward 2000). Within the above scene, Aggiss can be conceived as a femme fatale, a key figure in the noir tradition. The femme fatale is a desirable yet dangerous individual (Kaplan 1989) who, in a challenge to traditional filmic representations of women, is 'active, intelligent, powerful, dominant and in charge of her own sexuality' (Hayward 2000: 130). It is clearly Aggiss who commands control as she annihilates Beethoven's floral gift in one fell swoop, an act that is filled with multiple meanings. Her destruction of the flowers, an offering culturally invested with notions of romantic desire, is a sharp rebuff to Beethoven's affections. This gesture also plays on the metaphoric concept of 'deflowering' a woman. In a subversion of the idea that it is the male who 'takes' a woman's virginity, Aggiss seizes control over this symbol of sexuality by literally 'deflowering' the plant in a display of female empowerment. From another perspective, her actions can be interpreted as a direct reference to the castration complex (Parry 1994, Penman 1994).

It is notable that expressionist film is littered with Freudian references and influences, based on the notion that expressionism is a representation of the psyche (Eisner 1973).[4] Hayward (2000: 172) states that expressionism 'mirrors to a degree the efforts in psychoanalysis to bring the workings of the unconscious to the fore, to the level of consciousness where the malaise or hysteria can be expressed'. An androcentric reading of the above scene might suggest that Aggiss plays out the cliché of the 'hysterical' woman hell-bent on destruction.[5] Yet an alternative interpretation rooted in Freud's notion of castration anxiety might conceptualize Aggiss as a figure of female empowerment. In psychoanalytic terms, the female represents a castration threat since she is marked by the visible absence of a penis and thus the male fears the loss of his member in the form of castration anxiety (Kaplan 1990, Caughie and Kuhn 1992, Stam *et al.* 1992). As a means to deal with this anxiety, the male disavows the threat of castration by fetishizing objects as penis replacements. For instance, in film noir, phallic objects such as guns, stiletto heels and cigarette holders are classic examples of castration disavowal (Place 1989, Hayward 2000). In *Beethoven in Love*, Aggiss represents a castration threat par excellence when she appears with her shears. In this instance, however, there are no signifiers of disavowal as she carries out the symbolic castration without a hint of remorse. On the one hand this comical act of defiance sends out a potent feminist statement; yet on the other, it could be read as a horrific gesture of mutilation. This ambiguity is typical of a postmodern dance tradition in which multifarious and competing meanings co-exist (Banes 1987, Mackrell 1991). The conflict of humour and disgust also call attention to the grotesque.

Themes relating to film noir and Freud also continue with the third song. In this section Beethoven conducts a chorus of singers that perform a piece which is lyrical and calm (DVD 13:4). The power balance between Aggiss and Beethoven has now shifted and it is Aggiss who is obsessed with him. As he attempts to lead the chorus, she begins to study him with a meticulous degree of attention, making small adjustments as she goes along: she removes imaginary flecks of dust from his jacket, cleans his shoe with a lick of her thumb, checks his face with a magnifying glass, plucks a hair from the centre of his brow, inspects his nails, dusts him down and so on. Eventually, her increasingly obtrusive behaviour causes him to knock over his music stand to the audible shock of the chorus. Her interference easily plays to the stereotype of a woman being the downfall of artistic genius. This idea perhaps also alludes to the classic film noir scenario in which a femme fatale obstructs the male protagonist in his narrative quest (Kaplan 1989). In this instance, it is Aggiss who stands in the way of Beethoven and his music.

Although Aggiss's meddling could be interpreted as a female obsession with a powerful male, another reading might regard such intimate handling as being that of a maternal figure. In the case of the latter, Freud's notion of the Oedipal complex, in which a child experiences feelings of a sexual desire for the parent of the opposite sex, can be read into this relationship (Stam *et al.* 1992). Beethoven's explicit sexual desire exhibited towards Aggiss in the previous song is translated into an incestuous Oedipal moment in this third song as she arguably takes on the role of a mother figure. Indeed, this idea is carried through to the final song during which Beethoven positions Aggiss's arms so that he can climb into them like a baby. The final image shows her rocking him in what could be interpreted as his ultimate Oedipal fantasy (DVD 13:5). A sense of the grotesque also enters into this third section. On the one hand, Aggiss's micro bodily inspection is comical, but, on the other, the indignity of her intrusion is distasteful and obscene.

The above analysis identifies an abundance of references to expressionist art, cinema and the grotesque in *Beethoven in Love* and similar concerns emerge in *Motion Control*.

Motion Control

Hayward (2000) notes how early expressionist films contain limited camera action and sparse editing, whereas later ones employ fast camera work to reflect the speed and technology of modernity. Interestingly, the same transition occurs between *Beethoven in Love* and *Motion Control*. Although the camera and cut play a significant role in the construction of meaning in *Beethoven in Love*, their presence is relatively understated compared to the dynamic filmic style that characterizes *Motion Control*. Most of the film is shot on a state-of-the-art 'motion control camera', a piece of equipment which has all of its movement pre-programmed. The automated dynamic, elaborate spatial trajectories and sheer force of speed that can be achieved with this camera result in an intense physicality that would be difficult to replicate on a manually operated machine. The film was a collaboration with David Anderson, with choreography by Aggiss and Cowie, and music by Cowie, and is divided into three sections.

The opening scenes of the film are shot purely from the 'point of view' of the camera and its quality of movement, in combination with the images that it produces, endow it with a character of its own (DVD 13:6). Initially, it appears to emerge from underground amid flying debris and, when it reaches ground level, scurries through some cobbled streets hurriedly glancing from one direction to another. The feeling of urgency is heightened by the soundtrack which employs electronic samples of screeching, buzzing and racing feet. There is a sense of the supernatural as this 'being' is not revealed as human, but as a 'presence' that has risen from below and moves along the ground at lightning speed. Themes of horror continue as it enters an old house, rushes up a flight of stairs, fleetingly surveys the landing, races up another level, shoots down a corridor, startling a cat on route, to arrive at a door on the left. Notably, staircases and corridors are key features of the architectural landscape of expressionist film (Eisner 1973, Quaresima 1997). The signifiers of an 'inhuman presence', an apparently deserted house and a frightened cat, also allude to the classic gothic horror, a genre of film which has its roots in expressionist cinema (Gledhill 1996, Hayward 2000). Further allusions to gothic horror are seen as the camera enters the room. The candelabras and gilt-edged mirrors which hang from the dark cerise walls, in conjunction with the bare floorboards and minimal furniture, suggest a fading grandeur, while a stuffed crow on the dressing table creates a macabre edge. In the centre of the room is a large wooden bed and strewn across the bottle green sheets is a body. It is Aggiss dressed in a heavy grey gown with a shock of orange lining to match her henna-dyed hair.

As Aggiss's hand drops off the edge of the bed, the camera flies overhead to gaze down upon her as she shifts around in an uneasy sleep. As she tosses and turns, it slowly rotates so that the image rocks back and forth in what could be described as a duet between dancer and camera. Quaresima (1997) states that, in expressionist film, the camera plays an important role in organizing space and as a protagonist of the action, and the same can be said of Motion Control. The manner in which the camera might suddenly move towards or away from Aggiss, sharply circle her or purposefully shift from side to side makes it a key participant in the dance. The image cuts briefly to several shots of Aggiss trapped in a box cut into the side of a white wall, which is perhaps the subject of her unsettled sleep. Again, references to expressionism lie in these images of horror and nightmare (Eisner 1973, Hayward 2000). Without warning, the camera jerkily zooms down towards her and, with her face framed in close-up, her eyes flash open. She stares menacingly at the camera in a moment of unsettling direct address. The magnification of her sunken dark eyes and razor-sharp features position her as a figure of horror.

Slowly, Aggiss rises to sit on the edge of the bed. In the movement sequence that follows, Aggiss performs the most private and personal of acts. She twists her body into strange contortions and her expression of unwavering concentration is comically juxtaposed with all kinds of creaks, rattles and squeaks. A harsh scraping accompanies her as she strains to uncross her knee and as she awkwardly straightens her back the sound of a spring bursts. Immediately her head and spine collapse. She pulls her head to the side with a painful creak, only to push it back to the sound of bones cracking noisily. The concept of 'motion control' not only refers to the camera used in filming, but also to the stiff and rigid movement that comes about as she tries to manipulate her body. As Aggiss (2000) herself recognizes, she does not conform to the stereotype of the lithe and youthful dancer and this exaggerated image of an old and creaking body clearly plays on the grotesque.

Through time, the solo becomes increasingly intimate, neurotic and disturbing. She obsessively itches her arm with one hand and her cheek with the other and then violently scratches her nose. The camera moves to a close-up as she cleans her upper teeth with her index finger to the noise of a rubbery squeak and, with a sharp click, 'flosses' her centre two teeth with her nail. The idea that she makes such private moments public, and the crude manner with which she treats her body, clearly call attention to the mirth and disgust characteristic of the grotesque. Thomson (1973) describes how the grotesque has a vivid physicality and this is evident here from the preoccupation with the body's foibles, the sound score which serves to magnify Aggiss's physical defects and the mobile camera which seeks to inspect her corporeality from multiple angles and positions. The phrase is brought to an abrupt end as she hawks in the direction of the camera followed by a loud spit. Bakhtin (1984) writes that the grotesque body is a basis of impertinence, of which spitting is a typical example. This section also shares similarities with the expressionist film aesthetic, which features distorted bodies and gestures that are mechanical and abrupt (Hayward 2000). The awkward con-tortions and manic repetitions performed by Aggiss are even further heightened by the jerky and automated movement of the motion control camera.

Themes of horror and torment continue with the remaining sections, both of which are based on 'nightmare scenarios'. The second section plays on notions of entrapment and claustrophobia and is adumbrated earlier in the film in the brief clips of Aggiss trapped in the wall cavity (DVD 13:7). Hence this section may represent the dream content of her uneasy sleep from before. Once again, there are obvious Freudian references relating to dream work as a manifestation of the unconscious (Stam et al. 1992). The scene opens with a long shot of a pure white wall and, as the camera zooms in with three sudden jolts, it reveals Aggiss squeezed into a small white box shape that is cut into the wall. Wearing only a brief slip dress, she seems isolated and vulnerable in this minute space. Initially she appears to be curled in a foetal position with her hands flat against the left side and the tips of her feet touching the right. As the camera slowly rotates, however, the image revolves so that all sense of perspective is sent askew and the spectator has little idea of what is actually upright and what is not. This rolling device continues and although she sometimes appears to be upright in the frame, her move-ment suggests that she is working against the pull of gravity as her bright red hair flies out at abnormal angles and her use of weight is distorted.

Aggiss edges around the cramped space in which she is almost bent double. She adjusts her limbs, tiptoes her feet along the wall, slides her back from side to side, awkwardly twists around and occasionally reaches out into the white infinity. This form of entrapment again plays on the idea of 'motion control'. The overwhelming sense of torment and restriction that pervades this scene is echoed in the electronic soundtrack which contains samples of tense breathing, the low moan of a wind resonating through a barren space, odd creaks, mumbles and rattles and short bursts of dramatic female vocals. The nightmare intensifies as one of the walls slowly begins to move inwards, eventually leaving Aggiss no option but to leap into the blank abyss or else be crushed to death. Prolonged in slow motion, the spectator witnesses a sight of pure horror in which Aggiss's gaping mouth emits a silent scream of terror. The image is replete with expressionist anguish (Eisner 1973, Müller 1973).

In the third section, Aggiss is again located in fantastical circumstances that speak of dread and horror. It commences with her lying on her back with her knees flexed, dressed in a scarlet gown with a spiky hem that is pinned to the ground (DVD 13:8). She is surrounded by folds of brilliant white curtains and a crumpled ice-blue floor, all of which conjure up a foreboding chill. A female vocal dramatically accompanies the introduction of a pulsing electronic riff followed by a breathy spoken sequence that evokes fear: 'Fright, fright, jostling near the edge, dark night, way down there below, hold me tight, is it time to go now, might, might, think that I was rather scared.' In a single movement, Aggiss comes to standing and it is immediately clear that her feet are rooted to the spot. This is confirmed as she slowly leans forward in an unnaturally off-balance position with her body at a 45-degree angle to the floor. This freaky ability hints at the supernatural as she continues to twist and contort her body into a series of peculiar and impossible positions.

On the one hand, Aggiss is subject to this physical nightmare in that her motion is literally controlled; she cannot leave this spot. On the other, she is also the subject of this nightmare. Her face is deathly, with its blackened eyes and ghostly complexion, and her unhuman physicality is sinister and unnerving. Overt references to the horror genre and its fascination with the unnatural are followed through in other actions (Hayward 2000). As the camera moves into close-up she opens her mouth widely. Whereas in the last section this gesture spoke of fear and vulnerability, in this instance it is bold and intimidating as if she could happily consume all that she sees before her. In another instance, she holds her hand as a claw and drags it down her face in a menacing action of self-mutilation. Suggestions of supernatural forces are made as she blows towards the camera and, as if subject to a spell, it revolves so that she suddenly turns upside down. The section is brought to an end as the camera pulls back and Aggiss stands with her arms raised above her head in a gesture of bold female omnipotence.

Engaging with the filmic medium

The themes of expressionism and the grotesque that have come to characterize Divas' live stage work are equally evident in the dance films of the company. Yet I would argue that this is not simply a case of transferring stage concerns to the screen. Alternatively, I suggest that Aggiss and Cowie draw on a variety of cinematic traditions in order to express these interests. The type of filmic language that *Beethoven in Love* and *Motion Control* employ includes both intertextual references to specific cinematic subject matter and to formal features of the screen apparatus, such as particular styles of camera work, lighting and editing techniques. Therefore the two films do not simply borrow the themes of expressionism and the grotesque apparent in Divas' theatre work. Instead Divas' dance films demonstrate an extension of these concerns through their interaction with the filmic medium.

Both *Beethoven in Love* and *Motion Control* are littered with cinematic references to the expressionist film tradition. First this is apparent in subject matter. Themes of anxiety and torment shade the mood of the two films and this is carried through into their explicit content. *Beethoven in Love* deals with notions of obsession, genius and madness, while *Motion Control* focuses on horror and nightmare. These key expressionist themes are echoed though the music, set, costume and movement. In *Beethoven in Love*, the shrill female vocals evoke an air of hysteria, and in *Motion Control* the electronic score of rattles, creaks and breathy panting creates an uneasy edge. While *Beethoven in Love* uses musty old rooms and dark corridors as part of its bleak environment, *Motion Control* draws on unsettling dream-like locations. In both films, Aggiss is presented as a figure of dramatic visual impact with her floor-length gowns, scorching orange hair, pale visage, dark-rimmed eyes and blood-red lips. She is a potent female figure and this is followed through into her movement style. Her gestures are sharp, angular and two-dimensional. Further testament to the influence of expressionist film is apparent in references to related cinematic traditions, most notably film noir in *Beethoven in Love* and gothic horror in *Motion Control*. Likewise, allusions to Freudian metaphors concerning psycho-sexual complexes and the dream work of the unconscious are also typical of the expressionist film style.

Yet in spite of this grim subject matter, there is often a strong comedic element, especially in relation to images and scenes of the grotesque. Within each film, there are key moments that provoke simultaneous sensations of mirth and disgust. In *Beethoven in Love*, the composer's clownish attempts to woo Aggiss are set in painful contrast to her utter disdain, and her hilarious inspection of Beethoven's dress and body are countered with a sense of awkwardness over the inappropriate intimacy of the situation and the humiliation that he endures. Similarly, in *Motion Control* it is laughable to see Aggiss attempt to bully her cranky old body into action, but equally vulgar to witness her private bodily acts. In both films, the grotesque is paraded rather than masked. The overt focus on Aggiss as an older dancer, complete with lined face and a generous layer of flesh, is a bold act of defiance against the lean and supple stereotype of the female dancer. Indeed, within these two examples, Aggiss plays several 'screen divas' that challenge accepted notions of femininity. In *Beethoven in Love* she is a femme fatale and in the final section of *Motion Control* she is a figure of horror. Typical of the ambiguity of postmodern dance practice, these images can be dialectically read as monstrous constructions of femininity or as potent symbols of female empowerment. It is also significant that the open mouth is featured in both films as a symbolic expression of the grotesque.

References to expressionism and the grotesque do not simply remain at the level of content, but the formal cinematic apparatus is employed in order to explore these themes further. In *Beethoven in Love*, the high contrast lighting calls attention to expressionist film and, in both works, the striking use of colour to heighten visual impact is typical of expressionist art. It is the camera work, however, that particularly plays on ideas of expressionism and the grotesque. At times, the camera frames the performers like the two-dimensional subjects of expressionist portraiture. In other instances, the oblique angles create skewed perspectives that seem to echo the slanted view of reality that is part of the expressionist film paradigm. In both films, the camera is clearly a protagonist of the action, which again reflects the expressionist film style. In the second section of *Beethoven in Love*, the camera work and editing construct a silent dialogue between Beethoven and Aggiss during their eccentric courtship, and in *Motion Control* the dynamic camera movement enters into a duet with Aggiss.

The close-up shot is a key device that is employed to magnify and exaggerate facial expression. The flashing eyes and gaping mouth of Aggiss enlarged across the screen suggest a form of excess that is characteristic of the grotesque. Indeed, the importance of facial expression to 'silent cinema' in general is articulated by Coates (1991). In a study of expressionism and horror in German cinema, Coates states that the absence of language allows the spectator to concentrate on the visual, hence the importance of facial expression. He describes facial communication as a kind of 'wordless soliloquy'. In the dance films studied here, the close-up camera work allows the spectator to study the facial language in depth. In *Beethoven in Love*, there is Beethoven's look of wonderment and intrigue upon first seeing Aggiss, and her duplicitous raise of the eyebrows before brandishing her shears, and in *Motion Control* images of determined concentration flash across Aggiss's face as she manipulates her stiff and creaky body.

The two films under investigation are replete with thematic and stylistic traits of the expressionist film tradition. Yet I do not want to suggest that *Beethoven in Love* and *Motion Control* are expressionist films as such. Instead, Divas operates within a postmodern paradigm through calling upon aspects of expressionism as a source of humour and critique. On the one hand, the blatant and exaggerated references to the expressionist aesthetic can work to parodic effect. The dramatic imagery, Aggiss's severe demeanour and the angst-ridden physicality all contribute to a comic acknowledgement of the genre. On the other hand, Aggiss also draws on expressionism to make comment upon different aspects of social existence. Her bold display of the grotesque confronts the constructed nature of social tastes and norms, in particular ideas concerning the ideal body. Likewise, infused with expressionist themes, the female figures that she creates are complex women that both maintain and subvert received notions of femininity: they are powerful, destructive, monstrous, vulnerable, hysterical, manipulative and dangerous to know. In *Beethoven in Love* and *Motion Control*, it is through drawing on particular cinematic traditions, both in terms of form and content, that allows Aggiss and Cowie to explore and comment upon themes of expressionism and the grotesque.

Notes

1   This is not to suggest that Aggiss is a modernist as such, but rather she makes a postmodern comment on the expressionist tradition through devices such as irony, humour and critique.
2   Aggiss (2000: 31) comments, 'I am convinced that despite Tommy's learning difficulties there could never have been another Beethoven such as his.'
3   This device of the performer's body reflecting the formal organization of the mise-en-scène is also evident in the fourth song. In an angst-ridden solo, Aggiss's manic and tormented movement is sharp and angular in design.

Seated on a step, she throws her clasped hands out only to stab them back into her chest, hugs her torso with her elbows stuck out, thrashes her upper body back and forth and splays her legs at 90-degree angles.

4   Also of significance is that the work of Hilde Holger, with whom Aggiss trained, was informed by Freudian thinking (Aggiss 2002a).

5   Images of hysteria are also apparent in the movement content of the fourth song, which is described briefly in note 3 above.

chapter 14

reconstruction

or why you can never step into the same river twice

liz aggiss

They say your past catches up with you. Reflecting over the 25 years of collaborative performance history between Aggiss and Cowie, a truer word has not been spoken. Either through invitation, or commission, some notable performances were reconstructed in 1999 including: work by the The Wild Wigglers (1982–1990), *Grotesque Dancer* (1986) and *Die Orchidee im Plastik Karton* (1989); *Bird in a Ribcage*, made for Transitions Dance Company in 1995, was reconstructed in 1999; *Vier Tänze*, a collection of dances choreographed by Hilde Holger in the 1920s and 1930s, was reconstructed on Aggiss in 1993.

> Reconstruct: to construct or build again, recreate a lost or damaged original form, deduce from fragmentary evidence.
>
> (*Penguin English Dictionary* 1965: 588)

The challenge of reconstruction depends on many components, and in the case of Divas' work, video documentation, personalized notation, motivation and memory have all aided the process. However, the American Repertory Dance Company considers that:

> reconstruction falls into three categories: reconstruction is when multiple methods or resources are used; revival is when work is directed by the choreographer on his/her own company, and recreation is when a complete documentation does not exist and the dance must be built through available research, artistic sensibility and educated guesswork.
>
> (Terry 1980)

These are useful sub-headings for this essay but they are only the tip of the iceberg.

The Wild Wigglers: Not just written on, but carved into the body

In 1999 I returned to that established hedonistic Mecca for youth, The Zap Club in Brighton, where, in 1982, The Wild Wigglers had originally premiered. This visual dance cabaret act had been a significant embryo for the collaborative artistic future of Aggiss/Cowie. Here we were, nearly twenty years on, the now sagging, ageing original Wild Wigglers – Ian Smith, Neil Butler and myself[1] – straining against the same fading, spiralled yellow and black leotards, and battered pointy hats, jumping mercilessly up and down in rhythmic syncopation in the same micro scummy performance space. The air still reeked of 'night before' – beer, fags and sweaty bodies; Cowie's scant music large and loud in huge bass cabs; the audience, reminiscent of 1980s punk, jammed up against the stage, hearing our grunts, smelling our sweat, seeing every microscopic visual, physical and aural nuance. What a fearsome somatic audience experience!

Inspired by music hall, vaudeville, pantomime and punk, 'Wiggling' involved a 20-minute set of interchangeable visually connected simple dances, titled to do 'exactly what it says on the tin': Dance One, 'Hop on Pops', inspired by Dr Seuss (Figure 14.1 DVD 14:1); Dance Two, 'Coughing Wiggle', inspired by Dada and the Absurdists; Dance Three, 'Walking the Dog', inspired by Spike Jones, and Wilson, Keppel and Betty (DVD 14:2); Dance Four, 'Birdies', inspired by Max Wall and Danny Kaye; Dance Five, 'Kicking the Red Dress', inspired by the Georgian State Dance Company and synchronized ice dancing; Dance Six, 'Sagging Hats', inspired by comic deflation and misery generally. These simple animated gestures – hopping, jumping, scuttling, rummaging, skittering, blobbing, slugging – were grasped and choreographically 'worried to death' in succinct three-minute visual performance wonders which locked into immediate engagement with the audience.

Performance opportunities in 1980 for an experimental dance outfit like The Wild Wigglers were limited to sharing a stage with other 'alternative artists' of the day – John Hegley, Rose English, Roy Hutchins, Anne Seagrave, Desperate Men, Ivor Cutler, Women with Beards, Open Secret, John Cooper Clarke – at such places as The Zap and London's Cast Tour, or with punk bands like Birds with Ears and The Stranglers on larger stages like Wembley Arena.[2] And we did all of this, and more, with 'a splendid dead pan humour. The three dancers hopped with mad fanatical precision . . . The approach was highly personal with its own witty madness' (Hall 1983: 15).

Survival in this particular arts marketplace meant: demand only the smallest space in which to perform (usually on a 'sixpence' just in front of a drum kit), secure five minutes to 'tech', enjoy your alien audience for whom contemporary experimental dance is not a buzz-word, be prepared to perform at midnight, be seen and above all learn to

Figure 14.1 'Hop on Pops' – Liz Aggiss, Ian Smith and Eva Zambicki in The Wild Wigglers.
Photo: Billy Cowie, 1982.

perform. This guide to visual and performance literacy in hindsight
marks the beginnings of a collaborative artistic direction for Aggiss/
Cowie for whom 'uncompromising' or 'subversive' has since become a
recognized identity.

Issues concerning the dance vocabulary, technique, performance
skill and choreographic content that Aggiss/Cowie chose to develop in
1980 within the context of The Wild Wigglers, including 'whether or
not all that hilarious jumping and swaying with feet tied together really

qualifies as dance, I'm not sure' (King 1983: 4), were repeatedly commented on by critics. 'It was certainly movement of a highly entertaining kind, to be remembered with gratitude by a critic so often threatened with drowning in a sea of self-indulgence, pretentiousness and insipidity' (King 1983: 4).

And so, let us return to the Wiggler devotees who staggered along to The Zap in 1999 to witness this 'epitome of cartoon avant-garde' (Hutera 1991: 63); or maybe to marvel at gravity defying menopausal breasts, thickening waistlines, or tightly packed testes stuffed into mildewed leotards; or maybe to reorientate or revisit themselves socially, politically, physically with this fragmentary evidence of past. For them and us, we wiggled, jumping and hopping relentlessly; but, in truth, 19 years on, we barely left the ground. Amazingly, not one single step, not one gasping grimace, not one tiny flicker of an eyelid was forgotten.

So why reconstruct? 'To mark the end of an era, or is it the ear of an ender?' (to quote from Divas' live work, *Divagate*, 1997). Revisiting The Wild Wigglers signified how anarchic, original and formative this work had been and how it informed and shaped our subsequent choreo-graphic and performative language. Performing this revival testified to an embodiment of performance skill and craft developed from hundreds of performances, not just written on, but carved deeply into the body. It also clarified that The Wigglers could be revived and, like Divas' work, required strong performance personae and anarchic physicality to enhance the already bizarre movement content; Butler and Smith, gangly, super-confident and both over six feet tall, and Aggiss, 'she of the anarchically gleeful onstage grimace' (Hutera 1991: 63), five foot squat, hard and muscular. The revived The Wild Wigglers, in 1991 and again in 1999, was an affirmation that this distinct work had informed a sub-sequent artistic direction for Divas: a vivid physical language and identity that embraced intense sculptural grotesque physicality, emotional poetic expression and strong performance skill.

In hindsight, it is no surprise that Aggiss/Cowie's work sits queasily in dance. It invents and reinvents itself. It defies category. It crosses discip-lines. It is all at once dance, dance/theatre, cabaret, visual performance, live art. The work is always driven by issues, ideas and questions about performance and the performer. Latterly it experiments with interdisci-plinarity; it uses text and film projection but the music, live or otherwise, was always embedded into the expressive movement language. In Christy Adair's book, *Women and Dance: Sylphs and Sirens*, in the chapter 'The Subver-sives', of women's dance practice Adair says:

The description the critics use of Aggiss and Cowie's work indicates the subversive nature of much of it. Their reaction to the work has varied from incomprehension to sarcasm to enthusiasm and an understanding of a new approach. In terms of challenging the expectations of mainstream dance, the work is uncompromising. Aggiss/Cowie are concerned with making pieces which are relevant to today's audiences.

(Adair 1992: 214–215)

Since 'today' is ever-shifting this provides a key to the way much of the 'reconstructed' work has been approached and developed.

Grotesque Dancer: Same tune, different violin

In 1999, nestling up to the millennium, it seemed as appropriate a place as any to relocate performance histories, to contextualize current performance practice and to ask the question: Has anything really changed? The issue of reconstruction in the case of the solo, seminal work Grotesque Dancer (1986) asks these questions, to myself as the performer and similarly to the audience. In 1986, this solo was a shocking, provocative presentation of femininity, made from an intuitive and impassioned performance position. We were commissioned with £200 to create a work for the single performance arch at The Zap Club, Brighton. This diminutive, grubby performance space whose history was Wiggler-imprinted on my body, and from where I had been inspired by seeing much performance experimentation, fired me up to research into my dance lineage. The results consequently formed a patent for the next tranche of work. The Zap space championed subversive alternatives and could be considered a contemporary melange of Weimar/Dadaesque/Cabaret Voltaire. Thus I researched early European solo female dancers and discovered photographs of Valeska Gert, Niddy Impekoven, Gret Palucca and, latterly, Dore Hoyer. The simple photographic portraits were inspirational, full of character, visuality and performativity. These women personified independence; they were dancers, choreographers, authors and in charge. Valeska Gert stood out. Lewitan (quoted in Koegler 1974: 6), the critic, said of her, 'The dancer of the grimace, dominating in all of her performances is the pathos of protest . . . she has the courage to present this world and she presents it strong and great, insofar as her dance technique allows.' I related to all of this and read on. Subsequently, Grotesque Dancer emerged like a quote, and like a mixture of homage and competition and all that implies. The performance acknowledged its histories and provided a grounding for a future personal artistic direction.

Grotesque Dancer was made without respect to dreary dance clichés and it developed from where The Wild Wigglers had left off. 'The piece's excessive contorted movements, its parodic style, transgression of gender boundaries and plays with performer/audience relationships suggest associations with the grotesque and Carnivalesque' (Briginshaw 2001: 165). I was the subject, object, author, performer, choreographer and owner of the work. *Grotesque Dancer* was aware of its context and was uncompromising. It politicized past and present. It divided critics, most notably into gendered responses. Not only did I have an expressive physical language but also a voice (*sprechgesang*) as a tool to support movement imagery. Having an audience to share these ideas with was a luxury, so why waste the opportunity? Why compromise? Art is not about complacency.

Thirteen years later, in April 1999, *Grotesque Dancer* was revived and reconstructed by invitation for the Purcell Room at London's South Bank Centre (DVD 14:3). So in post-performance hindsight, what are the conclusions? Well, nothing much has changed: the work is still challenging, still provocative. The piece has stood the test of time but it is not the same work. A new resonance informed by extensive performance experience pervaded the work. Where it was amusing it now could be very funny. Where it was emotional, it is now driven by a deeper understanding. Back in 1986 I performed intuitively. Now I know what I am doing and how to do it. In short, I can objectify, manipulate audiences, tug the appropriate heartstring and tickle the laughter gland, and I can now make my age and my body, with all its physical shortfalls, invest in the sentiment (DVD 14:4). Same tune, different violin. Being invited to reconstruct is testament to a confidence with an established body of work. As Valeska Gert said:

> My favourite dance is the one I can change the most. What is permanent and never changes is the basic structure of steps and movements. Each time the same steps follow each other in the same order: what is changing however is the emotion out of which the dance grows. I experience the dance anew each time.
>
> (Gert 1931c: 14)

Reconstruction is like conservation. As a practice associated with museology, conservation is concerned with ideas of fragility. Since performance is temporal, reconstruction is one opportunity in which a certain fragile 'truth' can be determined. *Grotesque Dancer* was made as an inclusive piece of dance performance; the 'non standard' performer addresses the audience with overt self-reflexivity and lays bare its subject. Now 20 years on, my knowing body must reacquaint and reinterpret. As author and subject, its absolute authenticity is conserved but not preserved. *Grotesque Dancer* was never singularly about dance steps but responded to contemporary dance circa 1980. It challenged, championed and resisted the dominant visual aesthetic, mostly sweatpanted pedestrian workwear. It disobeyed the current vogue of breathy-gentle-touchy-feely-considerate tactile dance language that was infusing the contemporary dance world. As Christy Adair says in *Women and Dance,*

> in terms of the new and post modern dance works which evolved in the late 1960s and early 1970s. Many of these works disregarded the visual aesthetic and concentrated on the sensation and experiences of the performer, with contact improvisation being a prime example.
>
> (Adair 1992: 77)

The context from which *Grotesque Dancer* emerged in 1986 is critical to how it engendered critical review: 'A refreshing new aesthetic . . . here tragedy is not allowed to become beautiful the way it often does in mainstream contemporary dance' (Constanti 1987a: 20); 'There are two points worth noting, first they are trying to develop a style of their own and second they raise questions about accepted values that in turn make an audience stop and think' (Nugent 1987b: 17); 'It says a lot for English audiences that the spectators watched this whole offering politely and even applauded' (Percival 1987: 42). Interestingly, in 1999 the critics chose to dwell on descriptive comment, continuing to find the issue of this female aesthetic complex: 'black bloomers, sensible shoes . . . mannish haircut' (Levene 1999: 8); 'lesbian games mistress, weird puff ball shorts, contorted poses' (Gilbert 1999: 8); 'anarchic ageing crooner in a satin frock' (Sacks 1999: 55).

Heading into the millennium, and reacquainting myself with *Grotesque Dancer,* I refocused, overhauled and reconstructed. Certainly, I could not now justify shaving my head for this performance (Figure 14.2). This had visually marked the two halves of the performance in 1986,[3] making a coherent statement within the context of the performance climate, 'the mixture of humour and horror, dignity and absurdity disturbs' (Jordan 1987: 2). In 1999, the hair issue as a signifier had moved on, but most importantly I had moved on and my new long red hair was part of a new performance persona associated with other work. This sounds so facile, but there is a method to this madness. Our (Aggiss/Cowie) work depends on clear visual trajectory and research that works in tandem

Figure 14.2 'Pantomime' – Liz Aggiss in *Grotesque Dancer*. Photo: Billy Cowie, 1986.

with the underlying theme. I always know what I will look like – hair, clothes, shoes – before I dance a step. I always know who I am before I know what I do. I always decide what I am before I learn how to do me. The reconstruction with hair was no less dramatic: 'thirteen years later, the provocation, strength, vulnerability and the power to shock are still evident. In this reworking Aggiss is a more experienced performer and the piece now has live music which allows more fluidity between music and the dance' (Adair 1999: 12).

Over and above, what is interesting is that the work has inspired a good deal of academic enquiry. In her book *Dance, Space and Subjectivity*, Valerie Briginshaw discusses the piece thus:

> By mixing gender values and norms in her grotesque performance she achieves an ambivalent androgyny, 'making the top and bottom change places'. Her mixture of strength and vulnerability is a kind of 'positive negation'. Her performance challenges boundaries and binaries, going beyond hierarchical norms and values associated with a closed unified subjectivity, suggesting instead a more multiple, open subject connoted by her 'double body'.
>
> (Briginshaw 2001: 169)

There appears to be a value on many levels to reconstructing *Grotesque Dancer* as a socio-political, historical reference point; as a reminder that a dance performance can be an appropriate medium for an ongoing political debate. This piece appears to have stood the test of time because the form of the work is appropriate, because the work provides no solutions, no fait accompli, because, rather than disguise itself with each revival, it actively reguises itself appropriately, relevantly to the now.

Die Orchidee im Plastik Karton: Twisting perversity

Die Orchidee im Plastik Karton was made originally in 1988 for 13 women studying dance at Chichester University (DVD 14:5), revived in 1989 for the all-female company Divas (Figure 14.3, DVD 14:6), and reconstructed in 1999 for the Purcell Room on four men and Aggiss as Mistress (DVD 14:7). This hilarious and satirical dance performance was inspired by perverse gender biased phrases from a language lesson using a sampled female voice: 'InterCity is the train for the men,' 'The orchid in the plastic carton is the flower for the ladies,' 'And what shall we give the man?' 'Oh roses,' 'Then they go shopping, housewife and mother,' 'They come also with female secretaries,' 'Dusseldorf is a very discreet town.'

Figure 14.3 'Oh Rosen' – Liz Aggiss, Maria Burton, Ellie Curtis, Virginia Farman and Sian Thomas in *Die Orchidee im Plastik Karton. Photo: Billy Cowie, 1989.*

Despite adhering strictly to the steps, form, and content, this deliberate 'regendering' in reconstruction shifted meaning. The men looked 'infantilised' and 'conformist' in their costume, and produced 'an avalanche of exquisitely camp synchronised manner that brought the house down' (Sacks 1999: 55). What had, in 1989, been a strident and funny feminist performance – 'Divas do away with conventional aesthetic. Behind their intentional dilettantism lies the high professionalism. In order to be amused, one must have a leaning towards their harsh black humour' (Löblich 1990b: 37) – had morphed, in 1999, into a dandified event. The original performance was a comic etiquette of acceptable bourgeois behaviour which satirized social stereotype. By dressing the company in red lederhosen and constructing an ugly aesthetic, these women were certainly not ladies:

> Movement is staccato, grotesque and funny. Dann geht sie einkaufen – hausfrau und mutter, then she goes shopping housewife and mother, is a woman in a crab position walking backwards and forwards on palms and feet; the endless repetitive work action delivered dead pan, was answered with female laughs of recognition.
>
> (Pascal 1989: 35)

Each reworking reaps new readings: on the original line-up of 13 women in 1988, dressed uniformly in vest and pants, read automaton and the debate on body objectification, 'the gaze'; on the subsequent revival on six women at the Vienna Festival in 1990, read the aesthetic grotesquerie as political and provocative ('A daring trapeze act indeed, very close to the edge of the preposterous which just manages to stay within the boundaries of the acceptable' (Zamponi 1990: 13, translated by the author); on four men and a mistress in 1999, read as camp and hilarious. The point of reconstructing on men was not to appropriate power simply by role reversal, but to acknowledge that in 1999 patriarchy requires a new satire. Revisiting such politicized performance history as *Die Orchidee* provided the chance to retain her-story and required new direction to sharpen the point. Reconstruction here became a useful tool to theorize, to put into perspective current practice and contextualize process. In my role as school 'mistress', I underpinned the ridiculousness and often hopelessness of female representation in language but in an altogether more accessible and less alienating manner. I deliberately stereotyped my own role, provocatively dressed in power suit, stockings and stilettos, carrying a cane, my instrument of punishment and pleasure and I succumbed to a stereotype sadistically flourishing my weapon, pushing my men on in their relentless, repetitive, harsh, uncluttered movement commentary: 'They also come with female secretaries,' 'Dusseldorf is a very discreet town.' I am the ironic observer as they complete the final orgasmic jolt on the ridiculous insult, 'I am eating pig's liver.'

The early all-female cast, though funny, was a strident, serious political work that tried hard to remove sex from the stage. However, in 1999 female empowerment and sex was given creative licence and it seemed appropriate to regender to develop the commentary. The reconstruction did not dwell on deliberate ugliness as a dominant aesthetic but conversely used sex and sexiness in juxtaposition to content.

Bird in a Ribcage: A faithful reconstruction

The year 1999 was one for consolidating practice and understanding the demands of reconstruction. The most faithful prize must go to Transitions Dance Company for their reconstruction of Bird in a Ribcage (1995). Watching this four years on at the Bloomsbury Theatre, Cowie and I were aware that this piece had stood the test of time. Its uncompromising form and content, and the development of per-formance skills, had been faithfully adhered to by Transitions. Having established a very specific dance aesthetic, movement language and deliberately confrontational visual and spatial relationship with an audi-ence, this opportunity to reconstruct on an established contemporary dance company sited within the established Laban centre affirmed a recognition, a place in history, an acceptability. Reconstruction on a company with a new cast enabled our particular brand of dance choreography and performance style to be aired to a dance audience associated with a more accessible, acceptable face of contemporary dance.

We have rarely sought reassurance but the odd nod of assent can be gratifying. Reconstruction of such a fragile work gave respect to the conservation of that work.

Hilde Holger: Reminding us of the place of a vibrant history

It is important to touch base. Having trained in an expressionist tradition with Hanya Holm, Alwin Nikolais and Murray Louis, and consequently established a personal choreographic and performance signature that strives to locate an outer expression from an inner ferment of feelings, meeting and studying with Hilde Holger in 1988 was the start of a significant friendship that has cemented theory and practice. Holger, an original member of the Gertrud Bodenwieser Tanzgruppe in Vienna, found success as a soloist for her own work in the 1920s and 1930s. In 1992, Holger revived four simple, brief and moving choreographies from her repertoire: The Golem (1937), Le Martyre de San Sebastien (1923), Mechanisches Ballett (1926), Die Forelle (1923). The success of our partnership was no accident; we shared common ideas – the necessity to charge steps with belief, both physically and emotionally; the need to promote challenging and provocative work and deny dance clichés, to say what you have to say and then stop, and if you have nothing to say to not even start.

Historical revivals are so different from reconstructing your own work, but being tutored from the horse's mouth was a distinct advantage. The American Ballet Company maxim – 'recreation is when a complete documentation does not exist and the dance must be built through available research, artistic sensibility and educated guesswork' – struck home. This was 80 years later, though there is a contemporized timelessness about Holger's work. Unlike in ballet, where revivals secure its tradition, contemporary dance has arrived at a place where history brings the current practice into perspective. Murray Louis (1980: 113) said: 'Nostalgia, sentiment and the safety of distance can be disastrous for revivals. To revive a work properly, one cannot bring the work out of the past to create it, but instead one has to go into the past to recreate it.'

A successful reconstruction depends on many components, not the least of which is casting the right dancer. Alwin Nikolais, when watching a reconstruction of Martha Graham's Primitive Mysteries with Besse Schoenberg, 'agreed that the dancers couldn't dance the work as it needed to be danced. They were overtrained and could not restrain themselves enough to dance simply although the choreography for its time was very rich' (Louis 1980: 112). Critic and dance historian Walter Terry (1980) also said in the Smithsonian that 'the old timers did not have today's highly developed techniques but were intensely gutsy and communicated what Graham has called "that urgency to action" '.

Hilde and I were a successful partnership in recreating her work. Our faith in each other's understanding and our commitment to this 'urgency to action' was what mattered. It was a privilege to present Hilde, represent her choreography and find a way to do justice to her her-story, a way to honour the expressionists whose art threatened the Nazis, a way to embody history. 'Together all four pieces danced with great sensitivity and aplomb by Aggiss accompanied by Cowie on piano, provided a fascinating insight into the lost Ausdruckstanz of central Europe' (Constanti 1993: 3–4).

Conclusion: Golden rules: Reconstruction, revival, overhauling

Only reconstruct what is worth reconstructing and choose carefully who will perform this duty

We chose performers who brought appropriate physicality, strong performance presence and a desire to perform politicized work. We have been ruthlessly uncompromising in our choice and it required a strong character to subvert the tide. 'The performers in Aggiss/Cowie's company Divas often use long moments of stillness to edge the performance into open confrontation, either cowering before us in harsh pools of light or snarling in frozen abuse' (Mackrell 1987: 11). 'This rule-breaking was met by critics' scathing sarcasm and her choreography was described by one critic as "horrors" ' (Adair 1992: 77).

Consider the appropriateness of the context in which work was originally created and the context in which it is reconstructed

It would be easy to slip into oblivion following negative press – 'determinedly ugly in dress and in movement they [Divas] seem as untrained as they are unattractive' (Clarke 1987: 21) – but failure to secure good press is no reason to stop. Failure to secure any press might be a better reason. So much has been written about *Grotesque Dancer* – 'the whole performance hovers brilliantly between invitation and repulsion' (Mackrell 1987: 11) – all of it a valuable record of a history that clearly continues to strike a nerve. 'Seems I've totally missed the point of this piece (which I would gladly nominate as one of the most unbearable events I've ever sat through) . . . Aggiss galumphs around as if she were a transvestite refugee from one of the nightclub routines in *Cabaret* (presumably she's being awful and gross on purpose)' (Robertson 1987: 54).

All reconstructions are reinterpretations so each performance is a reconstruction

What *Grotesque Dancer* stands for is written on my body. In politicizing my inscribed body, I make the meaning in my own image and my performance must surpass and subvert itself through the very issues and regimes of representation. If this is one of the objections of the work from the critical press, then all the more reason to continue to reconstruct, reinterpret, revive, overhaul. The question is: Could *Grotesque Dancer* be reconstructed on another performer? Delightful as this seems to preserve an imprint on the artistic ether into the next millennium, I am not sure how relevant or even possible this would be. Rather it is better I take this one to the grave with me. There are no 'mini-mes' who would want to shatter their bodies and minds. To live in the annals of history as a subversive soloist might be more appropriate. I might even choose to continue to perform Grotesque Dancer into my second age should I survive that long. Its survival in reconstruction depends on appropriate thematically reflective permutations. It must therefore always be current.

Conserve history as a way to inform the present

Heading into the millennium, the seminal work Grotesque Dancer that informed our (Aggiss/Cowie's) trajectory inspired us to try to solve the problem of posterity through documentation. This publication goes some way to fulfil this, and maybe marks the end of a particular era. The most recent live show presented under the banner of Divas, Divagate (1997), was a dance reference to Watergate. Maybe it is time to come clean, expose and agitate other sanctified performance zones?

Acknowledgements

This article was first published in the summer 1999 edition of animated magazine and is reproduced by permission of the Foundation for Community Dance. This article has been reconstructed for this publication.

Notes

1   The Wild Wigglers, visual performance trio, in their various permutations have included the following performers: Liz Aggiss, Ian Smith, Neil Butler, Ralf Higgins, Patrick Lee, Simon Hedger, Eva Zambicki, Jane Bassett and Billy Cowie. Liz Aggiss has been the one consistent member throughout their history.
2   The Wild Wigglers in their heyday performed on various Saturday morning children's TV shows including Going Live and No 73. They met The Stranglers whilst boogying in the No 73 basement and were consequently invited to tour with them to Wembley Arena, Oxford Apollo, Brighton Centre and Zenith Paris. From pub audiences of 100 to TV audiences to stadium gigs of 6,000-plus punk aficionados, we became bored with the format, realizing there was nowhere left to go, only more of the same. We subsequently formed Divas Dance Company in 1986 in a ploy to find fertile ground for our work.
3   At the 1987 showing at The Place London, on tearing off my wig, I heard a sharp intake of breath from the audience and then my father audibly mutter, 'Good God!' He simultaneously wept and ranted at my brother throughout the journey home: 'Why does she have to make herself so ugly, my beautiful daughter?'

anarchic dance

billy cowie

Many titles were suggested for this book, some fairly standard, some pretty obvious, others quite possible – but when Aggiss came up with *Anarchic Dance* it seemed entirely appropriate. In this essay I would like to examine just why this appellation seems so relevant to this body of work and what if anything it actually means.

Anarchic is a rather complex word with many interpretations. The original derivation from the Greek simply means 'without a leader', but the term has become associated with groups of people who wish to see the removal from society of government and laws. One faction sees the change as a gradual and peaceable shift with a resulting state of affairs in which everyone behaves responsibly to each other; government is in effect simply made redundant. Another more impatient wing would like to speed up the overthrow of governmental control using such tools as assassinations and bombs. This second group has obviously caught the public's attention and anarchy is now associated most readily, in the general view, with violence, terrorism and an ensuing disorder, chaos and lawlessness. More recently, especially since the punk movement (and of course the infamous 'Anarchy in the UK' by the Sex Pistols), the term is frequently associated with fashion and pop culture and appears almost as a kind of badge of rebelliousness and newness.

So what could anarchic dance possibly be? Is it leaderless? Is it anti-government? Is it chaotic? Is it violent? Is it rule breaking? Anti-authority? Is it a fashion statement? Or is it all these things at different times? And just how does Aggiss/Cowie's dance work slot into this world of definitions? To examine this question I propose to look at these ideas in relation to three different works: *Eleven Executions* (1988), *Drool and Drivel They Care!* (1990) and *Divagate* (1997).

Eleven Executions: Breaking the rules

At first sight, The Wild Wigglers dance-bites (DVD 15:1) with their in-your-face aggression, unconventional overall structuring,[1] pogoing punk movements and a complete absence of any conventional dance vocabulary (and heavy boots) might seem anarchic, but with regard to breaking the rules, context is everything; the Wigglers were after all totally outside of any conventional dance arena – there literally were no rules. Similarly, *Grotesque Dancer* (1986) inhabits a cabaret world which has its own conventions and structures. The two early Divas pieces from 1986, *Torei en Veran Veta Arnold!* and *Dva Sa Momimomuvali* (Figure 15.1) attracted some rather lurid headlines (such as 'A wardance in under-pants' by Judith Mackrell [1987: 11]). They started to put in place a new unconventional movement vocabulary and manifested Aggiss and Cowie's (somewhat contentious) determination to use dancers for their performance skills rather than for any conventional dance training they might have. It is, however, with *Eleven Executions* in 1988, followed closely by *Dorothy and Klaus* in 1989, that we clearly see the emerging Divas' pattern, i.e. that there is no pattern; each work will reinvent itself relentlessly.

Eleven Executions is based on fragments from the work of Frank Wedekind (and also one text from Bertolt Brecht) – letters, poems and sections from the plays (Figure 15.2). On stage we have a mixture of Wedekind's invented figures (Lulu, Moritz – the dead youth from

Figure 15.1 'Fall in Love!' – Rachel Chaplin, Ellie Curtis, Virginia Farman, Kim Glass, Kay Lynn and Amanda Tuke in *Dva Sa Momimomuvali*. *Photo: Billy Cowie, 1986.*

Figure 15.2 'Lulu and the Strongman' – Maria Burton and Sian Thomas in *Eleven Executions*. *Photo: Ginny Munden, 1988.*

Frühlings Erwachen), some archetypes (the ringmaster, the strongman) and three real historical characters (the Kaiser, Wedekind himself and Wedekind's mistress's dog Fischmann). These seven performers take part in a series of 11 tableaux. The work is fractured like a cubist painting, and like a cubist face with several noses we seem to see the same things over again from different angles: we have Wedekind's sombre death as reported by Brecht butted against the howling fury of the funeral of Moritz, the dead youth who participates in his own burial; we have the Kaiser's waltz pitted against the fairy story of the Queen without a Head. And above all we have manipulation. Nearly everybody is manipulating someone else: Aggiss the ringmaster whips her performers into shape; Lulu abuses the dog; the Kaiser dictates to his subjects; Moritz the dead youth plays with the strongman's head like a ball; and, of course, Wedekind is writing the script – is forcing his words into all their mouths.

Lulu is perhaps the central character of the piece and in her solo (performed by Maria Burton) we can see many of the characteristics that will thread through the Aggiss/Cowie work of the following years (DVD 15:2). First the lip-syncing: Lulu delivers one of her key speeches from the play *Erdgeist* in which she addresses her husband Dr Schön, who has manipulated her life and whom she will eventually kill. It is actually Aggiss who speaks the text from the side of the stage in darkness using her microphone, while Burton merely mouths the words. This technique allows the speech to have an intimacy even in a large theatre; it is as if Lulu is whispering in your ear. Furthermore, it brings to the fore the already mentioned theme of manipulation – the ringmaster (or should we say ringmistress?) is literally putting words into Lulu's mouth, just as the playwright puts his words into hers. Finally, the working together of the two performers in a live situation produces an exhilarating effect, almost like two jugglers throwing their clubs to each other. Aggiss and Burton feed back from each other's timing, not only the words but the expression; at any one stage it is impossible to say who has instigated a certain tone of voice or a certain expressive look.

The second important characteristic of the solo is the focus on the upper body, the head and the face; apart from a little walk forward at the beginning and lowering her body towards the end, Lulu's feet don't move. The head becomes the central character, the arms become frames that constrain it and are manipulated by it and, in turn, manipulate it back. At one startling place Lulu (re)moves her head backwards, leaving the empty frame of her arms (a Queen without a Head?). The whole section explores the malleability of the body, at times ductile (an arm is pushed into a shape and holds its position), at times resilient (pushed to the limit and released, the head springs back to its original position). And all the time the section explores and exposes Lulu's character: her vulnerability, her acceptance, her knowingness.

Another solo, the 'Letter to the Dog Fischmann', is one of the most shocking sections in the work. Here, Aggiss as ringmaster addresses Fischmann the dog directly (using text from a letter Wedekind wrote to his mistress's dog) in a heightened *sprechgesang* fashion (DVD 15:3). This is as close as Aggiss gets to 'dancing' in the whole work – a series of electroconvulsive shocks, manic twitchings and some ominous invasions of personal space. Fischmann responds with equal neurosis and after receiving his letter, approaches his mistress (now conflated with Lulu). Rather than initially comforting him, she subjects him to a series of brutal sexual assaults; the abused becomes abuser? Her final petting of him and his acceptance of it is one of the most disturbing aspects of the scene. The whole is accompanied by a manic, dislocated sound score that distorts operatic voices into almost animalistic sounds – all at extremely high volume.[2]

The whole of *Eleven Executions* is a mixture of opposites: comedy/tragedy, brutality/tenderness, harmony/grating dissonance, contemplation/rage. With its brilliant all-white costumes and stark lighting, the work is recognizable from any five-second excerpt; it is totally unlike any Divas piece before or after.

Drool and Drivel They Care!: Politics with a capital P

The expression of political views and concepts through the medium of dance has never been straightforward. Dance frequently deals with sexual and racial politics, but politics with a capital P is more problematic. There are obvious exceptions – for example *The Green Table* by Kurt Joos from 1932 (which received a small homage, if that is the right word, in the all-women Divas piece *No Man's Land* [1993] [DVD 15:4]). The main sticking point, however, would seem to be that while movement is very adept at expressing emotional content, it is not really geared up for the imparting of hard specific information or political facts. The marrying of text and dance, however, opens up a whole new dimension and as, apart from the early Wigglers' pieces, nearly all of Aggiss and Cowie's works use text, either spoken, sung or lip-synced, they are clearly in a position to exploit this marriage.

In 1990, Margaret Thatcher had been in power for around eleven years. Her daily dominant media presence and quotable language proved irresistible. Using her more famous quotations, chopped up, looped and accompanied by banjo as musical score (in a somewhat similar manner to *Die Orchidee im Plastik Karton* [1989]), each phrase formed one of seven sections. Rather than a single Thatcher figure she was cloned, and all five

Divas dancers of the time (including the male dancer Ralf Higgins) were dressed in appropriate twin-suits, pearls, handbags and wigs (Figure 15.3). The piece became known as *Drool and Drivel They Care!* from a Thatcher quotation in an interview with David Dimbleby, where the interviewer asked if she really thought that people who expressed concern for others were really just drooling and drivelling they care. In the section that used that quotation, an impression of Thatcher's unending busyness accompanied by her inflexible stiffness was given by a choreography (borrowing heavily from Irish dancing) where the upper body remained immobile while the legs performed a hopping, puppet-like sequence. The dancers were also performing, unknown to the audience, each with a mouthful of milk and, at the appropriate moment, they let it drool from their lips – this also referred to Thatcher's infamous withdrawing of school milk earlier in her career (which had earned her the soubriquet of Margaret Thatcher, Milk Snatcher).

In another section, 'Moaning Minnies' (DVD 15:5), two of the Thatchers performed en pointe a choreographed rubbish distribution and collection sequence. Thatcher had engineered a photo opportunity

Figure 15.3 'Five Thatchers' – Liz Aggiss, Jane Bassett, Virginia Farman, Ralf Higgins and Sian Thomas in *Drool and Drivel They Care! Photo: Billy Cowie, 1990.*

in a park where she intended to pick up some litter to launch a litter awareness scheme. On arriving the park had already been cleaned. A man was therefore despatched with a black plastic bin bag to litter the park up again in order to give her something to pick up.

Near the opening of the work, a section entitled 'This Government Keeps its Promises' was presented with a morphing choreography that commenced with a parody of the then seemingly ubiquitous contemporary dance movement of striking the forehead with the heel of the hand and letting it fly off. The sequence gradually changed into a Pinocchio nose-stretching movement – thus undermining the repeated vocal sentiment. Later on, the words are distorted into a kind of tiger snarl, adding a certain viciousness to the parody. What seemed like a fairly simple idea on the surface gained a certain power with the endless repetition of the phrases, and brought to the forefront the heartlessness of Thatcher's premiership.

The world premiere of the piece was scheduled for the Zap Club in Brighton on 22 November 1990. As that date approached (after around six months of Divas planning, choreography and rehearsal), Thatcher's position as leader of the Tory party began to look increasingly unstable. Around the country it seemed that almost everyone was willing her to resign – apart, obviously, from Aggiss and Cowie who were literally praying for her survival.[3] As things turned out she abandoned us on the day of the premiere – the opening night was a celebratory success marred only by the whispered comment, 'Nice piece, bad timing.' Aggiss and Cowie managed, however, to inject some new life into the work by having the five Thatchers magically transform themselves into five John Majors for the last section, a repeat of the opening 'This Government Keeps its Promises,' with the hapless Majors mouthing Thatcher's words – hinting at a 'plus ça change' theme (DVD 15:6).

After the premiere an article appeared in *Dance Theatre Journal*:

Liz Aggiss and Billy Cowie's choreography is highly politicised and calls on cartoon allegory for its punches. It has the ironic humour of an Otto Dix sketch, the dark wit of a painting by George Grosz. The company takes its influence from a mix of cultural clichés and a tradition of performance expressionism. It has long been a problem for dance programmers, funders and critics alike. How to take seriously dance that does not seem to take itself seriously? How to criticise content performed with such technical nonchalance? The Divas attract rave appreciation whenever they perform. What they have become are the darlings of the anti-dance world, eschewing the more contained experimentalism of the recognised 'cutting edge'. In this sense the Divas are the DaDaists of dance.

(Phillips 1991: 46)

The question of effectiveness must always arise, however, with any political artwork: what difference do a few dance pieces, with their very limited audiences, ever achieve? Precious little, it must be admitted. Aggiss and Cowie offered the *Drool and Drivel* piece to the Labour party as part of its election campaign, an offer that was welcomed by the then leader John Smith, who sadly died before anything could be arranged. One should of course always be careful what you wish for. Writing this approaching a third term Blair government, it is tempting to think that a revival of the piece would now even more appositely than five John Majors feature five Tony Blairs mouthing Thatcher's universal political lie 'This Government Keeps its Promises.'

Divagate: Who's in control?

The 'leaderless' aspect of anarchy when applied to dance might be interpreted as the abandoning of choreographic control, the allowing of the performers to do their own thing, perhaps even 'improvise'. Paradoxically, improvisation plays almost no part in Aggiss/Cowie's performance work; the pieces are tightly scripted, choreographed and directed. Indeed, one of Heidi's seven commandments from *Hi Jinx* (1995) is: 'Thou shalt not improvise, keep your improvising for the bathroom!' In the ironically entitled 'Improvisation Section' from *Divagate* (a full-scale piece commissioned by the South Bank Centre in 1997), the two male characters in the work (Neil and Lorca[4]) playfully discuss the concept of improvisation (DVD 15:7).

Lorca: Neil! Do you ever improvise in this show?
Neil: What? Improvise? You mean make up something new . . . spontaneously . . . on the spot . . . that kind of thing?
Lorca: Yeh. Well do you?
Neil: Well not normally. I could do if I wanted to but generally I choose not to.
Lorca: But you could if you really wanted to?
Neil: Of course I could.
Lorca: . . . Well . . . Go on then.
Neil: What now, right now, you want me to improvise something?
Lorca: Yeh prove it . . . Improvise.
Neil: What . . . a movement phrase, an improvised movement phrase?

Lorca: [Nods]

Neil: [Executes lengthy three-minute pre-choreographed phrase]

Lorca: Not bad. I'm impressed. Ever done any duet improvisation?

Neil: Nooo but I'll give it a try. [They do exactly the same piece in unison]

Neil: . . . Lorca, something's bothering me.

Lorca: Yeh.

Neil: Last night . . . when we did the improvisation bit . . . it was . . . exactly the same as tonight . . . Well. . . . . .how can two improvisations be the same?

Lorca: Chance . . . you know, probability, that's what it must have been.

Neil: But it must be millions to one.

Lorca: Listen Neil, if it happens again tomorrow night . . . then we start worrying, OK?

Neil: Fair enough [Lorca starts walking away]. But Lorca, didn't you say that . . . last night?

As it turns out, not only are the two boys scripted and choreographed to within an inch of their lives but also one of the perpetrators of this insult (Aggiss) is actually on stage with them – lording it over them, in fact. The actual literal dictionary definition of 'divagate' is explained early in the piece, i.e. 'to wander aimlessly from one thing to another' – an invitation that Aggiss/Cowie have always found hard to resist. However, the title also obviously plays on the merging of Divas and Watergate (and all the other something-gates that followed Watergate) and refers to the political power struggle in the piece. This hierarchy is most clearly demonstrated by the way that whenever Aggiss says Neil's name, the other three performers (Lorca, Neil and Estelle, the opera singer played by Melanie Marshall) must fall to their knees. Throughout the piece, though, rebellion is fermenting in the ranks and towards the end it boils up and the three decide to impeach Liz.

Lorca: Well I didn't write this – she makes me say it, she even made me say this . . . You know, we're all just her puppets.

[Liz comes off phone at last]

Liz: And where are all my little puppies?

Neil: He said puppets.

Liz: Puppets, puppies, it's all the same to me. I love you all, especially you NEIL

[they do kneel sequence].

Lorca: [On knees] Puppets [under breath].

Estelle: [Nudged forward by other two] Liz? The three of us have been talking and [Liz's glance halts her] and we decided some things . . . We . . . took a vote you know, democratic and . . .

Liz: And what Estelle?

Estelle: Well, we sort of decided to impeach you, you know, like that Nixon.

Liz: I see. OK. So I'm not in charge any more.

[Three all nod slowly]

Liz: The monkeys want to run the zoo, do they? Fine by me, fine . . . by . . . me . . . I'll be seeing you then [leaves stage].

[Three look at each other for a while]

Neil: I didn't think it would be that easy.

Estelle: I was quaking in my boots.

[Long pause]

Lorca: So what do we do now?

Neil: We carry on. We do a number of course. You got any more songs Estelle?

Estelle: [Thinks] Well, I have got a song about the Permafrost.

Neil: What?

Estelle: Permafrost, the arctic, the tundra.

Neil: Look, I can't do a dance about 20,000 square miles of land mass. I need a character to work with. Ice, it's not really me.

Lorca: Neil. I think you're being a little too literal. Think obliquely, at a tangent, add another layer, a gloss. Dance doesn't need to be the slave of words or music. Magnify with cross references, the chance relationships.

Estelle: You swallowed a book have you?

Lorca: Only trying to help . . . Let's do it then.

[Permafrost song and dance]

Neil: Where are we performing this thing next?

Lorca: I think it's Darlington.

Neil: Oh God no – that's the middle of nowhere.

Lorca: Well, I wouldn't say it was quite as central as that, it's more like you get to nowhere and then you've got a two-hour bus journey.

Neil: The edge of nowhere then?

Lorca: That's about it.

Neil: [Thinks for a looooong time] But isn't the edge of nowhere nearer to somewhere than the middle of nowhere?

Lorca: Well it is on this side but not on the opposite side.

Neil: Of course.

Estelle: Lorca! come over here . . . I think you should apologise to Neil. You were really patronising to him just then.

Lorca: Poor little Neil.

Estelle: Just because he's not that bright, you've no need to treat him like she does. In fact you're starting to behave a bit like her. This is all turning into *Animal Farm*.

Neil: I think we should get her back. At least she knows what she's doing.

Lorca: Well, I don't.

Neil: [Shouts] LIIIIZ! [Nothing] LIIIZ!

Liz: [Enters] That was much better. I think that you could be a little more petulant Lorca when you say, 'Well, I don't,' a bit more like this, 'Well, I don't.' [Lorca glowers at her] But you were excellent, Neil. [The three do the kneel sequence]

So it appears that even the impeachment was scripted and rehearsed (as of course it was in real life) just as the earlier improvisation was choreographed. Ironically, even Liz herself is entrapped in the theatrical straightjacket and bound to the construction of the piece as much as the others.

Conclusion

This tendency to deny performers in their work certain improvisatory freedoms might seem to disqualify Aggiss and Cowie from any anarchic pretensions. However, a little clarification on this subject is necessary. The two have always maintained that the tighter the choreographic structures are, the greater are the performers' opportunities to express their own personalities and individualities. It is surprising in many contact impro-visation pieces just how anonymous the performers are, whereas in the Divas pieces one feels that one actually learns something of what it must be like to be a Richard Knight, a Tommy Bayley or a Maria Burton, or indeed Aggiss herself. Aggiss and Cowie even took this strictness into their work with performers with learning difficulties, where a certain looseness is more the norm. Ben Pierre in *The Surgeon's Waltz* (2000) per-forms a head banging sequence with an inflatable heart; the music stops

and the text booms out – 'My heart, my heart, my heart went . . .' –
he drops the heart which 'smashes'. His extemporized response to the
audience's vocal sympathy for the smashing of his heart is a joy to behold
(DVD 15:8).[5]

In 1990, the magazine Freedom – anarchist fortnightly contained a half-
page article entitled 'DIVAS: Britain's only Anarchist Dance Company',
written by James Ellis:

> Making something new in modern dance is difficult. Convention is
> rampant, criticism can be damning. But Divas have now managed to
> tear aside the shrouds of tradition to such an extent that bookings
> for next year are crowding the diary. 'We never get invited to
> Number Ten' admits Liz Aggiss. 'We've never met the Education
> Minister or Thatcher. What they symbolise is a sickening sort of
> hidden repression – and some of it is not exactly hidden. We have
> moved into a position of becoming anarchists in the arts as a practical
> and positive revolt against what is happening . . . throughout the
> country.
>
> (Ellis 1990: 7)

The bulk of the article focuses on money, subsidy and sponsorship.
Indeed it was often said to Aggiss and Cowie by other choreographers
that their companies' funding structures would not allow them to make
such overtly party political works as Drool and Drivel. Truth be told, Aggiss
and Cowie were not refusing public or private money from a moral
standpoint, they were simply not being offered it. When, in 1989, Canon
Fax wanted to use parts of Die Orchidee in a corporate film about their new
plain paper fax machines, Aggiss and Cowie jumped – though it must be
said more for the excitement of working with the co-star of the film, Rik
Mayall, than for the pittance that was offered. Herr Mayall was duly kitted
out in matching Divas' lederhosen (although bright green rather than
regulation red) and gamely entered into that little world of German
anarchy.

In 1990, Divas had performed Die Orchidee and Dorothy and Klaus at the
Hannover Festival Tanz und Theater. The following review appeared in
the Braunschweiger Zeitung, under the headline of 'Happy Anarchism, Funny
Ugliness':

> With a shrill and hectic mechanical sound the Divas from Britain
> prepare their public for a quite unconventional evening of
> entertainment. The dance style of this company refutes any accepted
> ideals of beauty. They make ugliness their business. These British take

no-one seriously least of all themselves. Their anarchical dilettantes' dance expresses anything but amateurism. This group performs dance theatre in a totally free and unencumbered fashion, a tongue in cheek parody. With the Divas the different forms of communication are analysed with the surgeon's knife and the brutal ridicule is well worth the search.

(Löblich 1990a: 9)

The ugliness/beauty debate runs through many of Divas' reviews – sometimes as a stick to beat them with and sometimes as a source of praise. Many of the critics offended by 'ugliness' have ballet backgrounds and one can see that in that world where so much effort is spent on flawless perfection, beauty, effortlessness – the entrance of a bunch of performers willing to let it all hang out, be honest about their imperfections, be themselves above all rather than some idealized fiction must come as something of a shock. It must be said that this superficial ballet 'beauty' after a while wears thin and becomes tawdry, whereas the 'ugly' performance contains within it a deeper, truer beauty that sustains.

So, finally, what is anarchic dance, or rather, should we say, what is it in relation to Aggiss and Cowie, for there must obviously be as many flavours of anarchic dance as there are of anarchy? Perhaps the simplest thing is to attempt a definition and to paraphrase that old anarchist of language Humpty Dumpty: we should make it mean whatever we want it to mean.[6]

Anarchic dance: a choreographic style that reinvents itself at every 'turn', that knows its boundaries only so that it may transgress them and that respects no masters. A genre that plagiarizes relentlessly and is never the same twice. A movement, in both senses of the word, that is deadly serious but refuses to ever take itself seriously.

Notes

1   A programme was constructed by piecing together a series of short, self-contained three-minute dances much as a pop band builds a set from a series of songs.
2   After the premiere, Aggiss and Cowie were summoned by an ex-member of the audience who happened to be a professor of hearing at the nearby university. He informed them that the music was so extreme and the volume so great that he had to leave. He was concerned that the audience was in danger of permanent ear damage. Aggiss and Cowie naturally replied in unison with the only possible response: 'What?'
3   Aggiss categorically denies that she prayed for Thatcher's survival.
4   In the premiere, Lorca was played by Sebastian Gonzalez and Neil by Richard Knight. It was with great sadness that we learned of the death of

Richard, one of the most exceptional dancers and performers that we have worked with.

5   It could be argued in a parallel analogy that in the 'real' world laws and government similarly provide a structure that enables greater personal freedom and expression than the world of anarchy.

6   'When I use a word,' Humpty Dumpty said in rather a scornful tone, 'it means just what I choose it to mean – neither more nor less.'
        'The question is,' said Alice, 'whether you *can* make words mean different things.'
        'The question is,' said Humpty Dumpty, 'which is to be master – that's all.'

                                                        (Carroll 1976: 274)

afterword

liz aggiss and billy cowie

Sifting through mountains of photographs and videotapes to provide the documentation for this book we came across some surprises: pieces forgotten, never seen and rarely discussed. Two of them stand out, *Stations of the Angry* and *Cafeteria for a Sit-Down Meal*. In fact, browsing through the chronology of our work, amongst a plethora of bizarrely titled performances, one might think it would be folly not to go and see work titled with such spectacular visually inscribed clues and perplexing wordplay.

All that remains of *Stations of the Angry* is a photo (Figure Afterword.1). This solo work, performed by Aggiss, explored a musical collision of Bach's *St John's Passion* and the words of Worzel Gummidge, and was premiered and 'endiered' (if that is the word) at the Institute for Contemporary Arts (ICA) in 1989. The two central characters, Jesus and Worzel, share a gift for homespun knowledge and a penchant for the cruciform position. In the photograph, Aggiss is wearing one of her most

Figure Afterword.1 'Station One' – Liz Aggiss in *Stations of the Angry*. Photo: Billy Cowie, 1989.

spectacularly unusual costume traps. A series of blocks on arms, feet and head allow her on the one hand to take up an enchainment of abstract geometrical forms, cubes and parallelograms, and on the other hand show her physical entrapment within the crucifix. A post-show discussion with bemused students revealed that they hadn't a clue what it was about and had not twigged what Aggiss and Cowie had considered the most obvious synaptic link embedded into the title. Cowie maintains the piece was ahead of its time, Aggiss that it was a valuable learning experience. In any case, it was never seen again.

Cafeteria for a Sit-Down Meal is another kettle of fish. In 1992, Aggiss snapped her Achilles tendon (three days before a sold out premiere of Hilde Holger's reconstructions at the ICA). Aggiss remained in plaster for six months and was unable to walk properly for a further six. Never one to take things lying down, this new piece was constructed for the Zap Club in Brighton that year. In the piece, Aggiss remains seated (of necessity since at the premiere her leg was in plaster) for the entire show – thus continuing a tradition (often blamed on the armchair choreographer Cowie) of the seat in the performances (Wigglers' 'Coughing Wiggle', La Soupe's 'Sit-Down Dance', the chair sequence in Falling Apart at the Seams).

Aggiss plays the world's greatest 'classical' classical pianist, Stanislaw Bartkovitch, going through his daily dysfunctional functions. The piece had as many performances as Stations of the Angry (i.e. two), and we firmly believed that there wasn't even a photo of it. However, nestling at the bottom of a filthy box: 'What's this? Divas at Zap? Stick it on.' And voilà. The complete video, well recorded, plenty of close-ups; Aggiss appearing drawn from her surgical operation but giving a sterling performance with shades of Hilde in the choreographic vocabulary and the make-up. We watched the entire piece transfixed; ten years disappeared. Judge for yourselves (DVD 16:1).

How did Cafeteria get its unusual name, you ask? Well, Aggiss and Cowie have spent much of their lives in committee meetings at the venerable University of Brighton. Most of this time has been devoted to discussing the esoteric concepts of 'criteria for assessment' – these being a set of arbitrary rules that attempt to pretend that the marks given to the students' works of art, pieces of music, choreographies, etc. are not merely the result of whimsical subjectivity but are actually rationally produced, objective results. In one of the papers Cowie presented to a meeting, he substituted 'cafeteria for a sit-down meal' for 'criteria for assessment'. Despite the phrase occurring more than twenty times, the paper went through and probably is still somewhere in the bowels of the university. Regarding their films and performances presented for this book, Aggiss and Cowie feel their criteria for assessment of their own pieces are as nebulous as ever – but still manage to maintain an immense pride in this body of work.

In conclusion, this 25-year retrospective could seem like the end of an era. We, however, prefer to see it as simply the tidying up of some loose ends, leaving us with some nice clean space to start the work of the next 25 years. We would like to dedicate this book to passion, commitment, the delight in still being able to do something we love and, hopefully, making a difference. This of course goes hand in hand with applause ringing in our ears and a well-earned post-performance (or post-screening) drink slamming onto the backs of our throats.

list of works

All works (except *Vier Tänze*) were made by the collaborative partnership of Liz Aggiss and Billy Cowie.

*Asterisked performers appear on the DVD documentation.

The Wild Wigglers (1982–1990)

Cast: Liz Aggiss,* Jane Bassett, Neil Butler, Billy Cowie, Ralf Higgins,* Simon Hedger, Patrick Lee,* Ian Smith, Eva Zambicki

The Wild Wigglers is a visual comic trio emerging from the back end of punk with a suite of interchangeable three-minute simple cartoonesque dance bites which could be performed on stages, in tents, in stadiums and on television. The basic costume is a spiral yellow and black stripe that emphasizes each performer's size.

Premiere: 29 August 1982, Edinburgh Fringe Festival.

Grotesque Dancer (1986)

Original cast: Liz Aggiss*
Reconstruction cast: Liz Aggiss*

Commissioned by Zap Arts, Brighton, *Grotesque Dancer* is a relentlessly monochrome solo performance inspired by avant-garde German grotesque dancer Valeska Gert. This defiant and muscular work explores female sexuality, mixing humour, absurdity, dignity and vulnerability. The work features a series of connected expressionist dance vignettes accompanied by German cabaret-style instrumentals and songs, using poetry from Goethe, Morgenstern and Dehmal. The reconstruction featured live music from Billy Cowie* (piano), Gerard McChrystal* (saxophone).

Premiere: 6 December 1986, The Zap, Brighton
Reconstruction: 9 April 1999, Purcell Room, London

Torei en Veran Veta Arnold! (original title: *The Daughter of the Regiment*) (1986) *Le Mieux Servez Moi and Kakarella Ka Diva!*

Cast: Rachel Chaplin, Ellie Curtis, Virginia Farman, Kim Glass, Kay Lynn, Amanda Tuke, Louise Rennison, Jeanne Ayling
Lighting: Christina Ure

Torei en Veran veta Arnold! (a phonetic translation of the accompanying sampled music) explores the individual performer stage presence using pedestrian, habitual and repetitive gesture. Wearing tailored suits and high heels, 'power dressed' women claim the stage space and demand attention.

Premiere: 4 October 1986, Chisenhale Dance Space, London

Dva Sa Momimomuvali (1986)

Cast: Rachel Chaplin, Ellie Curtis, Virginia Farman, Kim Glass, Kay Lynn, Amanda Tuke
Lighting: Christina Ure

From hobbyhorse to competitive racehorse, six women in men's Y-fronts and vests jockey for space, chase their own tails, toe the line, jump on the band-wagon, compete and drive themselves on with optimism, collective spirit and individual identity.

Premiere: 4 October 1986, Chisenhale Dance Space, London

Eleven Executions (1988)

Cast: Liz Aggiss,* Maria Burton,* Rachel Chaplin,* Ellie Curtis,* Virginia Farman,* Kay Lynn,* Sian Thomas*
Costume and lighting: Christina Ure

A full-length dance theatre production loosely based on texts by German expressionist playwright Frank Wedekind. Each performer embodies a character/archetype: Wedekind, Lulu, Kaiser, Moritz, Holtoff the Strongman, Fischmann the Dog. This 'performance within a performance' is overseen by a raging Ring Mistress. Each character confronts the sexual hypocrisy and bourgeois values that informed Wedekind's writing. The structure of the performance is organized in precise sections that give each character a solo whilst the group takes on a chorus role. All performers are dressed in white and the production uses sculptural or frozen moments to ensure images are burnt into the space.

Premiere: 15 February 1988, Spring Loaded, The Place, London

Dead Steps (1988)

Cast: Scott Ambler,* Kaye Brown,* Sarah Barron,* Lindsey Butcher,* Chantel Donaldson,* Madeleine Ridgeway,* David Waring*

Musicians: Elizabeth Davis (percussion), Stephanie Nunn* (accordion, vocals), Nicolas Ormrod (percussion), Mary Plumb* (clarinet, saxophone), Clive Scrivener* (percussion)
Costume and lighting: Christina Ure

Commissioned for Extemporary Dance Theatre by Emilyn Claid, *Dead Steps* (*Die Totenschritte*) was made specifically for the front apron of any stage. Using texts from Frank Wedekind, Gustav Hochstetter and Kurt Eisner, and set to music, this work is a bleak, bizarre bridal dance that displays seven androgynous brides dressed in slate grey satin who become a nightmare anarchic anti chorus line, stripping themselves physically and emotionally bare. The costume contributes to this idea as it is gradually ripped and shredded during the performance.

Premiere: 28 May 1988, Harlequin Theatre, Redhill

Stations of the Angry (1989)

Cast: Liz Aggiss

An ironic solo performance amalgamating Bach's *St John's Passion* and the *Best of Worzel Gummidge*.

Premiere: 9 January 1989, The Ripple Effect, Institute of Contemporary Arts, London

Dorothy and Klaus (1989)

Cast: Liz Aggiss,* Jane Bassett, Maria Burton,* Ellie Curtis,* Virginia Farman,* Sian Thomas,* Ralf Higgins, Barnaby O'Rourke
Costume and lighting: Christina Ure

Dorothy and Klaus is a 45-minute cock-eyed, crazy dance opera. The narrative follows the tale of the obsessive composer Klaus, his rich wife Dorothy, whom he exploits and leaves once he has achieved success, and his three composer friends. The entire performance is lip-synced to prerecorded and synthetically treated voice.

Premiere: 12 October 1989, The Zap, Brighton

Die Orchidee im Plastik Karton (1989)

Original cast: Liz Aggiss,* Jane Bassett,* Maria Burton,* Marisa Carnesky, Ellie Curtis, Virginia Farman,* Ralf Higgins,* Barnaby O'Rourke, Sian Thomas,* Fiona Wright.
Reconstruction cast: Liz Aggiss* (schoolmistress), Adrian Court,* Sebastian Gonzalez,* Stephen Kirkham,* Ralf Higgins*
Costume and lighting: Christina Ure

A language lesson in nine interludes, taking as its starting point the study of a foreign language, in this case German. The instructor is on blackboard and the pupils are swathed in red lederhosen. Both the sampled words and the connected movements are cut up, collaged and repeated. The choreography deconstructs and explores the subversive nature of language from a feminist perspective.

Preview: 1988 by 13 students of West Sussex Institute of Higher Education, now University College, Chichester
Divas premiere: 12 October 1989, The Zap, Brighton
Reconstruction: 9 April 1999, Purcell Room, London

Banda Banda (1989)

Cast: Carousel Dance Company (an integrated company): Joyce Francis, Eric Grantham, Edna Guy, Debbie Hartin, Sarah Jackson, Martin Lake, Veronica Lee, Jac Mathews, Clare Matthews, Alison Mills, Colin Richardson, Valerie Rowe, Margaret Stamp, Gill Wilcox
Costume and lighting: Christina Ure

Banda Banda is an integrated performance that explores individuality within a carnival atmosphere of energy and music sung in Sierra Leonese by Daphne Scott-Sawyer. Each performer was invited to share an aspect of their life with the group. This information was recorded, used to inspire the choreography and in some sections embedded into the music.

Premiere: 12 May 1989, Sallis Benney Theatre, University of Brighton

Time Out/Dance Umbrella Award 1990

La Soupe (1990)

Cast: Divas – Liz Aggiss, Jane Bassett, Virginia Farman, Sian Thomas, Ralf Higgins, Parmjit Pammi (singer); and Carousel Dance Company – Joyce Francis, Eric Grantham, Edna Guy, Jane Hanson, Debbie Hartin, Sarah Jackson, Martin Lake, Veronica Lee, Jac Mathews, Clare Matthews, Alison Mills, Colin Richardson, Valerie Rowe, Margaret Stamp, Gill Wilcox (entire cast *)
Costume and lighting: Christina Ure

La Soupe is an exotic dance/opera, inspired by the Outsider Art collection housed at La Fabuloserie, Dicy, France. The piece is based on the writings and poems of the cast. The setting in the Music Room at the Brighton Royal Pavilion reads as a powerful statement about privilege, exclusion and appropriation of culture. *La Soupe* is about liberating performance structures and points towards a rethinking of social and political boundaries.

Premiere: 16 May 1990, Music Room, Brighton Royal Pavilion

Brighton Festival Alliance and Leicester Award 1990

La Petite Soupe (1990)

Cast: Liz Aggiss, Jane Bassett, Virginia Farman, Edna Guy, Martyn Lake, Ralf Higgins, Sian Thomas, Parmjit Pammi (singer)

Costume: Christina Ure

This mini touring version spin-off from *La Soupe* brought together members of Divas and Carousel.

Premiere: 22 May 1990, Eurodanse, Mulhouse, France (who also commissioned the work)

Drool and Drivel They Care! (1990)

Cast: Liz Aggiss,* Jane Bassett,* Virginia Farman,* Ralf Higgins,* Sian Thomas*

Commissioned by Zap Arts, this is a political satire on Mrs Thatcher's years in power. The music is composed using samples from her political speeches and brought to life by a quintet of Thatcher look-a-likes. Ironically (or is it tragically?), this work premiered on the evening she resigned. The final section was swiftly reworked, with the wall of Maggies transforming into five John Majors still intoning relentlessly from Thatcher's speeches.

Premiere: 22 November 1990, The Zap, Brighton

French Songs (1991)

Cast: Tommy Bayley, Maria Burton
Live music: Billy Cowie (piano), Cathryn Robson (voice), Lucie Robson (voice), Anne Stephenson (violin), Sian Bell (cello)
Costume: Tig Evans
Lighting: Robert Clutterham

This is a suite of dances and songs using Verlaine's poetry.

Premiere: 15 May 1991, Gardner Arts Centre, Brighton

Vier Tänze (1992)

Cast: Liz Aggiss*

This suite of four dances was originally choreographed and performed by Hilde Holger. Accompanied on piano by Billy Cowie,* these reconstructions hail from pre-war Vienna; *Die Forelle* (1923), *Le Martyre de San Sebastien* (1923), *Mechanisches Ballett* (1926), *Golem* (1937). Costumes reconstructed by Tig Evans.

Premiere: 29 February 1992, Manchester Festival of Expressionism, Green Room

El Puñal entra en el Corazón (1992)

Cast: Liz Aggiss* and Daphne Scott-Sawyer*
Live music: Billy Cowie (accordion), Deborah Hay* (guitar), Lucy East* (cello)

Costume: Tig Evans
Lighting: Robert Clutterham

Commissioned by The South Bank, London, El Puñal entra en el Corazón is a 35-minute performance based on texts by the Spanish writer Gabriel García Lorca. The work explores Lorca's macho world and the romanticism of death.

Premiere: 20 January 1992, Queen Elizabeth Hall, London

Cafeteria for a Sit-Down Meal (1992)

Cast: Liz Aggiss* and Jeddi Bassan*

Liz Aggiss broke her Achilles tendon on 4 July 1992. Cafeteria for a Sit-Down Meal was made as a sit-down performance in response to the Achilles tendon break. The piece considers the life of the world's greatest fictitious pianist, Stanislav Bartkoviak. The narrative focuses on an unseen narration into which Bartkoviak interjects and performs his impossible piano compositions.

Premiere: 6 November 1992, The Zap, Brighton

Falling Apart at the Seams (so it seems) (1993)

Cast: Liz Aggiss* and Naomi Itami* (soprano)
Costume: Tig Evans
Lighting: Chris Umney

Commissioned by the Gardner Arts Centre, Brighton, Falling Apart at the Seams explores the onset of the ageing, fleshy body in a self-parodying, hilarious and surrealistic satire. The poems, which cover topics such as falling apart, dead friends, ageing and babies, are embedded into the operatic and spoken duets, and realized by the glamorous, slapstick double act. The production team included visual artist Gary Goodman and writer/comedienne Louise Rennison.

Premiere: 28 October 1993, Gardner Arts Centre, Brighton

No Man's Land (1993)

Cast: Marilu Achille, Bianca Adefarakan (singer), Liz Aggiss, Liesje Cole, Tig Evans, Hazel Finnis, Leonora Green, Lisa Haight, Siou Hannam, Doris Harman, China King, Mim King, Soile Lahdenpera, Nusara Mai-Ngarm, Pauline Rennison, Emily Shaw, Lois Underwood (entire cast *)
Live music: Juliet Russell (lead singer) and Marjorie Ashenden, Anna Copley, Lucy East, Gret Hopkins, Emma Stevens (cellists)
Costume: Christina Ure

Commissioned by the Gardner Arts Centre, Brighton, No Man's Land is a performance for 17 women aged 9 to 60 accompanied by Polish poems set to music, sung live and accompanied by cellos. The piece is a celebration of difference and diversity, and the collective and individual presence.

Premiere: 28 October 1993, Gardner Arts Centre, Brighton

Film: *Beethoven in Love* (1994)

Director: Bob Bentley
Cast: Liz Aggiss, Tommy Bayley
Choir: Jeddi Bassan, Sharon Curtis, Lisa Haight, Chris Hallam, Ralf Higgins, Andrew Kaye, Mim King, Sal Robarts, Maggy Burrowes, Mark Harrison (entire cast *)
Music: Elizabeth Woollett (soprano), Juliet Russell (mezzo), Thomas Kampe (tenor), Ian Needle (bass), Billy Cowie (piano)
Costume: Christina Ure

Beethoven in Love is a 15-minute screen-dance funded by a BBC/Arts Council of England Dance for Camera Award. Shot on 16mm film, it derives inspiration from the composer's difficult relationships with women and explores the nature of the outsider. Black humour and an expressionist dance vocabulary combine with the romantic lyricism of Billy Cowie's music to evoke images of the eighteenth century, though the central questions of the outsider and unrequited love are relevant to contemporary thinking.

Television premiere: 6 January 1994, BBC2

Absurditties (1994)

Cast: Liz Aggiss*
Costume: Tig Evans

Absurditties is about performance. In this solo, the performer has only her wits and body with which to entertain the audience. The performance is devoid of lighting, music or special effects and is a collage of precise sculptural choreography, absurd gesture, sharp humour, wordplay and visual gags.

Premiere: 6 May 1994, The Zap, Brighton

Hi Jinx (1995)

Cast: Liz Aggiss,* Aikiko Kajihara,* Lea Anderson*
Singers: Rowan Godel,* Liz Aggiss,* Sarah Jane Dale*
Costume: Kate Strachan
Lighting: Chris Umney

Commissioned by the University of Surrey's Choreographic Laboratory, this dance lecture performance is based on the experimental dancer/choreographer Heidi Dzinkowska (also known as Hi Jinx). The work parodies the desire to create icons from the past and includes film clips and reconstructions from Heidi's artistic back catalogue.

Premiere: 20 April 1995, Border Tensions Conference, University of Surrey, Guildford

The Fetching Bride (1995)

Original cast: Liz Aggiss (Bride), Chloe Wright (Groom)
Reconstruction cast: Colette Sadler (Bride),* Liz Aggiss (Groom)*
Live music: Billy Cowie (piano),* Anne Stephenson (violin),* Sian Bell (cello),*
    Amanda Morrison (soprano)*
Costume: Kate Strachan
Lighting: Jeff Baynes

Commissioned by the University of Surrey's Choreographic Laboratory, The
Fetching Bride is an erotic black satire and an exploration of sadism and
masochism, charting a downward spiral from innocence and naivety, through
to corruption and death.

Premiere: 20 April 1995, Border Tensions Conference, University of Surrey,
    Guildford
Reconstruction: 4 February 1996

Bird in a Ribcage (1995)

Original cast: Becky Brown, Lucy Dunden, Wei-Ying Hsu, Akiko Kajihara,*
    Kathinka Luhr, Rachael Read, Colette Sadler
Reconstruction cast: Hsiao-Chen Fang, Iris Fung Chi Sun, Maria Yuk Fung Law, Rose
    Payne, Jess Ward, Trude Jegstad
Costume: Suzie Holmes
Lighting: Anthony Bowne

Commissioned by the Laban Centre for Transitions Dance Company, this all-
female work is based on a set of poems written by Billy Cowie and Mine Kaylan
and sung in Turkish by Rowan Godel. It is a heart-rending and unconventional
portrayal of love, anguish and isolation.

Premiere: 9 February 1995, Bonnie Bird Theatre, Laban Centre, Laurie Grove,
    London
Reconstruction: 9 May 1999, Bloomsbury Theatre, London

Divagate (1997)

Cast: Liz Aggiss,* Richard Knight,* Sebastian Gonzalez,* Melanie Marshall
    (soprano)*
Costume: Tig Evans
Lighting: Bill Deverson

Co-commissioned by the Gardner Arts Centre, Brighton, and The South Bank,
London, Divagate is a Watergate of excuses. Based on the Latin definition 'divagari'
to digress, this interdisciplinary work includes specially created dance films
made in collaboration with Jeff Baynes, and slide projections created by visual
artist Jane Fox.

Premiere: 10 October 1997, Gardner Arts Centre, Brighton

The 38 Steps (1999)

Cast: Eve Caille, Young Soon Cho, Vahine Ehrensperger, Claudia Evans, Karen Foley, Alicia Herrera Simon, Allison Higgins, Melissa Hunte, Anette Iverson, Margun Kilde, Renate Kohoutek, Kaori Murakami, Marissa Nielson-Pincus, Emma Ribbing, Dawn Ritchie, Janine Skidmore, Annabel Smart, Khadifa Wong (entire cast *)
Costume concept: Aggiss/Cowie, realized by Linda Rowell
Lighting: David Goldsworthy

Commissioned by London Studio Centre for InToto Dance Company, 18 dancers fall in, out and in love again. Their 38 steps are set to bubblegum pop sung by Jenny Lee Potter. Their costumes owe inspiration to Mondrian.

Premiere: 13 July 1999, Bloomsbury Theatre, London

The Surgeon's Waltz (2000)

Cast: Sunah Al-Husainy, Ingrid Ashberry, Julia Burcham, Andrew Franks, Irene Mensah, David Mileman, Maria Pengelly, Ben Pierre, Andy Saunders (entire cast*)
Costume: Holly Murray
Lighting: Sean Phillips

Commissioned by Carousel for their integrated company High Spin, the cast are initially dressed in surgeons' gowns, rubber gloves and surgical masks. The work developed through collaborative workshops with the company in which different parts of the body were considered as sites for expression and meaning. The work is constructed in movement poems that are titled by the company, for example 'Skeleton Baby', 'Winterface', 'I Give you my Heart', 'Valentine', 'Don't Touch my Lemons', 'Rib Dance' and 'Coughing Ballerina'.

Premiere: 3 March 2000, Komedia, Brighton

Rice Rain (2001)

Cast: Julia Burcham, Rainna Crudge, Andrew Franks, Becki Hodgson, Irene Mensah, David Mileman, Maria Pengelly, Ben Pierre*, Mark Richardson, Andy Saunders
Singer: Kaori Murakami*
Costume: Holly Murray
Lighting: Sean Phillips

Commissioned by Carousel for their integrated company High Spin, the work developed through collaborative workshops with the company in which visual images of Japan were explored. The performance was divided into two parts. The first half used sea and ceremony, the second half city life and karaoke.

Premiere: 8 March 2001 at De La Warr Pavilion Bexhill

Film: *Motion Control* (2002)

Choreography: Aggiss/Cowie
Director: David Anderson
Costume: Holly Murray

In May 2000 Liz Aggiss's appendix burst and she was hospitalized. The film shoot was held over to May 2001. *Motion Control* is a BBC/Arts Council of England Dance for Camera Award. It specifically and uniquely examines the synergy of camera and performer. Shot on 35mm at Shepperton Studios, it is unique in its use of motion control camera and animation techniques. This film explores, from the camera's point of view, the physical and emotional entrapment of the ageing and glamorous dancer in her private and personal spaces. This is truly a dance for the camera. The film is notable for the hypersound foley work, overlaid with text and electro-opera.

Television premiere: 3 March 2002, BBC2

Czech Crystal award for best original dance and music made for television, Golden Prague International Television Awards, 2002
Honourable Mention, Paula Citron Award for Choreography for the Camera, Moving Picture Film and Video Awards, Toronto, 2002
Special Jury Golden Award, World FilmFest, Houston, 2003
Best Female Film, Mediawave, Hungary, 2003

Film: *Anarchic Variations* (2002)

Directors: Cowie/Aggiss
Costume: Holly Murray

Anarchic Variations, an Arts Council of England Capture 2 Award, aims to confound and disorientate the spectator's reality of space, scale and sound based on the choreographic and music idea of theme and variations. The underlying physical concept centres on dislocation and the splitting of the body into independent and separate units through the use of optical illusion. The audience actively engages in the film by problem solving – asking the questions who is doing what to whom, and how, and just who is in control?

Premiere: 17 December 2002, The Place, London

Scripted to Within an Inch of Her Life (2002)

Cast: Liz Aggiss*
Costume: Holly Murray

A solo installation performance that deconstructs the film *Motion Control*. Both multiple projections of the re-edited film and performer become literally installed: physically, textually, performatively and emotionally strapped into the work as Aggiss embraces the physical synergy between camera, sound and movement.

Premiere: 30 January 2004, British Dance Edition, Kettles Yard

Men in the Wall (2003)

Cast: Jeddi Bassan,* Sebastian Gonzalez,* Thomas Kampe,* Scott Smith*
Director/choreographers: Aggiss/Cowie
Text: Cowie
Costume: Holly Murray

This is an Arts Council of England Capture 3 Award and received support from the Centre for Research and Development (Arts and Architecture), University of Brighton.

This is a four-screen, three-dimensional stereoscopic installation which redefines dance screen practice. Four men's shared, framed lives are a public quartet of private differences.

Premiere: 23 February 2004, Institute of Contemporary Arts, London

Doppelgänger (2005)

Doppelgänger is a Capture 4 screen dance installation, co-commissioned by the Arts Council of England and the New Art Gallery, Walsall, and supported by the Centre for Research and Development (Arts and Architecture), University of Brighton. This installation of looped projections, made specifically for and in the New Art Gallery Walsall site, explores the notion of nano-choreography and the distillation of photographic fragments.

Premiere: 10 February 2006, New Art Gallery, Walsall

Break (2005)

Break, choreographed by Aggiss and Cowie, is a dance for camera film commissioned by Channel 4 for its 4Dance 2005 series.

bibliography

Adair, C. (1992). *Women and Dance: Sylphs and sirens.* Basingstoke: Macmillan.

Adair, C. (1999). Resistant revelations. *Dance Theatre Journal,* 15 (1), 12–15.

Aggiss, L. (2000). Juggling not struggling. *Dance Theatre Journal,* 15 (4), 29–33.

Aggiss, L. (2002a). Obituaries: Hilde Holger. *Dance Theatre Journal,* 17 (4), 45–46.

Aggiss, L. (2002b). Telephone interview with author, 28 August.

Aristotle. (2005). Rhetoric. Online. Available HTTP: <http://www.public.iastate.edu/~honeyl/Rhetoric/> (accessed 4 April 2005).

Bakhtin, M. (1984). *Rabelais and his World.* Bloomington: Indiana University Press.

Banes, S. (1987). *Terpsichore in Sneakers.* Hanover: Wesleyan University Press.

Barthes, R. (1975). *The Pleasure of the Text.* Oxford: Blackwell.

Bhatti, S. S. (1989). Nek Chands testament of creativity: The Rock Garden of Chandigarh. *Raw Vision,* spring, 1, 22–31.

Bowen, C. (1991). Dance of a culture vulture. *The Scotsman,* 11, 27 May.

Briginshaw, V. (1988). The wiggle goes on – A profile of Liz Aggiss and Billy Cowie. *New Dance,* summer, 44, 7–9.

Briginshaw, V. (2001). *Dance Space and Subjectivity.* London: Palgrave.

British Council. (2005). Liz Aggiss and Billy Cowie. *Performance in Profile.* Online. Available HTTP: <http://www.britishcouncil.org/arts-performance-in-profile-2005-liz-aggiss-and-billy-cowie.htm>. (accessed 4 April 2005).

Brooks, P. (1976). *The Melodramatic Imagination: Balzac, Henry James, melodrama and the mode of excess.* New Haven: Yale University Press.

Burt, R. (1998). *Alien Bodies: Representations of modernity, 'race' and nation in early modern dance.* London: Routledge.

Butler, J. (1993). *Gender Trouble: Bodies that matter: On the discursive limits of sex.* New York and London: Routledge.

Caputo, J. D. (1997). *Deconstruction in a Nutshell: A conversation with Jacques Derrida.* Edited with a commentary by J. D. Caputo. New York: Fordham University Press.

Cardinal, R. (1972). *Outsider Art.* London and Praeger, New York: Studio Vista.

Carroll, L. (1976). *Through the Looking-Glass.* London: Puffin Books.

Caughie, J., Kuhn, A. and Merck, M. (eds) (1992). *The Sexual Subject: A screen reader in sexuality.* London: Routledge.

Cixous, H. (1995). From the place of crime, the place of pardon. In R. Drain (ed.) *Twentieth-century Theatre: A sourcebook.* London and New York: Routledge, 340–344.

Clarke, M. (1987, May 1). Forward motion. *Guardian,* 21.

Clements, M. (1989). Carousel and Virginia Farman ICA. *Time Out,* 6–13 December, 72.

Coates, P. (1991). *The Gorgon's Gaze: German cinema, expressionism and the image of horror.* Cambridge: Cambridge University Press.

Constanti, S. (1987a). Easing the load: The Spring Loaded season at The Place, *Dance Theatre Journal*, 5 (2), 26–29.

Constanti, S. (1987b). Divas/Grotesque Dancer. *Spare Rib*, July, 180, 33.

Constanti, S. (1993). Dancing diva: Hilde Holger's choreography reaches the British stage at last – and triumphs. *Guardian*, 9 June, Arts Section 3–4.

Craine, D. and Mackrell, J. (2000). *The Oxford Dictionary of Dance*. Oxford: Oxford University Press.

Critchley, S. (1992). *The Ethics of Deconstruction: Derrida and Levinas*. London: Blackwell.

Cross, D. (2003). Article. *Artist's Newsletter*, January, 27.

Dandeker, C. (2001). Dance. *Disability Now*, April, 28.

De Keersmaeker, A.T. (1981). Valeska Gert. *Drama Review*, Fall, 25 (3), 55–66.

De Lauretis, T. (1987). *Technologies of Gender: Essays on Theory, Film and Fiction*. Blooomington and Indianapolis: Indiana University.

Derrida, J. (1968). 'La Différance' lecture given in 1968, reprinted in *Margins of Philosophy*. Translated by A. Bass (1982). Chicago: University of Chicago Press.

Derrida, J. (1981). *Positions*. Translated by A. Bass. London: Athlone Press.

Derrida, J. (1988). *Limited Inc*. Edited by Gerald Graff. Translation by S.Weber and J. Mehlman. Evanston: Northwestern University Press.

Eisner, L. (1973). *The Haunted Screen*. London: Secker and Warburg.

Ellis, J. (1990). Divas: Britain's only anarchist dance company. *Freedom – anarchist fortnightly*, 27 January, 51 (2), 7.

Farman, V. (1987). Review of Dartington Dance Festival. *New Dance*, summer, 41, 20–21.

Foucault, M. (1978). *The History of Sexuality, Vol. 1*. Translated by R. Hurley. New York: Pantheone Books.

Gert, V. (1926). Mary Wigman und Valeska Gert. *Der Querschnitt*, May, 6 (5), 361–363.

Gert, V. (1931a). *Mein Weg*. Leipzig: Devrient.

Gert, V. (1931b). Wie wird man 'Tänzerin'. *Der Tanz*, April, 4 (4), 5.

Gert, V. (1931c). Dancing: Valeska Gert from a talk given at Radio Leipzig. *Shrifttanz*, June, 1V (1), 14.

Gert, V. (1979). *Ich bin eine Hexe*. Reinbek bei Hamburg: Rowohlt.

Gert, V. (1995). I am a witch. In R. Drain (ed.) *Twentieth-century Theatre: A sourcebook*. London and New York: Routledge, 33–34.

Gilbert, J. (1999). Divas. *Independent on Sunday*, 11 April, 8.

Gledhill, C. (1996). Genre. In P. Cook (ed.) *The Cinema Book*. London: BFI, 57–112.

Grosz, E. (1987). Notes towards a corporeal feminism. *Australian Feminist Studies*, summer, 5, 1–16.

Hall, F. (1983). Splendid variety. *Daily Telegraph*, 31 October, 15.

Hamilton, S. (1990a). In the soup together: *La Soupe* by Carousel seen at the Brighton Pavilion 16 May 1990. *Dice Magazine*, July, 12, 11–12.

Hamilton, S. (1990b). Authentic voices: Stanley Hamilton looks at some recent dances for and by people overcoming disadvantages, and suggests a need for further development. *Dance and Dancers*, September, 486, 18–21.

Harpe, B. (1991). *Banda Banda*, St Helens. *Guardian*, 6 February, 36.

Harpe, B. (1992). Divas: Manchester. *Guardian*, 2 March, 33.

Hayward, S. (2000). *Cinema Studies: The key concepts*. (2nd edition). London: Routledge.

Hermann-Neisse, M. (1926). Endlich eine Revueparodie. *Der Kritiker*, April, 8 (4), 60–67. In F. M. Peter. (1987). *Valeska Gert: Tänzerin, Schauspielerin, Kabarettistin*. Berlin: Edition Hentrich.

Hildenbrandt, F. (1928). *Die Tänzerin Valeska Gert*. Stuttgart: Hädecke.

Hirschbach, D. and Takvorian, R. (1990). *Die Kraft des Tanzes: Hilde Holger: Wien: Bombay: London*. Bremen: Zeichen & Spuren.

Hoggard, L. (2003). Different class. *Observer Review*, 26 October, 5.

Holger, H. (1990). *Die Kraft des Tanzes: Wien, Bombay, London*. Zeichen & Spuren.

Hull-Malham, N. (2000). For one night only. *Disability Times*, May, 10.

Hutera, D. (1991). Divas. *Time Out*, 15 March, 63.

Hutera, D. (1999). Spring Loaded. *Dance Europe*, June/July, 18–21.

Irigaray, L. (1981a) This sex which is not one. Translated by C. Reeder. In E. Marks and L. Courtivron (eds) *New French Feminisms*. Brighton: Harvester Press (Briginshaw), 99–106.

Irigaray, L. (1981b). And the one doesn't stir without the other. *Signs: Journal of Women in Culture and Society*, 7 (1), 60–67.

Irigaray, L. (1985). *This Sex Which Is Not One*. Translated by Catherine Porter. New York: Cornell University.

Jordan, S. (1987). Beyond the umbrella. *New Statesman*, 27 February, 113 (2918), 2.

Jordan, S. (1992). *Striding Out: Aspects of contemporary and new dance in Britain*. London: Dance Books.

Kaplan, E. A. (ed.) (1989). *Women in Film Noir*. London: BFI.

Kaplan, E. A. (ed.) (1990). *Psychoanalysis and Cinema*. London: Routledge.

Keidan, L. (1990). Personal communication, 2 February.

Kelly, O. (ed.) (2002). *The Portable Kristeva*. New York: Colombia University Press.

King, J. (1983). Bonked by The Wild Wigglers. *Morning Star*, 11 November, 4.

Koegler, H. (1974). Shadow of the swastika: Dance in Germany 1927–1936. *Dance Perspectives*, 57, 6.

Konegan, H. (1990). Fröhlicher Anarchismus, komische Hässlichkeit. *Braunschweiger Zeitung Hannover*, 11 September, 11.

Kuhn, A. (1992). *The Power of the Image: Essays on representation and sexuality*. London: Routledge.

Kuhn, A. (1996). History of the cinema. In P. Cook (ed.) *The Cinema Book*. London: BFI, 2–56.

Laban, R. (1975). *Life for Dance: Reminiscences*. London: Macdonalds & Evans.

Levene, L. (1999). Divas Dance Theatre. *Sunday Telegraph*, 11 April, 8.

Levi, P. (1958). *If This Is A Man*. London: Abacus.

Lewitan, J. (1932). Bankrupt: A few words on formlessness and stupidity. *Der Tanz*, June, 5 (6), 4–6.

Löblich, E. (1990a). Happy anarchism, funny ugliness. *Braunschweiger Zeitung*, 11 September, 212 (45), 9.

Löblich, E. (1990b). Tanz und Theater International '90 Hannover. *Ballet International*, December, 13 (13), 37.

Louis, M. (1980). *Inside Dance: Essays by Murray Louis on revival*. New York: St Martin's Press.

Lyotard, J.-F. (1984). *The Postmodern Condition: A report on knowledge*. Manchester: Manchester University Press.

Mackrell, J. (1987). A war dance in underpants. *Independent*, 16 February, 11.

Mackrell, J. (1991). Post-modern dance in Britain: An historical essay. *Dance Research*, spring, 9 (1), 40–57.

Mackrell, J. (1992). *Out of Line: The story of British new dance*. London: Dance Books.

Morris, W. (1882). *Hopes and fears for art: Five lectures delivered in Birmingham, London and Nottingham, 1878–1881*. London: Ellis & White. Online. Available HTTP: <http://etext.library.adelaide.edu.au/m/m87hf/chap3.html> (accessed 1 April 2005).

Müller, H. (1985). The twisting spiral. *Ballett International*, March, 16–21.

Müller, H. and Servos, N. (1984). Expressionism? 'Ausdruckstanz' and the new dance theatre in Germany. *Dance Theatre Journal*, 2 (1), 10–15.

Müller, J. (1973). *A Dictionary of Expressionism*. London: Eyre Methuen.

Mulvey, L. (1989). *Visual and Other Pleasures*. London: Macmillan.

Mumford, M. (2001). Performing national identity: From the greater wholes of German Ausdruckstanz to the gaping holes of Bausch's Tanztheater. *Grounded in Europe: German Expressionism in Tanztheater*, International Conference in London, sponsored by the Centre for Performance Research.

Murphy, R. (1998). *Theorizing the Avant-garde*. Cambridge: Cambridge University Press.

Niehoff, K. (1962). Rede zum wirklichen, zum endlichen Tod der Valeska Gert. Stimmt es – Stimmt es nicht? Porträts, Kritiken, Essays 1946–1962. In F. M. Peter. (1987). *Valeska Gert: Tänzerin, Schauspielerin, Kabarettistin*. Berlin: Edition Hentrich, 122–124.

Norris, C. (1982). *Deconstruction Theory and Practice*. London and New York: Routledge.

Nugent, A. (1987a). Springing into life: Ann Nugent on a season of new dance at The Place. *Dance and Dancers*, May, 447, 18–20.

Nugent, A. (1987b). Divas. *The Stage*, 19 February, 17.

Nugent, A. (1992). The Green Table and Café Müller. *Dance Now*, autumn, 1 (3), 34–41.

Parry, J. (1994). Strange fish to goggle at. *Observer*, 9 January, Review, 12.

Pascal, J. (1988). Let's tanz. *Guardian*, 29 January, 19.

Pascal, J. (1989). Divas: Cockpit. *Guardian*, 3 July, 35.

Penguin English Dictionary. (1965). Second edition. London: Penguin.

Penman, R. (1994). Dance and the camera. *Dancing Times*, February, 497.

Percival, J. (1987). Applaud the audience. *The Times*, 14 February, 42.

Peter, F. M. (1987). *Valeska Gert: Tänzerin, Schauspielerin, Kabarettistin*. Berlin: Edition Hentrich.

Phelan, P. (1993). *Unmarked: The politics of performance*. London: Routledge.

Phillips, A. (1991). Dada dance. *Dance Theatre Journal*, 8 (4), 46–47.

Phillips, J. (2000). Dance's spin doctors. *Evening Argus*, 6 March, 23.

Place, J. (1989). Women in film noir. In E. A. Kaplan (ed.) *Women in Film Noir*. London: BFI, 35–67.

Ploebst, H. (2001). *No Wind No Word: New choreography in the society of the spectacle*. Munich: K. Keiser.

Poggi, C. (1992). *In Defiance of Painting: Cubism, futurism and the invention of collage*. Newhaven and London: Yale University Press.

Potter, T. (2001). Beethoven. In S. Sadie (ed.) *The New Grove Dictionary of Music and Musicians*. London: Macmillan.

Prinz, H. (1930). The Valeska Gert phenomenon. *Der Tanz*, March, 3 (3), 21–22.

Quaresima, L. (1997). Expressionist film as an 'Angewandte Kunst'. In S. Barron and D. Dube (eds) *German Expressionism: Art and society*. London: Thames and Hudson, 90–98.

Rainer, Y. (1965). 'No' to spectacle. *Tulane Drama Review*, 10 (2), 178. Also in S. Banes (1986). *Terpsichore in Sneakers: Postmodern dance*. Middletown, Connecticut: Wesleyan University Press.

Rhodes, C. (2000). *Outsider Art: Spontaneous alternatives*. London and New York: Thames and Hudson.

Robertson, A. (1987). Wendy Houstoun/Liz Aggiss: ICA. *Time Out*, 29 April–6 May, 54.

Robertson, A. (1995). Transitions. *Time Out*, 3–10 May, 64.

Robertson, A. and Hutera, D. (1988). *The Dance Handbook*. London: Longman.

Sacks, A. (1999). Divas, Purcell Room. *Evening Standard*, 8 April, 55.

Sanchez Colberg, A. (2001). Traditions and contradictions: From Ausdruckstanz to Tanztheater. *Grounded in Europe: German Expressionism in Tanztheater*, International Conference in London, sponsored by the Centre for Performance Research.

Scheier, H. (1987). What has dance theatre to do with Ausdruckstanz? *Ballett International*, January, 12–17.

Smee, S. (2003). It's a scream. Expressionism was one of the 20th century's key movements. So why is it so unfashionable today? *Guardian*, 16 June. Online. Available HTTP: <http://www.guardian.co.uk/arts/features/story/0,11710,978161,00.html> (accessed 1 September 2003).

Stam, R., Burgoyne, R. and Flitterman-Lewis, S. (1992). *New Vocabularies in Film Semiotics: Structuralism, post-structuralism and beyond*. London: Routledge.

Stapleton, A. (1989). Review: Manic, moving, marvellous. *Care Weekly*, 24 November, 6.

Stein, A. (alias Rumpelstilzchen). (1932). Nu wenn schon! *Berliner Allerlei*. vol.12. Berlin: Brunnenverlag, 230.

Synder, A. and MacDonald, A. (1983). *The fire that dances between two poles*. Film.

Terry, W. (1980). ARDC and the art of reconstruction. *Smithsonian*. Online. Available HTTP: <http://www.ardc-la.org./art.html> (accessed November 2003).

The Reader's Digest Great Encyclopaedic Dictionary. (1964). Second edition (Fourth impression). London: Reader's Digest.

Thiele, M. (c.1988). Personal communication between Frau Mathilde Thiele and the author, Waterport, NY.

Thomson, P. (1973). *The grotesque*. London: Methuen.

Torok, A. (1919). Dance evenings. Der Merker. In Oberzaucher-Schüller, Vernon-Warren and Warren, 21. Online. Available HTTP: <http://www.danceadvance.org/O3archives/bodenwieser/page8.html>.

Vogt, P. (1980). Introduction in *Expressionism: A German institution 1905–1920*. New York: Solomon R. Guggenheim Foundation.

Watson, K. (1991). Warmth in the Soupe. *Hampstead and Highgate Express*, 22 March, 22.

Watson, K. (1995). Winging it . . . *Hampstead and Highgate Express*, 19 May, 44.

Wolfreys, J. (1998). *The Derrida Reader: Writing performances*. Edinburgh: Edinburgh University Press.

Wordsworth, W. (1984). Lines written a few miles above Tintern Abbey. In S. Gill (ed.) *The Oxford Authors: William Wordsworth*. Oxford: Oxford University Press, 131–135.

Zamponi, L. (1990). Das Gute kommt von außen. *Die Presse*, 29 October, 13.

Index